C000176302

SKY+ BT BUSINESS NHS BLOOD AND TRANSPLANT MAGNERS CHANGE4LIFE ALLI O2 WAITROSE KFC MCDONALD'S HOVIS BRITISH GAS AUDI MARKS & SPENCER VIRGIN ATLANTIC DULUX SAINSBURY'S PEDIGREE THINKBOX HARLEQUINS MORE TH>N UPS WALKERS AVIVA EBOOKERS SHELL ICI PAINTS CHANNEL 4 BRITISH HEART FOUNDATION KEEP BRITAIN TIDY ARIEL MARKETING EXCELLENCE 2

Copyright © 2010 The Marketing Society

The Marketing Society
1 Park Road
Teddington
London TW11 0AR

Telephone: +44 (0)20 8973 1700
Fax: +44 (0)20 8973 1701

Email (for orders and customer service enquiries):
membership@marketingsociety.co.uk
Visit our Home Page on www.marketing-society.org.uk

British Library Cataloguing in Publication Data
A catalogue record for this book is available from The British Library

ISBN: 978-0-9563959-1-7

Project managed by 26 Marketing, Bath
Designed by So Design Ltd, Bristol, UK
www.so-design.co.uk

Printed and bound by Butler Tanner and Dennis Ltd, Frome

Marketing Excellence 2 can be purchased for £45.00 via
The Marketing Society or from selected retailers and distributors.

Marketing Excellence 2

Award-winning companies reveal
the secrets of their success

in association with

sponsored by

Contents

As consumers become
more sophisticated
and demanding and the
media for communicating
with them ever more
diverse, the standards
for marketing excellence
change and in turn become
more demanding.

Roisin Donnelly,
President of The Marketing Society

Foreword

By Roisin Donnelly,
President of The Marketing Society

What is marketing excellence?

Roisin Donnelly
President of
The Marketing Society

Corporate Marketing
Director and Head of
Marketing at Procter &
Gamble UK and Ireland

Marketing excellence can drive breakthrough business results for the short and long term. Marketing excellence requires great strategic thinking, great creative thinking and perfect execution.

But how do we assess *marketing* excellence? First we choose brilliant industry judges who are all experienced and successful practitioners of excellence and we ask them to pick out the cases which they see as remarkable. We ask them to look for two key qualities from our winners: creativity and effectiveness.

But marketing continuously changes and evolves, as consumers become more sophisticated and demanding and the media for communicating with them ever more diverse. So the standards for marketing excellence change and in turn become more demanding.

We believe that The Marketing Society Awards for Excellence in association with *Marketing* set the standard of marketing excellence in the UK. They have established this reputation over a period of more than 25 years, and they have always been based on the principle of searching out the best examples of different marketing techniques in action, that showcase great strategic thinking, great creativity and perfect execution.

In order to be a winner of one of the Society's Awards, marketers have to demonstrate that what they have done is outstanding in comparison with marketing in all industries not just their own particular sector.

If a marketing story has been good enough to impress our judges, then all marketers can learn from it – however senior they have become. The collection of case histories brought together in this book is the best of the best from the past four years of our Awards, and I am confident that it truly demonstrates *marketing excellence*. I have been truly inspired by these case studies and I hope you will be too.

Introduction

By Hugh Burkitt
Chief Executive of The Marketing Society

The first volume of *Marketing Excellence* was published in 2006, and this second edition contains thirty four new case histories, selected from the last four years of The Marketing Society Awards for Excellence. Four years is a long time in marketing — about twice the average tenure of a marketing director — and it is instructive to reflect on how the marketing landscape has changed since our first edition.

The banking crisis of 2008 caused a shockwave to run through many markets. After a long period of boom, marketers had to get used to bust. But good marketers thrive in adversity and two of the case histories in this book are examples of an effective response to difficult times – Sainsbury's 'Feed Your Family for a Fiver' and Waitrose's introduction of its essentials range. Both not only worked tactically but also helped re-assure shoppers about the value for money of the whole store, and both, in different years, were winners of the Society's Grand Prix.

A more important long-term influence on all marketers has gathered pace in the past four years. There is now a consensus in society that we all need to live more "sustainable" lives. The release of Al Gore's film 'An Inconvenient Truth' in 2006 has had a major influence on this. Suddenly we were all aware that global warming caused by human behaviour was not just a possibility but a fact. Now the word 'sustainable' has supplanted words like 'ethical' and 'responsible' and we have a new category in our Awards for brands which can demonstrate that they have encouraged 'sustainable consumption'.

Sir Stuart Rose and his team at Marks & Spencer (M&S) were certainly influenced by Al Gore, and they have subsequently given an admirable lead. The story of M&S's journey towards their goal of becoming a completely sustainable business can be found in Chapter 11. There you will also find the story of Ariel's 'Turn to 30°' campaign which has helped reduce energy consumption in many UK households by encouraging consumers to wash at lower temperatures.

Another trend in marketing which has become more visible in the past four years is the increase in social marketing. Marketing skills are increasingly being used to encourage consumers to change their behaviour for the benefit of society. Chapter 10 on social marketing includes Channel 4's campaign with Jamie Oliver to raise the nutritional standard of school dinners, Keep Britain Tidy discouraging young men from making a pig of themselves with fast food litter, and the British Heart Foundation encouraging teenagers to avoid obesity through the slightly ironic medium of an online game.

Hugh Burkitt
Chief Executive of
The Marketing Society

The last four years has seen a steady increase in the importance of the internet as a medium of communication and as a channel for trading directly with the public. Examples in this edition include ebookers brand re-launch and Walkers' online invitation to their customers to invent new crisp flavours.

As well as some new trends we can also see some fine examples of long running brands that have sustained their brand promise. In Chapter 5, two leading brands celebrate their success over 25 years: Audi gives an impressive account of how they have steadily pulled away from their competitors in the premium car market and Virgin Atlantic tells us how they are 'Still Red Hot'.

The last four years has also seen some great recovery stories. Perhaps the most impressive of these is McDonald's whose brand was under major attack four years ago, following the film 'Supersize Me'. You can read how it tackled every part of its marketing mix to put it back on track with consumers in Chapter 4 on brand revitalisation. It also re-examined the brand from an internal perspective and you can discover how it improved staff motivation in Chapter 9 which discusses Getting into Shape for Good Marketing.

New brands which have been winners during this period include Magners Cider which transformed a previously moribund category by encouraging consumers to drink cider over ice; and Change4Life which was introduced by the Department of Health as a new kind of brand which different partners could join to encourage a healthier lifestyle.

If I am allowed a personal favourite story in this book it would be O_2's brilliantly successful brand extension into the world of live music via the previously excoriated Millennium Dome. This achieved the commendable double whammy of strengthening the brand loyalty of O_2 customers and creating a new world-class music venue that made proper use of Richard Rodgers' iconic building. And I must also profess a personal enthusiasm for More Th>n's success in creating greater customer loyalty by offering that wonderfully old-fashioned concept — a personal claims manager! How often recently have I wept tears of frustration at having to deal with automated and impersonal call centres.

Finally, for those marketers concerned with business-to-business marketing excellence there are three fine examples in this book. UPS offered its shipping manager customers a downloadable "lovable, hardworking helper"; BT Business provides a model example of the role of customer insight; and Thinkbox recounts how it persuaded cynical marketers and media buyers that television is still the most effective advertising medium.

To help draw out the lessons from our case histories we have been fortunate to have the comments of eleven leading marketing directors who have judged the Awards. They were chosen because they are all successful marketers and their comments show that they have found reading these cases a rewarding exercise. I am sure that you will too.

Hugh Burkitt, Chief Executive Officer,
The Marketing Society

Acknowledgements

On behalf of the Society I would like to thank all the companies and agencies who have allowed us to publish their winning entries. We have occasionally been asked to omit some sensitive financial data, but in all of the cases which we have selected, the marketing problem, the solution and the success come across clearly. While we have used the original submissions as the basis for the case studies, we have reworked, edited, embellished and in some cases updated them to transform them into case studies suitable for the book. A complete list of winning companies, their agencies and the awards won is included in the Appendix.

The Marketing Society's partner for more than a decade has been *Marketing* magazine, and we are grateful to all the team at Haymarket who have helped us build the scope and stature of the awards during this time.

We could not have put this book together without the support of Jan Gooding of Aviva and Suzi Williams of BT, who have kindly sponsored its production.

Laura Mazur of Writers4Management has done a brilliant job in persuading the entrants to part with their material, chasing up the illustrations and editing the final manuscript in a timely and thoughtful manner. Ann Gould of 26 Marketing has kept us all to schedule, and Claire Watson has made it financially possible. Thanks also to Gemma Greaves and Sharon Conway from The Marketing Society for all their valued input.

The original "editors" of this book are, of course, the judges who choose the winners in each year. We are very grateful to all of them for the time they have given during the awards process each year, and especially so to those who have added their comments at the beginning of each chapter.

We would also like to thank all those who have entered the Marketing Society Awards for Excellence in association with Marketing in the past four years. There have been many excellent cases written, which we have not had space to include. Without these entries there would have been no competition.

We also extend our thanks, in anticipation, to our readers. If you can draw lessons from these cases that help you develop your own marketing success story, then you will be helping us prove that marketing excellence is indeed a key driver of business growth.

Chapter 1
Customer Insight

Fiona McAnena
Brand Director,
Bupa Group

An insight is never an end in itself. An insight is only an insight if you are able to do something with it. At Bupa we define an insight as 'an enlightening discovery of people's underlying needs and motivations that our business can address to create customer value and competitive advantage'.

There are a number of key words in there. Insight has to be enlightening. It has to discover underlying needs. And it has to be something we can address. Too often people come along and say they have so much 'insight'. But what they have is so much information.

What these three case studies highlight is that with almost any big piece of data analysis or market research you end up with only a few critical things to act on. They all discovered a lot of things along the way which were true but then turned out to offer a false promise because they wouldn't lead to effective action. So they kept digging — because the best insights never come easily.

For example, NHS Blood and Transplant experienced a number of false dawns in trying to get more people to sign up to the organ donor register. They finally made the enlightening discovery which the organisation could address: that people responded not to guilt but to understanding the potential benefits for themselves of receiving a donated organ if they needed one.

Sky thought if it explained the benefits of Sky+ it could persuade people to sign up to it. Well, it didn't work. Potential customers only listened to other customers about how good the service was. Sky's insight was that it had to 'tell, not sell'.

BT Business found that IT isn't important to small businesses — until it goes wrong. But it didn't use that to try and preach to small businesses. Instead, it chose to work with the right insight — which is that small businesses are passionate about what they do and BT Business can help them fulfil their dreams. This was not only true but it connected emotionally. BT Business was big enough to understand its true place in its customers' lives.

You have to keep digging to get real insights. It won't be those which seem powerful and game-changing to you. It will be those which resonate emotionally with the customer.

Sky+

01

Finding the right route to an elusive audience

Snapshot

Customer insight helped Sky engage successfully with a new and hard-to-reach audience for the Sky+ brand.

Key insights

- The compelling insight that Sky gained about its new target audience — that it resisted the hard sell — formed the basis of a demonstrably effective campaign.

- Using celebrities who would resonate with this audience to enthuse in their own words about the brand set the right tone.

- Tying this all up into a multi-channel, integrated campaign made the whole far more than the sum of its parts.

Summary

Sky operates the most comprehensive multi-channel television service in the UK and Ireland, offering movies, news, entertainment and sports channels and interactive services on Sky digital to over 9.7 million households. One of its major services is Sky+, a personal video recorder launched in 2001, which allows up to 40 hours of TV to be recorded and watched later.

This case study shows how Sky was able to appeal to a new audience by understanding that sometimes it is more powerful to get your customers to tell your story. Face-to-face sessions with customers revealed how much more compelling advocacy can be over a conventional brand selling approach. The company replicated this powerful tool by using celebrity testimonials to accelerate advocacy and get people talking about Sky+ through a multi-channel, integrated campaign.

The campaign brought a new audience to the channel and produced the strongest fourth quarter net additions in five years.

Coping with a changing market

At the beginning of 2008, Sky had just under nine million customers. With a public target of 10 million customers by 2010, there was a lot to play for. But with the growth of the Freeview base to over 14 million households, convincing people to pay for TV was becoming increasingly challenging. (Launched in October 2002, the Freeview service provides free-to-air digital TV channels, radio stations and interactive services through an aerial. It is owned and run by its five shareholders — BBC, BSkyB, Channel 4, ITV and Arqiva.)

In 2007, the value-driven sales message of 'See, Speak, Surf' promoting broadband and talk alongside TV had successfully grown Sky's market share. But the company could no longer rely on value alone to attract new customers. Appealing to a new, harder-to-reach audience was essential in order to achieve its targets.

Research indicated that many Freeviewers did not think that Sky was relevant to them. They saw Sky as delivering 'more TV' rather than 'better TV'. Moreover, they were already satisfied with their free digital channels.

The demographic profile of available customers was also changing. In particular, there was a group of older 55+ Freeviewers. They were harder to reach, with more barriers to advertising and to the Sky brand. The company worked closely with Dr Ken Dychtwald, an expert on ageing-related issues, to understand how to engage them. They appreciated authenticity and ideas that reflected their lives. They rejected complex and metaphorical creative concepts, but were also patronised by ads that they felt were too obviously targeted at their generation. More than anything, they valued things that were useful rather than wasteful.

So Sky needed to find an approach that would make the service relevant to their lives. A quantitative study was designed to understand the key barriers and conversion triggers that could move Freeviewers to consider the service. Sky+ was found to be one of the most efficient triggers. It would revolutionise how they watched TV and help them feel more in control of their viewing.

Rethinking the marketing of Sky and Sky+

Since its launch in 2001, Sky+, a personal video recorder which allows up to 40 hours of TV to be watched and recorded later, had been an incredibly successful product for the company. In March 2008, just over a third of Sky households had Sky+. However, if portraying the benefits of Sky+ to its own customers was difficult, attracting new customers to Sky through Sky+ would be even harder. Sky had always struggled to unlock its attractions in a large-scale marketing campaign. The company knew from the enthusiasm of existing Sky+ customers that it was indeed a life-changing product, but had never been able to convey its magic to potential customers. There was thus a mismatch between high levels of customer satisfaction and unfulfilled sales potential.

The way it was

In the past, Sky had adopted two different marketing strategies.

- The technological benefits. In 2006, as part of the 'What do you want to watch?' campaign, clips of content were paused, rewound and fast-forwarded to illustrate the benefits of Sky+. But this did little to demonstrate the true capabilities of the service. It succeeded in communicating the functional benefits, but failed to highlight lifestyle benefits.
- The social benefits. In 2007, the 'Brain' campaign was designed to emphasise the emotional benefits

of control by showing how you can carry on your life without missing your favourite programme. But this over-stated the importance of television in people's lives: people didn't want to admit that TV was a greater priority than their social life.

The company thus needed to find a way that would balance the lifestyle benefits with the technological benefits, be simple and motivating and which would create desire for the product, while also showing how easy it was to use, particularly for an older audience.

Digging deeper to find the right answer

There was a paradox at the heart of the problem. Anyone who had Sky+ would tell you how it had revolutionised their life. But anyone who didn't have Sky+ couldn't see what all the fuss was about. Therefore, to get under the skin of what it was the owners loved about it, the company asked them (Figure 1).

Their stories were a combination of social and technological benefits, but it was the personal touches, enthusiasm and language that brought the benefits of Sky+ to life. The real breakthrough came, however, when the company carried out some 'customer closeness research'. Sky regularly held these sessions to give executives the opportunity to talk face-to-face with customers and prospects.

The research session was split into two halves. In the first half, Sky executives had the opportunity to explain the benefits of Sky to 55+ Freeview prospects. Nevertheless, the Freeviewers remained unmoved. In the second half, Sky customers were asked to explain the benefits of Sky and Sky+ to the Freeviewers. The mood of the room changed instantly. The customers were able to give the

Freeviewers real examples of how they used Sky+ and how it had improved their lives. By the end of the session, the Freeviewers wanted to know where they could sign up.

The power of advocacy

The solution became clear to Sky: tell, not sell. The most powerful approach would be to get customers to be advocates.

In the past, the company had encouraged customers to tell their friends on a smaller scale with a 'member-get-member' scheme which had proved very successful. In fact, before the campaign, 20% of Sky+ boxes had been sold by existing customers. This effort needed to be given a boost by broadcasting it. However, because a campaign using customers would not give the impact needed, the company decided to use celebrities to get people talking.

Sky had a major advantage: many celebrities had Sky+ because of their busy lives, and spontaneously praised the service in public. Celebrities were also a much easier way to have a conversation with 55+ Freeviewers. They were cynical about advertising messages, so the company sought to create a campaign that would feel more like a relaxed conversation with someone they respected. This mixed the impact of celebrity with the credibility of advocacy.

The celebrities selected were genuine Sky+ customers. They were real advocates and enjoyed the status of 'national treasures' as some of the country's best-loved celebrities and could reflect Sky's British heritage. Those chosen were straightforward, down-to-earth and whose point of view would be respected. In addition, the company chose celebrities

My mum phones every Sunday evening. I like to watch a film on Sunday evening. My mum can sense exactly when I start watching the film and calls me. I can pause TV now. I win.

It means I get to replay the goals from the Arsenal game as soon as I get home from watching the match live at the ground.

Series link is amazing. It makes hangovers fun. I can crawl to the sofa with my duvet and watch American Idol, Dragon's Den, Ramsay's Kitchen Nightmares USA or something like that...

It has meant I get to see my oldest son more — now he tapes his favorite programme (Rugby Club) and spends more time at home on Sunday afternoon watching it with me when he's back from (boarding) school...

It means I can watch the right programme to suit my mood — e.g. comfort food TV when late home after work, a good drama when I'm home early enough to watch something with Liz, two back-to back episodes of Uni Challenge if we want a quiz night...

My sister uses hers to rewind crime dramas to check if the clues were there the first time. Sad I know, but she's a solicitor.

I no longer have to watch ads. That buys me a good 15 mins in each hour of programming. I'm a typical 16 hours of telly a week guy (an hour or two each night and maybe more at the weekend) — that means I recoup four hours of my life each week through Sky+. Since I got it a year ago, that works out at 208 hours or almost 8.66 days. So Sky+ has effectively given me an extra week of holiday — what single thing bar teleportation can give me so much additional free time?

Figure 1. How does Sky+ change peoples lives?
Source: WCRS Qualitative

who hadn't done many other ads to emphasise their genuine enthusiasm for the service. They were the kind of people the target audience would love to have a chat with: Sir Michael Parkinson, Ross Kemp, Mariella Frostrup, Felicity Kendall and Kelly Brook.

There was also an analysis carried out of testimonial campaigns to establish the rules of how best to deliver the campaign (Figure 2).

GOOD		BAD
Real customer and advocate	NOT	Customer spokesperson
Natural conversation (from the heart)	NOT	Forced script
Human benefit of the product	NOT	Product attributes
My story	NOT	Product sell
Entertaining	NOT	Informing

Figure 2. What makes a good testimonial?

The creative and tonal approach chosen was deliberately 'un-Sky'. In the past, Sky communications had been quite information-rich and slick. The company purposely adopted a quieter and more pragmatic style. The intention was not to 'sell' the product, but to have celebrities genuinely enthuse about it.

To ensure authenticity, the celebrity interviews were completely unscripted. The company knew neither what they would say, or how they would say it. While this was a leap of faith for the company, it realised that their words would be more powerful than any words written for them.

The print ads were also designed to be simple and clean. The company realised that many people were worried that Sky+ would be too technological and complex to use, so the body language and campaign

message were designed to overcome this barrier (Figure 3).

Figure 3. The Sky+ campaign

A consistent and integrated approach

The media strategy was to target two key groups:

1. Three million Sky+ customers: the company realised that the best form of advertising would be to stimulate existing customers to evangelise about their love of the product.

2. Freeviewers: particularly focusing on the 55+ age group.

The campaign was integrated through-the-line and used TV, outdoor, national radio promotion (where Sky+ customers were encouraged to call in and speak to radio presenters about the benefits of Sky+), direct door drops, press, media inserts, online activity, public relations, point-of-sale and internal communications.

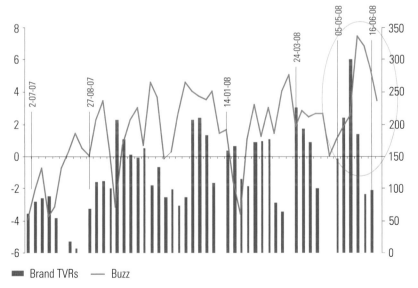

8

6

4

2

0

-2

-4

-6

2-07-07   27-08-07   14-01-08   24-03-08   05-05-08   16-06-08

350

300

250

200

150

100

50

0

■ Brand TVRs   — Buzz

Figure 4. Sky+ campaign created significant positive buzz around the Sky brand. Source: YouGov/Brand Index

Achieving record results

The campaign transformed the fortunes of the brand in a number of critical ways.

1. The campaign helped Sky to have its strongest final quarter in five years. Running for the majority of the fourth quarter in 2006, it was instrumental in helping Sky produce its strongest fourth-quarter net additions in five years. This was attributed to the success of the Sky+ advocacy campaign, which contributed more than 321,000 quarterly net Sky+ additions — only the third time ever that Sky had achieved such strong results.

2. The campaign changed perceptions of the Sky brand. The fresh, tonal approach of the campaign helped people to see Sky in a new way. Following the campaign the company saw statistically significant increases in the following measures:
   • "Sky makes life easier for its customers".
   • "Sky has the best technology".

   In qualitative groups following the campaign, people picked up on that change of tone: "It's not at all what you'd expect from Sky. It's much quieter, but it's much more likely to get my attention".

3. The campaign created unprecedented 'buzz' for Sky. An independent YouGov survey showed a significant increase in buzz for the brand during the campaign period (Figure 4), suggesting that the campaign was successful in creating accelerated advocacy. It also achieved high level of awareness.

4. The 'advocacy' approach attracted a new audience to Sky. Crucially, a record 55% of Sky+ additions were new to Sky (the highest number of new additions ever in a quarter, proving that the fresh

tonal approach appealed to a new base of customers). The appeal of Sky+ was clearly the driver as the proportion of new customers taking the service increased by 31% during the campaign. The brand also managed to attract the 55+ audience. At the start of the campaign there was a 90% increase in new customers who were 55+. By July 2008, 30% of all new additions were 55+.

5. The campaign strengthened the company's relationship with its customers. The number of customers intending to purchase Sky+ increased from 38% to 51% during the campaign period, and agreement with "Sky cares about its customers" and "..is a company I trust" increased. Sky+ was also an excellent retention tool: research showed that churn levels in Sky+ households were between 30-50% below average.

6. It was the most efficient campaign of the last two years. It achieved the lowest cost per acquisition (CPA) of all brand campaigns over the last two years and clearly out-performed the previous Sky+ campaign, 'Brain' (Figure 5). The campaign performed strongly across all media, showing the benefits of the integrated approach. There was also a direct correlation between media spend and additions (Figure 6).

Rewarding return on investment

Based on the proportion of new subscribers to Sky supported by the Sky+ campaign, the company stood to gain in the region of £100-plus million of additional revenue in the first year alone. This didn't include additional revenue gained from current Sky customers upgrading to Sky+ or the lifetime value of Sky+ customers, which is considerably higher than regular Sky customers because of lower churn rates. Based on this data alone, the total brand campaign more than paid for itself tenfold.

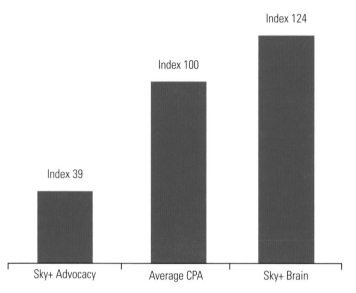

Figure 5. Sky+ advocacy had the lowest CPA of all brand campaigns in the last 2 years
Source: Marketing Strategy, September 2008

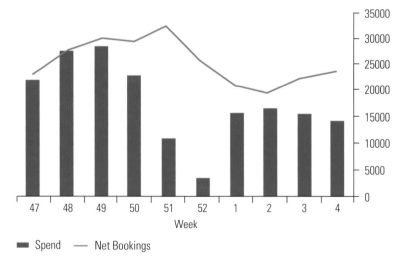

Figure 6. Net bookings vs marketing spend (brand, direct, online) during Sky+ advocacy
Source: Marketing Strategy, September 2008

All images appearing in this case study are reproduced by permission of Sky.

BT Business

01

Getting real-life people to make a real difference to the brand

Snapshot

A simple insight, articulated in a fully-integrated campaign, 'Do what you do best', revitalised BT Business and put it firmly on the SME map.

Key insights

- The determination to make BT Business the preferred partner for the IT needs of small and medium-sized businesses (SMEs) demanded turning current perceptions of the brand — very big and only in telecoms — upside down.

- Using real-life entrepreneurs in the communications captured the emotion and passion SME owners felt about their business and positioned technology as an enabler rather than something confusing and time-consuming.

- This proved to be the catalyst for changing attitudes to BT Business, building consideration of BT Business as an IT and communications provider by a significant 24 percentage points.

Summary

BT Business is part of BT Retail, itself part of the BT Group, one of the world's leading providers of communications solutions and services. The company was determined to become the partner of choice among SMEs for their information technology needs. But SMEs still saw BT Business as a telecommunications company that was too big to be relevant to them.

BT Business had to shift perceptions convincingly enough to grab the attention of these companies and become the preferred partner in a market worth £24.4 billion. Previous campaigns had achieved some increase in consideration of BT Business beyond telecoms but this had reached a plateau. A step change was needed. The resulting fully-integrated campaign using real entrepreneurs was a resounding success. Based on the insight that these customers wanted to pursue the passion that had taken them into business in the first place rather than worry about IT, it positioned BT Business as the best partner in finding the right solutions.

The campaign delivered impressive results — in particular, the rise in spontaneous brand consideration in IT and communications, which shifted from 33% to 58% in just over one year. It also increased positive perceptions of the BT brand overall.

Understanding the market basics

Technology was proving a double-edged sword for small and medium-sized businesses (SMEs). On the one hand it promised real commercial opportunities. On the other, it threatened to confuse and destabilise them. There was a world of IT applications and services that SMEs felt vaguely aware of but they didn't know where to start. The proliferation and convergence of services being offered by multiple providers were understandably causing these businesses to question whether they were making the right decisions, or who was best placed to help them.

Becoming the SME's first choice would prove highly lucrative to BT Business in a fiercely competitive market worth £24.4 billion. It would enable the company to retain existing customers, increase average revenue per user and acquire new customers.

To seize this opportunity, the company needed to address three significant problems:
• SMEs still saw BT Business as just a telecoms and broadband supplier. Therefore the challenge was to make them sit up and take notice of what BT Business could do for their business.
• SMEs did not find IT interesting, so they didn't spend much time thinking about or researching it unless something went wrong. This was a drain on resources, both in terms of costs and people.
• Sales people were coming up against scepticism among SMEs that BT Business could handle their IT needs.

Due to years of heritage and personal experience, SMEs still thought of BT Business as the big, reliable telco supplier. This was going to be a difficult perception to shift. Previous campaigns had achieved some increase in consideration of BT Business

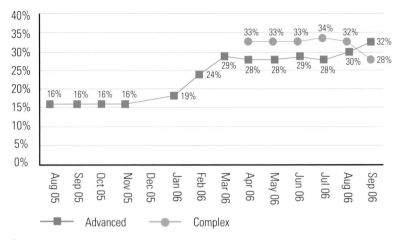

Figure 1

beyond telecoms, but this had reached a plateau. Figure 1 shows broadband consideration before the new campaign, where 'advanced' are mid-sized companies and 'complex' are larger organisations with more than 100 employees.

Choosing the best approach

Three key objectives were identified:
• Shift perceptions of BT Business from a telco to an IT and communications supplier.
• Create empathy with SMEs to show how BT Business could become an enabler, freeing them up from IT hassle.
• Generate a platform for change within the business itself.

The decision to make a step change in how SMEs saw BT Business meant that the company had to act very differently. The pillars of this new approach were:
a) Base everything on what the customers were interested in.
b) Seamless campaign integration.

A qualitative research programme found that, despite their self-professed distinctiveness, there were two common insights that applied to all SMEs. First, it took time, expertise and resources they didn't have. Just because IT and communications were important didn't mean they wanted to focus on them. So an approach that thrust technology in the face of SMEs wasn't going to work if BT Business wanted to be seen as a true partner.

Secondly, behind all stories of the tough times SMEs were having, what characterised them all were the passion, focus and dedication that it takes to succeed in small business. If the company was to make a real connection with SMEs, it needed to capture this emotion and passion of being in business. No one re-mortgaged their house or put their children's inheritance on the line to worry about their broadband lines. They did it because they had a vision.

Based on these two insights, BT Business saw an opportunity to play a genuinely useful role in helping SMEs. This would not be about the big company telling the little company how to do business. But it could be about acting as an enabler to their business success and become, for them, the company that looks after their IT and communications needs so that they could get on with what they loved about being in business.

Finding the perfect solution

The company decided to mount a major communications campaign to signify to the whole SME community (and not just BT Business customers) and its internal staff that BT Business was deadly serious about this major transformation.

A range of ideas was developed and tested with customers. Ultimately, the assertion that BT Business can help you 'Do what you do best' was seen as a perfect short cut to the insight, expressed in customer language. Research found the 'Do what you do best'

message was one that resonated in the hearts of all SMEs, being a powerful distillation of what they all fundamentally believe business success to be about.

It also struck the right note with the internal audience. BT Local Businesses, the principal channel to market for the target audience, saw it as expressing something that was important to their customers and as an aspirational statement about their own role. So they also recognised how this insight could turn sales conversations from being product-led to customer-led. Again, research found that for BT Business staff, this focus on success implied that 'helping business work' is what it did best. The result was real staff buy-in to an idea that enhanced the offer and empowered them to become valuable service providers.

Resonating with the audience

The best embodiment of this idea was to feature real-life successful SME owners who had worked their way up, had a genuine passion for business, were known as hands-on types and were growing and innovating.

The launch work, for example, featured Michelin-starred chef Gordon Ramsay, and was a general repositioning statement, supported by specific product messages (Figure 2). The second phase used Dragons'

Figure 2. Gordon Ramsay

Den star Peter Jones and showed how BT Business could liberate SMEs from IT 'gremlins' through 24/7 support and broadband reliability (Figure 3). This insight-driven approach was very different from the previous 'digital networked economy' campaign which centred on pushing products rather than trying to create a brand pull.

The £18.2 million above-the-line campaign redefined the position of BT Business in the minds of SMEs. TV, press, radio, and online advertising were supported by a microsite on bt.com, where the navigation was based on customer need and added depth of meaning to how BT Business really could help customers 'Do what they do best'. The campaign focused on reasons-to-believe provided by the IT manager proposition: a breakdown recovery service for IT which got the SME back to doing what it did best quickly. This was backed up by significant direct and electronic direct marketing.

Public relations (PR) was also a key pillar, with the development of major platforms such as Small Business Week, where customers were given the tools and advice they needed to do what they did best. But 'Do what you do best' was not just a communications campaign. It came alive in an innovative content programme which included a number of new offerings:

- *Upload*, a free offline and online magazine giving SMEs access to successful peers and industry experts who could help them get more out of their businesses.
- This publication was supported by Business Insight — an online tool providing guidance to SMEs based around what they wanted to achieve in their business (for example, move or grow it).

In addition, a completely new approach to the internal audience was adopted, with sales staff included as an integral part of the campaign launch. This led to the development of the online and offline 'Customer Dialogues' programme, which enabled the front-line sales teams to have customer-led conversations to help SMEs choose solutions that enabled them to 'Do what they do best'. In parallel to this, and to encourage adoption of the solutions-selling approach, a new communications programme, '4Sales' was launched with the sales community.

Figure 3. Peter Jones

This campaign was supported with internal communications engaging all 3,000 of the BT Business audience by explaining how they were critical to proving that BT Business could help customers 'Do what they do best'. Humorous viral featuring the BT Business managing director enabled the company to engage staff with the message. This was followed up with a booklet explaining how BT Business values could help staff customers 'Do what they do best'.

Reaching new heights of performance

As this was a repositioning campaign, the company focused on three principle sources of evaluation to track against its objectives:
1. Awareness and consideration of BT Business as a supplier of IT and communications.
2. Engagement with BT Business.
3. Staff engagement.

Underlying those objectives there was a series of key performance indicators (KPIs) based on pre-campaign tracking and business advertising benchmarks.

The campaign proved to be an extraordinary success, exceeding every one of its pre-set KPIs — in some cases by a factor of 10. Not only did spontaneous brand awareness (SBA) in IT and communications rise from 51% to 68%, but the most impressive result was the rise in spontaneous brand consideration (SBC), which shifted from 33% to 58% in just over one year, a significant achievement for an established brand such as BT Business (Figure 4).

Table 1 shows the actual results achieved against all key performance indicators (KPI).

	KPI objective	Actual result
Spontaneous brand awareness	60% (from 51%)	68%
Spontaneous brand consideration	43% (from 33%)	58%
Message take-out	60%	66%
Relevance	50%	59%
Visits to bt.com	+10%	>+50%
Campaign micro-site traffic	14,414 visits	160,000 visits

Table 1. KPIs vs. actual results achieved
Source: RSM Brand Tracker

The campaign also proved to have a fundamental effect on perceptions of the BT brand as a whole. Figure 5 demonstrates the increases in brand attributes across the board.

Increased awareness, consideration and favourability resulted in action. In tracking, 18% of SMEs claimed they had taken action as a direct result of the campaign (either talked to a colleague or contacted BT Business). The power of the campaign was also demonstrated through the fact that the sales people were enabled to have more and better conversations with customers. In February 2008, the company interviewed the managing directors of half the local

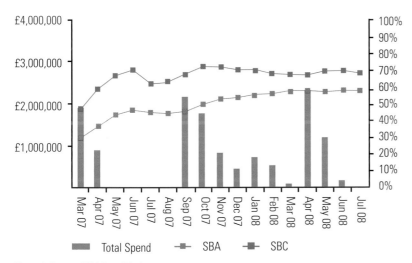

Figure 4. Source: RSM Brand Tracker

business base to gauge the impact of the campaign:
- 18/32 had had more enquiries since the campaign started.
- 24/32 said that businesses were interested in finding out more about the company's IT services as opposed to calls, lines and broadband.

Positive staff response

The following quotations reflect how positively the campaign was received internally:
- *"Customers are more open to hearing about what additional services we offer in the IT space."*
- *"It means improved credibility when speaking to customers."*

A correlation was also found between the spending on this campaign and broadband market share — crucial to growth. The campaign helped bolster broadband consideration dramatically which, in turn, increased market share (Figure 6).

Making the most of PR

The accompanying PR push also bore significant fruit. The campaign — in the spirit of imitation being the sincerest form of flattery — was spoofed by Rory Bremner, who showed Gordon Ramsay being distracted from what he does best by the pressures of running a multi-million pound business, not to mention starring in a BT ad.

Integrated PR platforms were also conceived to extend the campaign to the media, customers and other stakeholders.

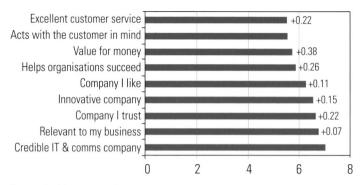

Figure 5. Ranking on score of 1-10
Source: RSM Tracker (results without numbers are new scores)

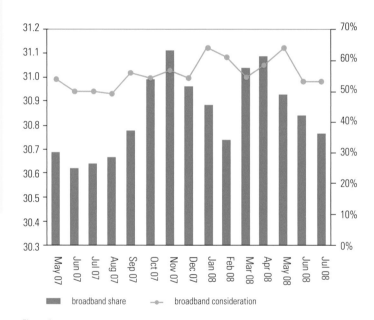

Figure 6

- The BT Business Experience was a week-long media, analyst and customer event held in London. As a physical manifestation of BT Business enabling businesses to do what they do best, customers could discuss with key BT Business representatives the challenges they faced and experience 'live' zones demonstrating BT Business services and their potential impact on their ability to compete and thrive. The event attracted over 1,000 customers and generated over £30 million in sales leads. Key media announcements surrounding the event, including the launch of the Peter Jones ads, attracted media coverage at an advertising equivalent of over £3 million. The event was translated into an online virtual tour, and became an enduring and valuable brand asset.

- Small Business Week brought together a coalition of public and private sector organisations, committing publicly to championing SMEs in the UK and enabling them to do what they do best. Over 350 pieces of media coverage, with 5.5 hours of broadcast coverage on launch day (advertising equivalent value of over £3.5 million) were generated along with whole-hearted support from a myriad of public and private sector stakeholders, including the-then Conservative Party enterprise spokesman Mark Prisk MP, who set out new VAT policies for small businesses at the event.

Crucially, not only did the campaign help reposition the brand for the future, but it has also had a short-term effect in terms of boosting BT's 'business as usual' product advertising. There was an increase of 20% in terms of response to the direct marketing activity while the campaign was on air. Meanwhile, as consideration rose, cost per response (CPR) to online advertising dropped by 30% and to press by an even more impressive 50%. Of course, other factors affect cost per response like the economy, competitive activity, refined media selection and the quality of the offer itself, but the trend was marked and consistent enough to imply a clear correlation.

That this was achieved for such an established brand and one associated 'just' with telecoms, highlights the power of the 'Do what you do best' idea — an idea that grew far beyond a tagline to become the central organising idea for the whole company.

NHS Blood and Transplant

01

Inspiring people to do the right thing

Snapshot

A campaign based on remarkable insights into the contradictions people feel about registering as organ donors dramatically changed attitudes to this difficult issue.

Key insights

- Getting people to reveal their true feelings about registering to be organ donors showed that focus groups only deliver reliable insights if the right questions are asked.

- Turning the tables by asking people if they would want an organ transplant if they needed one highlighted the confusion most people felt about such a sensitive issue.

- Playing on this 'right' sort of guilt kick-started a very successful campaign.

Summary

The National Health Service Blood and Transplant (NHSBT) was established to oversee the provision of a reliable, efficient supply of blood, organs and associated services to the NHS. Because the UK has one of the lowest rates of organ donation in Europe, there are 8,000 people registered for a transplant who face the dilemma of having to wait for an organ. 1,000 people die every year while waiting for a donor organ to become available.

To improve these shocking statistics the government set the NHS a target to increase the number of people registered with the Organ Donor Register (ODR) from 16 million to 25 million by 2013 — an extra nine million registrations in three years. To achieve this, the NHSBT commissioned a campaign to increase awareness and support of organ donation as an issue and convert this support into registrations.

Building the campaign on the insight that people give because they want to receive produced remarkable results. In the first five weeks the campaign generated 128,218 completed registrations, exceeding the estimated target by over 400%.

Setting the scene

The task was formidable. The UK had one of the lowest rates of organ donation in Europe. As a result there were 8,000 people waiting for a transplant, with 1,000 sadly dying before one became available. The NHSBT needed to boost the number of registrations on the ODR from 16 million to 25 million by 2013 — an extra nine million registrations in only three years. The specific goal was to generate 37,600 registrations in the first five weeks alone. This meant the campaign would have to be eight times more effective than the average health advertising campaign.

Quantitative research revealed that 90% of people in the UK said that they were 'in favour of organ donation' although only 27% had registered with the ODR. Interestingly, it was found that the main barriers to registration were largely rational: "I don't know how to", "I hadn't thought about it", "I didn't know about the ODR". So it looked at first sight that the campaign could be quite straightforward: remind the 63% of adults 'in favour' but not on the register to register. As one man pointed out in groups, "You don't wake up every morning thinking I must register to be an organ donor today".

Discovering a not-so-simple truth

So groups were held where respondents were set a simple task: to write down how they felt when they were told: "I just want you to register to donate your organs, today". This, it was felt, would create a sense of urgency and push them to do it. This, however, wasn't the reaction. Instead of agreeing it was a good idea, people were horrified and felt under pressure.

It turned out that thinking about organ donation was anything but straightforward. Instead, that question unlocked deeper and unsettling emotions about the idea of death and tempting fate. People needed to be given a more compelling reason why they should donate their organs.

More groups, representative of the British public, were then recruited to explore other possible approaches. At first, it looked as though guilt about the fact that three people were dying every day because of a lack of organs would be a powerful motivation. While this shocked people and struck a chord with them about the importance of organ donation, it also unlocked a 'bad guilt' which left people feeling angry that they seemed to be unfairly blamed for people dying.

After all, organ donation isn't like giving blood where the donation can help save lives straight away. With organ donation you need to die before your organs can be used, so it's unlikely your registration will help people on the register today. So while guilt was indeed a powerful emotion, it had to be the right sort of guilt: guilt about not being on the register.

So a different approach was tried: what about making people feel good about saving lives and leaving a legacy? After all, there is no better gift you can leave than the gift of life. While this resonated with people, it only put organ donation on the 'list of things to do before I die'. It lacked any sense of urgency.

Delving deeper found some submerged but strong superstitions. Seemingly rational people would say things like, "Well, I want to be buried whole, not walking around in heaven with my organs missing". These superstitions were confronted head-on by pointing out that they would be dead, and therefore didn't really need their organs. Although, when challenged, people agreed they were being irrational, these beliefs were so deep-set that they were simply not something that could be changed overnight.

Cracking the code

The fact that it had already been established that 90% of people were 'in favour' of organ donation and yet were so reluctant to register was a puzzle. A psychologist was brought in to try and explain what was happening. His story about vampire bats transformed the campaign approach.

Group help

Vampire bats need to feed on blood every two days or they will die. They get blood from other bats who regurgitate it for them. Because access to blood is vital, it seems vampire bats have decided it is in their interest to feed any bat in the colony, not just family members, even though that bat may not feed them in return. However, by feeding any bat, they are actually widening the pool of potential feeder bats, improving their chance of getting fed in return. This is known as reciprocal altruism.

Using the bats as a metaphor, the thinking changed to whether it would make more sense not to ask people if they would be willing to donate an organ, but would they be willing to *receive* one. Asking people in groups that simple question produced a response that was both surprising and uncomfortable to watch. Not only did people say that yes, of course they would take one but, as they answered the question they started to squirm, quite literally, and giggle nervously as the hypocrisy of their answer dawned on them.

As soon as they realised what was in it for them, their consciences got the better of them. After all, if they were prepared to receive an organ, shouldn't they be prepared to donate one? This had resonated with their inherent sense of fairness. Organ donation is not like charity where giving makes you feel good. It's about reciprocity. You give because you hope that when the time comes, you will receive. And research backed that up: 96% of people agreed that 'if they needed an organ they would take one'. This was not only the 'right' guilt, but it pointed the way to getting people to register.

Striking a dramatic tone

The campaign dramatised the contradictory nature of the issue: that if one of their loved ones needed a transplant, they would gladly take an organ yet would make excuses to put off registering. The campaign line 'If you believe in organ donation, prove it', posed a challenge to the viewers because the moment they answered 'yes' it would be very hard to argue against registering. This strategy also offered a new public relations (PR) angle to exploit: exposing the statistics behind the hypocrisy — that 96% of us are willing to take an organ yet only 27% are registered. This created a ripple effect across media channels, generating discussions about whether people would accept an organ or not and whether this reflected the attitudes of our society.

Figures 1 and 2 are examples of the press campaign, while Figure 3 shows some stills from the TV execution.

A key part of securing registrations was to give people time to connect with the subject, to talk about it with family or friends, but then 'act' by registering

Figures 1 and 2. Examples of the press campaign

Figure 3. Stills from the TV execution

as quickly as possible, before they talked themselves out of it. That led to a two-pronged media strategy: first to get consumers to 'connect' with the issue among friends and family; then to 'act'. The 'connect' phase involved 30-second TV ads in key media spots that attracted a captive family audience (e.g. Emmerdale, Murderland, ITV news) and large full-page press ads in the tabloids and broadsheets.

The 'act' phase converted intention into registrations as fast as possible, utilising online banners, pre-roll video ads, small-space press and 10-second reminder TV ads to prompt action. In addition, the website was streamlined and simplified to ensure registration could be completed in just two pages.

Surpassing targets

In the first five weeks the campaign achieved a total 187,820 responses, which converted into 128,218 completed registrations, beating the estimated target by over 400%. The advertising was well-recognised and achieved a prompted campaign awareness of 60% among adults, with 57% seeing two to five media channels. Importantly, strong support for organ donation as an issue increased from 36% to 54% among those who had seen the campaign.

The PR from the campaign generated an additional 110,851,094 opportunities-to-see (OTS) and the total coverage of the issue generated a total of 326,940,322 OTS.

All images appearing in this case study are reproduced by permission of NHSBT.

Chapter 2
Launching New Brands

Pete Markey
Marketing Director,
More Th>n

Launching a new brand is an exciting prospect for any marketer, and yet it is also one of the most challenging areas of marketing today. With the recession still very fresh in our minds, the potential risks and challenges to launching new brands in tough market conditions are more real than ever.

The three case studies in this section provide inspiring content, where marketing is seen as the engine room of success for the business. All of them faced seemingly impossible challenges in their target markets: for Magners, a declining market written off by experts, for Change4Life, the increasing national slide into obesity and for alli the launch of a new product into a highly sensitive market.

All three case studies show marketing at its best. All used solid research and consumer insight to define a tight and clear view of their target market. This strong research focus extended in some cases into product testing and regional, segment-focused marketing. Research was very much at the heart of the successful launch of all three brands, helping to deliver a strong and inspiring positioning.

What also marks out these case studies so strongly is their highly targeted and focused use of the marketing communications mix backed by powerful creative closely aligned to the brand positioning. alli's powerful use of digital, Magner's strong sponsorship strategy and Change4Life's community communications and engagement approach are just some of the highlights.

The results for all three organisations are the stuff of legend, and there is much to learn from Magners, Change4Life and alli. At the heart of all three is the craft of marketing delivered brilliantly, and a vital message for us all on the power great marketing can have to change the unchangeable and to deliver powerful business results — truly inspirational!

Magners

02

Refreshing the entire cider category

Snapshot

Magners defied industry analysts' negative views of the potential of the cider market with the successful launch of its new cider brand in the UK, which revitalised a moribund category.

Key insights

- The languishing cider market received an injection of new energy with the arrival of the Magners brand at a time when the industry had written the market off.

- The brand's strong point of differentiation of pouring it over ice brought a sense of freshness to the category, appealing to even the most jaded consumers.

- A multi-platform campaign, including advertising, outdoor, press and sponsorship made the whole much bigger than the sum of its parts.

Summary

Magners is the brand owned by Irish drinks company C&C Group. When the company began to research the possibility of launching its Irish cider into London in 2005, industry specialists warned the company that cider was a declining market which held little or no potential. Within 18 months of the launch Magners was not only the leading bottled alcohol brand in London, but it became a trendy beverage among young people.

What propelled Magners into such an elevated position in the UK was the integrated marketing programme for Magners Irish Cider, while the premium pricing strategy (+20% vs premium beer) supported the brand positioning. Its unique selling point was its service — a pint of Magners from the bottle was to be poured over ice — which established a point of differentiation in the cider market, offering consumers added value from both a premium drinking experience and prolonged enjoyment of the beverage.

The importance of sampling and the extensive programme undertaken accelerated trial and was a sign of confidence in the product, helping ensure faster consumer connection. This translated into a 332% increase in volume sales in just one year. This very success soon attracted aggressive competition, particularly from Bulmer's, which, ironically, copied the now-textbook marketing strategy outlined in this case study.

Making the initial foray

When C&C decided to launch its Magners brand into the competitive London market in 2005, it was keen to apply the learnings of its successful launch in Scotland. It had carried out extensive research in early 2002, launching in Scotland as a whole in 2004 with the Magners 'Seasons' advertising campaign (Figure 1). By 2005 it was ready to attack the hardest market of all, London.

There were a number of ambitious marketing objectives for London:
- Build brand awareness and generate sales.
- Become the number one bottled alcoholic brand within four years.
- Make each season as relevant as the next for a product which had traditionally been a summer-only drink.
- Position the brand as a premium product in the long alcoholic drinks market (LAD).

Research told the company a number of things:
- First, that the London market was likely to prove challenging but not insurmountably so.
- Secondly, that distance and its effect on time and transport costs shaped how Londoners drank.
- Finally, consumers were faced with so much choice that they had learned to edit their way quickly through the choices confronting them.

Analysis of the extensive consumer research conducted by RG Research led Magners to develop the following hypothesis to underpin its consumer insight: irrespective of economic or cultural differences, people would adopt and crave an ideology that opposed the routine and habitual. This was followed by what the company termed the 'connection' moment: 'The orchard is more than just a place; it's a sanctuary whose consistency is refreshing'.

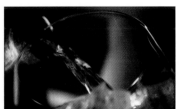

Figure 1. 'Seasons' ad campaign

Figure 2. 'Seasons' ad campaign

Finding the right balance

The research led the company to conclude that a brand which placed such a premium on 'time' and 'heritage' was exactly the antidote that these 'over-choiced' consumers needed. The 'Seasons' campaign was designed to reinforce the importance of time within another world — the orchard. It could serve to propel these consumers out of the monotony of being rushed and into an aspirational zone of 'lazing on a sunny afternoon' or 'enjoying the magic of a little ice around winter' (Figure 2,3 and 4).

Even though research had shown that the London audience was possibly the most cynical and hesitant in the world, due to the over-exposure of brands and messages on a continual basis, Magners felt that it would be more difficult to be cynical about something that was rooted in a product truth. Authenticity was a rarity in this market.

Because the London media marketplace in London was somewhat of a circus, it warranted a radical, innovative and completely integrated strategy to achieve maximum impact, with the 'Seasons' TV campaign acting as the lead media. This TV activity would communicate both the emotional and functional benefits of the Magners brand to the key target market.

The media brief was to create 'shock and awe' while remaining true to Magners and the integrity of the 'Seasons' campaign. What that meant, in essence, was bringing the Irish orchard to the concrete jungle.

The strategy was one of heavy, sustained attack in highly concentrated areas. Prior to launch, Magners had near-zero distribution in London. Its approach was to drop high-impact, highly visible advertising into new areas to build distribution quickly in pubs and bars. Put simply, in London, 'If the punters ask for

Figure 3. 'Seasons' ad campaign

Figure 4. 'Seasons' ad campaign

it the landlord has to get it'. Through the advertising campaign the company wanted to ensure talkability, thereby triggering consumer call for brand.

The 'Seasons' TV campaign, due to its immediately arresting visuals and highly evocative music tracks enabled Magners to achieve significant cut-through. However, it was felt that these visuals needed to be built on to bring the strategy to life.

Figure 5. Outdoor advertising

Figure 6. Magazine gatefold

Going the extra media mile

In order to overcome the negativity that existed in regard to cider and give permission to drink cider and, even more so, over ice — a new innovation in the UK cider market — significant media investment and TV media weights were added to the 'Seasons' advertising campaign. This was supported by continuous mainstream outdoor (Figure 5) radio and 'Seasons' press campaigns.

For example, in collaboration with the company's media arm, MPG, creative outdoor executions were developed to leverage the brand's 'natural apple' proposition by turning Waterloo Tube station into a virtual orchard by buying every poster site on the concourse. This original initiative not only created a visual feast but took an artificial man-made structure and naturalised it, thus bringing to life the Magners brand values of 'craft, tradition, naturalness, time and heritage'.

In addition, three-page seasonal pull-out gatefolds were placed in style magazines such as *FHM* and *Arena* to bring the orchard into an unexpected environment and arrest the audience's attention (Figure 6).

This was about bringing the consumer insight to life by giving this supposedly cynical audience, who were tied into their habitual choices, a refreshing snippet of a landscape that was far more engaging and which would motivate them even when they stood waiting for the train to take them to their 9-to-5 jobs. The aim was to create an image that would not be forgotten easily, but stay with them for the day.

To dramatise even further the contrast of the natural Magners world with that of the synthetic urban environment, the company devised a 'media first' with a 96-sheet poster which dispersed real apple blossoms. These showered down on passing human traffic, resulting once again in positive talk about Magners Irish cider (Figure 7).

Another media first took place at Heathrow airport, with the entire length and breath of the well-known Heathrow tunnel covered with authentic visuals of the Clonmel orchard, giving the appearance that you were, in fact, in the orchard itself (Figure 8).

A natural fit for sponsorship

Sponsorship became another essential way to deepen consumer relationships.

- Building on the success of previous sports sponsorships, Magners decided that London Wasps was the perfect fit for the brand. The 'natural' link with wasps and blossoms were inherently obvious and the very fact that the brand would team up with an emerging rugby side made the decision that bit more inspired. (The sponsorship ended after the end of the four-year contract in 2009).

- Further development of this equity association was the sponsorship of the Magners League, helping to extend the brand into Wales and lending even more weight, not to mention the increased column inches the coverage generated.
- The sponsorship of the Scottish Golfing Championship also enabled the brand to gain further respectability by seamlessly entering a territory which would normally never have been a mainstay for cider.

Beating every target

Research conducted prior to the launch of Magners Irish Cider in the UK market and industry trends at the time indicated that without Magners activity the market would have continued to decline. Existing brands in the market had resigned themselves to the fact that the market was failing because consumers had not been presented with any reason to consider cider as a potential beverage.

Figure 7. Poster

Figure 8. Heathrow tunnel

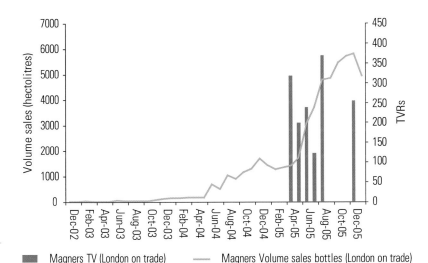

Figure 9. Direct correlation between TV commercials airing and Magners 285% increase in volume sales
Source: AC Nielsen

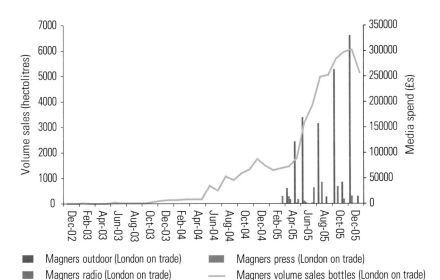

Figure 10. Direct correlation between Magners advertising activity and a 285% increase in their volume sales
Source: AC Nielsen

C&C estimated that Magners accounted for 75% of the growth in UK cider sales in 2006. Other notable results included:

- It became the no. 1 bottled alcohol brand, outselling bottles of Stella or Budweiser, the previous category leaders in London, after just 12 months — and three years ahead of target.
- There was a direct correlation between the airing of the TV ads in London and the hike in volume sales (Figure 9).
- The same was true for non-TV advertising (Figure 10).

Meanwhile, by September 2006:

- Magners was the no. 1 packaged LAD in the UK, with a 26% share and 30% share of total cider sales.
- Magners was the no. 1 packaged LAD in London with 27% share and 36% share of total cider sales.
- Magners was the no. 1 packaged LAD in Scotland, with 26% share, and accounted for 46% of total cider sales.
- Magners was the no. 1 packaged cider in the UK, with 77% share, rising to 90% of the Scottish packaged cider market.
- Packaged cider was the fastest-growing product and accounted for 37% of total UK cider sales and 51% of cider sales in Scotland.

Finally, Magners' brand success was key to driving the C&C share price from €2.26 at initial stock market quotation to €11.94 by 23rd January 2007, more than four times its original value.

Change4Life

02

Tackling a major public health issue by creating a new brand

Snapshot

The Change4Life brand was developed to target childhood obesity and promote a healthier lifestyle and has already made a measurable difference in attitudes and actions.

Key insights

- The Department of Health (DoH) marketing team realised that getting mothers to change the way they raised and nourished their young children would require an enticing carrot rather than a preachy stick.

- The resulting integrated campaign from M&C Saatchi created a new and colourful brand, Change4Life, and a number of flexible sub-brands which local and national partners could use and adapt.

- New products and services were developed to motivate families to change behaviours, while the most at-risk were enrolled in a customer relationship management programme to offer additional support.

Summary

On current trends 90% of adults will be overweight or obese by 2050, putting them at significantly greater risk of ill health and dying early. In response to this, the DoH embarked on an anti-obesity movement. The scale of the task was huge and the DoH did not believe that a traditional government information campaign would achieve this.

Instead, marketing resources were used to inspire and brand a societal movement, Change4Life, in which everyone who could help, including community leaders, teachers, health professionals, charities, leisure centres, retailers and food manufacturers, could play a part. The three-year marketing campaign, which began in January 2009, aims to prevent childhood obesity by helping change the diets and physical activity patterns of children who are at risk of becoming obese.

The campaign goal was for 200,000 families to join this movement in the first twelve months. By the end of the first year well over 413,000 had joined Change4Life.

A ticking time bomb

The rise in childhood obesity is one of the greatest health challenges facing society. Already, 30% of children and 60% of adults are overweight or obese. If the trend is allowed to continue, by 2050 only one in ten of the adult population will be a healthy weight.

Obesity is not a cosmetic issue. Becoming overweight or obese increases an individual's likelihood of developing (among others) cancer, type 2 diabetes and heart disease, leading to reduced quality of life and, in some cases, lives cut short. The cost to society of obesity-related illness is forecast to reach £50 billion per annum by 2050 at today's prices. Childhood obesity is particularly worrying, since there is a 'conveyor belt effect' whereby the majority of obese children grow up to be obese adults.

Change4Life was set up to combat this (Figure 1). It involved a complex array of issues:
- Creating a segmentation to allow resources to be targeted to those families who most need help.
- Providing insight into why those families behaved as they did.
- Creating a new brand identity.
- Providing 'products' (handbooks, questionnaires, wall charts, snack swappers) that families could use to change their behaviours.
- Signposting them to services (such as dance classes, accompanied walks and free swimming) and bringing together a coalition of local, non-governmental and commercial sector organisations to help families change their behaviours.

Figure 1. The new brand

What the department realised was that preventing childhood obesity required fundamental changes to the way families raised and nourished their children: the food they bought, how they prepared it, when and how much they ate, how they travelled and how they spent their leisure time. Expert opinion was that to achieve and maintain a healthy weight, children needed to:

- Reduce their intake of fat, particularly saturated fat (marketed as 'Cut Back Fat').
- Reduce their intake of added sugar ('Sugar Swaps').
- Eat smaller portion sizes ('Me-Size Meals').
- Eat at least five portions of fruit and vegetables per day ('5 A Day').
- Have three regular mealtimes each day ('Meal Time').
- Reduce the number of snacks they eat ('Snack Check').
- Do at least 60 minutes of moderate intensity activity during each day ('60 Active Minutes').
- Reduce time spent in sedentary activity ('Up and About').

(Figures 2a through 2h)

Before the launch of Change4Life, only 16% of mothers claimed that their children exhibited all of these behaviours.

Designing an effective campaign

In its first year, Change4life focused on families with children aged 5-11, especially those (identified via quantitative segmentation) whose self-reported attitudes and behaviours suggested that their children were at increased risk of becoming obese.

While 93% of these families saw childhood obesity as a problem for society, only 5% recognised that

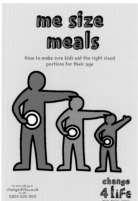

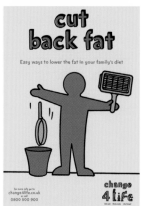

Figures 2a - h. Change4Life sub-brands

their own children were at risk. Parents viewed weight as a cosmetic rather than a health issue and seldom welcomed government advice on how to raise their children.

Change4Life supported the government's public service agreement (PSA) target to reduce the proportion of obese children to 2000 levels by 2020. Modelling indicated that, in order to meet the target, 200,000 families would be needed to commit to changing their behaviours through Change4Life by the end of the first year — of whom at least 33,333 families had to stay in the programme for at least six months.

Other published targets for the first year of activity were set, including reach, awareness, response, sign-ups and continued interaction with the programme.

For families to trial and sustain changes to their lifestyles, they needed powerful motivation, coupled with access to services and support. A traditional government information campaign wouldn't be able to do this. Instead, marketing resources were used to inspire a societal movement, through which everyone who could help, including community leaders, teachers, health professionals, charities, leisure centres, retailers and food manufacturers, could play their part in bringing about change.

Birth of a new brand

A new brand, Change4Life, was created by M&C Saatchi (along with a suite of sub-brands, such as Walk4Life, Cook4Life and Play4Life). Change4Life launched to the public in January 2009 with an integrated communications campaign, comprising national advertising and public relations (PR), bus stop posters (Figure 3), supported by a website (including a locally-searchable directory of services) and a helpline.

The Change4Life brand and its sub-brands were made available to local and national partners, so that they could market their own products and services (such as accompanied walks, free swimming, gym sessions, dance classes, new play facilities, healthy school meals, recipe books and cooking classes) within the movement.

Figure 3. Bus stop poster

Families were invited to join Change4Life. When they joined, they were sent a questionnaire (called *How Are The Kids*?) that asked about a typical day in the life of each child. This enabled Change4Life to send them a personalised action plan with advice for each child (Figure 4).

New products and offers were developed to prompt behaviour change. For example 250,000 'snack swapper' wheels were distributed to help parents negotiate with their children about healthier snacking and seven million free swims were provided by local authorities. 200,000 of the most at-risk families were enrolled in a customer relationship management programme which provided additional continued support.

Figure 4. Personalised action plan

A significant outcome

The campaign exceeded all published targets, as Table 1 shows.

Table 1

	Year one target	Year one achievement
Reach (% of all mothers of children under 11 who had an opportunity to see the advertising campaign)	99%	99%
Awareness (% of all mothers with children under 11 who recalled seeing the Change4Life advertising)	82%	87%
Logo recognition (% of all mothers with children under 11 who recognised the Change4Life logo)	44%	88%
Response to *How Are The Kids*? (total number of questionnaires returned electronically, by post or from face-to-face marketing)	100,000	346,609
Total responses (including website visits, telephone calls, returned questionnaires)	1,500,000	1,992,456
Sign-up (total number of families who joined Change4Life)	200,000	413,466
Sustained interest (total number of families who were proven to still be interacting with Change4Life six months after joining)	33,333	44,833

The campaign helped parents make the link between the behaviours that cause excess weight gain and poor health outcomes. For example:
- 85% of mothers agreed that the Change4Life advertising "made me think about my children's health in the long term".
- 81% agreed it "made me think about the link between eating healthily and disease".
- 83% agreed that it "made me think about the link between physical activity and disease".

Brand metrics were strong, especially when it came to being clear, trusted, relevant, adaptable to my lifestyle and supportive, not judgemental.

Getting everyone on board

Change4Life galvanised activity across communities. For example:

- 25,000 community leaders joined Change4Life as local supporters and used Change4Life materials to start conversations with over a million people about their lifestyles.
- 44% of primary schools, children's centres, hospitals, GP surgeries, town halls, leisure centres and libraries displayed Change4Life materials.
- NHS staff ordered over six million leaflets and posters to distribute to the public.
- 183 national organisations (including Asda, Tesco, Unilever, PepsiCo, Kellogg's, Nintendo and the Fitness Industry Association) spent their own money marketing Change4Life and supported the movement by, for example, selling bikes at cost, providing money-off fruit and vegetables and funding free exercise sessions.
- Primary schools generated over 50,000 sign-ups to Change4Life and created Change4Life-themed assemblies, lessons and healthy school menus.
- Local authorities and primary care trusts joined the initiative up with their own activities and created new ones, such as street parties and road shows, in support of Change4Life.
- Other government departments synchronised their activity and created new activity under Change4Life sub-brands (such as Swim4Life, Play4Life and MuckIn4Life).
- Three of the main health charities (Cancer Research UK, Diabetes UK and the British Heart Foundation) ran their own campaign in support of

Change4Life and other non-governmental organisations, such as Natural England and Sustrans, also supported the campaign.

Changing behaviours

Early results indicated that families were already changing their behaviours. In the tracking study, 30% of mothers who saw the advertising (equating to over a million mothers) claimed to have changed at least one thing in their children's diets or activity levels as a direct result of Change4Life.

Encouragingly, the number of mothers claiming that their children did all eight of the Change4Life behaviours increased from 16% at the baseline of January 2009 to 20% a year later. This equated to 180,000 more families claiming to do all eight behaviours. The proportion of families claiming to do at least four of the behaviours also increased from 77% to 83%.

While it's true that mothers may have claimed that their children did behaviours when they didn't, parental claims were backed up by sales data provided by commercial partners in the case of food-related behaviours:

- BrandScience analysed data from 7,000 households that were both on the SkyView panel and the TNS family food panel. The analysis compared the ratio of purchases between a selection of typically less healthy products (e.g. full-fat milk and cakes) with typically more healthy products (e.g. fruit and vegetables and pasta) for the full year 2009 and the full year 2008. Brand Science found that the ratio of healthy to unhealthy products improved significantly among C2DE families with children who had high exposure to the Change4Life advertising campaign. Penetration of healthier products increased by 20% in these households and volume of healthier products increased by 9%.

- dunnhumby analysed actual purchases (using the Tesco Clubcard database) of 10,000 of the families who were most engaged with Change4Life. The analysis compared purchases made at Tesco during September, October and November 2009 with the same three months of 2008 (i.e. pre-Change4Life). To factor out the impact of pricing and sales promotion, dunnhumby created a control group of 10,000 non-Change4Life families who were demographically comparable and whose purchasing in 2008 matched the intervention group. The analysis found a significant difference in the purchasing behaviour of the intervention group relative to the control. Specifically, Change4Life families bought more low-sugar drinks, more low-fat milk, more fruit and vegetables, more dried pasta and fewer cakes relative to the control.

Achieving cost effectiveness

The Central Office of Information's Artemis tool holds data for 54 government campaigns and enables government departments to assess the cost effectiveness of their activity. As Table 2 shows, *How Are The Kids?* (HATK) was the most cost-effective response mechanism in government.

Table 2

	COI Artemis average	COI Artemis forecast for HATKs	HATKs actual
Cost per response	£13	£5	£5
Cost per active response	£115	£22	£10
Cost per immediate conversion	£303	£27	£15

The DoH committed £75 million to the first three years of Change4Life. In addition to the free activity provided by local authorities, the NHS and community groups, the Change4Life movement attracted significant funding from partners such as, for example:

- £1.5 million from other government departments.
- £9 million spent by national partners.
- £12.5 million in free media space for the launch.
- £500,000 in free media with the sponsorship of Channel 4's *The Simpsons*.
- £200 million in future commitments by the Business4Life consortium.

Collectively, these gave a return on investment of £2.98 for every £1 spent. But the ultimate return on investment will be experienced in 2050, when children who avoid obesity today do not develop obesity-related illness, such as type 2 diabetes, cancer and heart disease in middle age, potentially saving society £50 billion per annum.

alli

02

Breaking new ground with a new weight loss brand

Snapshot
The company rewrote the rules of the weight loss category with the ambitious launch of a revolutionary new brand.

Key insights

• Launching a radical new product into such a sensitive area as weight loss meant establishing a positioning that was honest, credible and truthful about what could be achieved.

• Insights enabled the company to empathise with consumers' struggles by developing a number of initiatives, including offering them online forums and ensuring that pharmacists were well briefed on how to consult effectively about weight loss.

• The innovative campaign ran across a wide range of channels and paid off with high levels of consumer awareness and strong sales from the start.

Summary

GlaxoSmithKline Consumer Healthcare UK is part of GlaxoSmithKline (GSK), with headquarters in the UK and an estimated seven per cent of the world's pharmaceutical market. GSK's Consumer Healthcare UK is the UK's leading over the counter (OTC) company and home to a wide range of household brands.

In 2009 the company launched a new weight loss brand into the UK marketplace. alli was the first OTC medicine to be granted a single licence for sale across Europe as well as being the first non-prescription weight loss aid to receive a European licence. The UK launch was one of the company's most ambitious marketing campaigns ever, with a simultaneous pan European launch across 27 countries. The fully integrated, cross channel campaign was based on in depth consumer research and liaison with key experts.

In the UK within only a few months the weight loss brand had 56% prompted consumer awareness and strong sales, making it the leading weight loss capsule on the market.

alli 60mg capsules are a weight loss aid containing Orlistat. For overweight adults with a BMI 28 or over. Follow a reduced calorie, lower fat diet. Always read the label.

Gaining deeper insights

Before launching alli the company had spent a significant amount of time understanding its consumers and their needs and expectations for weight loss products. It had also liaised with key obesity experts to build the brand positioning in a credible and responsible way so that the launch could have a positive impact on public health.

This was critical, since obesity is set to overtake smoking as the biggest preventable disease within the next five to 10 years. So it was important that consumers were educated responsibly and with consideration for their needs.

The target audience for the brand were adults with a BMI 28 or more trying to lose weight and who claimed to have been overweight for a significant period of time. However, they often adopted a cycle of 'yo-yo' dieting as well as setting unrealistic targets. It was therefore essential to make sure they understood that the key to successful and sustained weight loss in the longer term was diet and exercise.

In addition, they suffered from low confidence and self esteem so it was important not to patronise them but also, from a brand point of view, ensure that the brand was not perceived as a 'scary medicine' which would be off putting to them. So the brand tone of voice the company developed was empathetic, supportive and based on an emotional connection, not just rational messages about the product benefit.

Because this was a category that had traditionally offered quick fixes, the brand positioning had to be honest, credible and truthful. The message throughout all the communications was based on the recognition that losing weight is not easy and

that alli is not a magic pill. Not only did consumers need support and advice to help them on their way to healthier habits for life through traditional media channels, but also through a dialogue with well trained and knowledgeable pharmacists.

How it works

alli works by stopping around a quarter of the fat you eat from being absorbed. So for every 2lbs you work to lose through following a reduced calorie and lower fat diet and introducing exercise, alli can help you lose 1lb more.

The role for the alli brand was to act as a spur and reward their hard work and efforts with increased weight loss (50% more weight loss than dieting alone). The company had found that giving them realistic expectations of the product could lead to an excellent experience, and, potentially, the adoption of healthier eating and lifestyle habits over the longer-term.

Figure 1

Forming close connections with prospective customers

The brand positioning was clear: *"alli is not just a pill because it comes with a programme of support. Added to healthy eating, alli can help boost weight loss by 50%. So for every 2lb you lose on your own, alli can help you lose 1lb more"* (Figure 1).

Once the company gained approval to launch, it initiated a programme called the 'alli first team' which brought 60 people from across the UK to preview the alli programme. They were given handheld video cameras, access to a blog and a connection to a pharmacist so the company could learn more about their experiences and ultimately ensure it was giving consumers the right support and information.

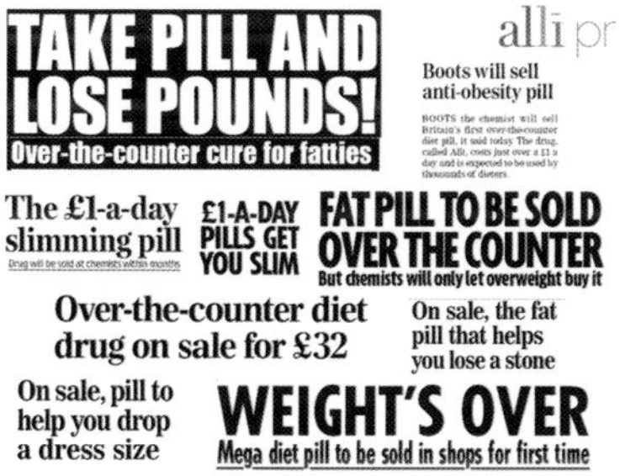

A lot was learned from following their journeys, and this insight informed the communications. An important finding was that community and peer-to-peer support would be critical. As a result, initiatives such as the discussion forum on alli.co.uk were put into place. Their videos were also shared online and with media partners, along with open and honest commentary about their struggles. Many of these participants were used for case studies in the media.

All this reinforced both the honesty and credibility the brand stood for also while also offering added value to consumers looking to try the product through increased information and resources.

Effective use of marketing resources

The launch plan was focused but also ambitious and designed to make a big impact. It included a number of elements.

Public Relations (PR)

PR was seen as a major contributor to consumer awareness and had three core objectives:
- Cutting through cluttered 'fad diet' reporting to establish a credible, clinically-proven product.
- Managing expectations: media over-hyping could have led to the wrong consumers buying alli.
- Providing the reassurance of pharmacists' expertise in weight management.

Many tactics were deployed, including medical media briefings, developing relationships with media journalists with long lead times, showcasing consumer successes as case studies and holding a huge press launch day event which received TV and press coverage (Figures 2 and 3).

Figure 2. Press coverage

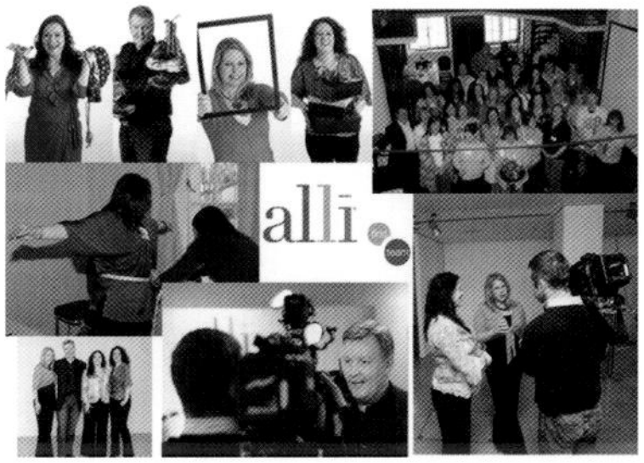

Figure 3. Launch day

Digital

Online is the first place that consumers go to search for weight loss information so it was important for alli to have a dominant presence, This was delivered through:

- A website with information and resources, including online recipe planners, weight loss trackers, case study videos and live discussion forums to engage with other consumers.
- Display advertising across key food and lifestyle sites.
- Partnerships with Channel 4 Food and Hearst Digital to amplify relevant content.
- Search activity.
- Visibility on many retail sites.

Many elements of the campaign were a first for the company. The most innovative element was the live discussion forum on the website at alli.co.uk/forum, which gave consumers an opportunity to discuss their experiences with others and share advice and support. This had to go through a complex regulatory approval process, with the company committing itself to moderating this content in a responsible way while still allowing consumers to speak freely.

Pharmacy support

Support from the pharmacy sector was crucial for a successful launch. The aim was to ensure that pharmacists and pharmacy assistants were well-prepared and engaged so that they could offer the best service and support to consumers. The plan included:

- Extensive training: hard copy, interactive and face-to-face training at 60 workshops.
- Advertising: display and advertorial content to educate about weight management.
- Support tools to aid discussion with consumers in store.
- A website for pharmacists with education and support.

The pharmacy campaign was the most ambitious ever and included many innovative elements, such as the face-to-face training in a series of 60 workshops across the UK. It involved using live action filmed scenarios together with handset technology to train pharmacists and pharmacy assistants

Films were played of consumers in pharmacies asking for alli in order to demonstrate how a successful consultation should take place. During the training live handset technology was used to allow trainees to vote on the right outcomes. In this way the company could monitor any confusion or misapprehension about the process and adapt the live training to address these areas on the spot. This was the first training of this type for an OTC launch that the company was aware of.

Figure 4. Press ad

Figure 5. *Cosmopolitan* promotion

Figure 6. *Good Housekeeping* promotion

Consumer communications

To raise consumer awareness and to establish the alli brand proposition the company put substantial investment into the media campaign, which included:

- TV: April-August on terrestrial and satellite channels with 30-second ads.
- Press display adverts in April in retailer magazines and national magazines titles (*She, Cosmo, Prima, Company, Good Housekeeping, Zest*) (Figure 4).
- Outdoor posters for key grocery accounts, with 6-sheets placed during May in Tesco, Asda and Sainsbury's.
- Publication of a supporting book — 'The alli Diet plan' — sold in pharmacies and retail chains.
- A year-long series of press advertorials in key titles showcasing successful users of alli and providing help and advice regarding healthy eating (Figures 5 and 6).
- Online partnerships and display activity with Channel4.com and Dietdiaries.com.
- Consumer starter guide handed out in stores.

Although many aspects of the plan were ambitious, the most innovative element of the consumer communications campaign was the extensive consumer advertorial series which the company ran with National Magazines Company from April 2009. These advertorials were developed to showcase key brand messages and share stories of successful users by following key first team members in different titles throughout the year.

They were used to help educate consumers about the alli lifestyle and ensure that they were well prepared to follow the reduced calorie and lower-fat diet. The close working relationship with National Magazines helped to make content relevant to the readers of each publication while still maintaining the brand style and messaging.

In-store visibility

The aim of the launch was for 100% visibility in pharmacies, which meant working with partners to place materials virtually overnight. The materials showcased the core 'Dieting? alli can boost your weight loss' claim and incorporated:

- Window displays in nearly every independent pharmacy window in the UK.
- In-store posters, floor media, display units, counter display units, counselling room kits, free-standing display units.
- Impressive secondary displays with all multiple customers including Boots, Tesco and Lloyds Pharmacy.
- Brand ambassadors in Boots stores throughout the month of launch.
- Online retail support materials.

The campaign in store was recognized as a gold standard OTC launch by many of the company's partners.

Hitting all the right targets

The launch of alli required significant input from all areas of the business, which worked as one team to engage with customers, develop marketing plans and to ensure that everything was the best it could be. Since launch in the UK the company has established a successful weight loss brand, with high levels of consumer awareness and significant sales results. It is already the number one weight loss capsule in share and value terms and has given a boost to category growth overall.

Over one billion impressions were generated through just under 400 articles ranging from press and radio to TV reports. PR was the main driver of sales at the early stages of launch. Digital activity saw a million visits to alli.co.uk, with thousands of registrations and active participation on the discussion forum. There was a high conversion to online sales through the website and commercial and media partners.

There was also an overwhelming endorsement of the pharmacy campaign, with 93% of UK pharmacies engaging in some form of training. Of those attending workshops, the overwhelming majority felt confident recommending alli. There were over thousands of registrations to the expert website, while the company was consistently voted the Best Pharmacy Support package in the OTC bulletin *Pharmacy* magazine and won numerous industry awards.

The consumer communications achieved high levels of awareness of the brand within the target group in just a few months, which was higher than any other OTC launch that the company monitored at the same period, including brand extensions. The diet plan book sold in excess of 20,000 copies. A satisfying number of users asked in a GSK/Millward Brown usage and awareness survey claimed to be 'very satisfied' or 'satisfied'. The company won supplier awards following its in-store activity from both Boots and Tesco for 'best product launch'. Finally, alli reached 98% weighted distribution after just three weeks of launch.

All images appearing in this case study are reproduced by permission of GSK.

alli 60mg capsules are a weight loss aid containing Orlistat. For overweight adults with a BMI 28 or over. Follow a reduced calorie, lower fat diet. Always read the label.

Chapter 3
Brand Extension

Jon Goldstone
Marketing Director,
Premier Foods

We all know the logic for launching brand extensions. Taking the equity of an existing brand into a new market or category is often much more profitable than attempting to launch an entirely new brand.

However, brand extensions are very difficult to get right and many turn out to be expensive failures. At their best they deliver incremental sales and profit while enriching the core brand with improved equity. At their worse they cannibalise sales from the parent brand, dilute margins and harm overall brand equity.

The two case studies featured here both got it right. So what made them work and what can we learn from their success? I think both adhere to four principles that any brand extension should follow:

1. Be remarkable. Both examples did something brave and remarkable in the truest sense of the word. People noticed them and remarked upon them. What was Waitrose, Britain's most premium supermarket chain, doing launching a value range? Why was O_2, Britain's coolest mobile phone network, going anywhere near the Millennium Dome?
2. Be on brand. Beneath the initial surprise both case studies had very clear and logical linkages back to their core brands and the marketing support for both was bang on brand. For example, Waitrose called its new value range 'essentials', not 'basics', and the packaging design had a pared-down elegance that was totally consistent with the core brand.
3. Be on trend. Both of these responded to shifts in trend (Waitrose to the recession, O_2 to the rise in popularity of live music) and were very much leaders in their respective markets. Those that followed with 'me too' initiatives were much less successful.
4. Be generous with your marketing support. The worst brand extensions are launched on measly budgets which are often 'stolen' from the core brand. Both of these case studies appear to have been generously supported with budgets that were incremental to the core brand.

O$_2$

03

Striking the right note with brand extension

Snapshot
O$_2$ undertook an imaginative brand extension into entertainment which increased customer loyalty and helped create the world's most popular music venue.

Key insights

- O$_2$ wanted to give its brand a more tangible feel and build closer customer relationships in a market notorious for churn.

- Although the decision to give its brand to what had been a national laughing stock — the Millennium Dome — was fraught with risk, partnering with a leading entertainment group made the venue world-famous for attracting big names.

- More importantly, it enabled O$_2$ to forge close bonds with its customers through a variety of customer benefits, including special areas for customers at the arena and priority booking.

Summary

O$_2$ is a UK leading provider of mobile and broadband services to consumers and businesses in the UK. Part of the Telefónica O$_2$ Europe group, it was formed in 2001, following the demerger from British Telecom of its former mobile business, BT Wireless. Since the concept of turning mobile networks into brands first

took hold in the early 1990s, operators have viewed brand extensions as a diversion from the job in hand: growing customer bases as quickly as possible. Even as market penetration reached 120% (because of multiple SIM card ownership), brand extension continued to be an unexplored option. Instead, operators continued to focus on acquisition by luring customers from rival networks with ever more attractive deals.

However, O$_2$ recognised that a brand extension could play a role, but not in the conventional sense of delivering a new revenue stream. Instead, a brand extension could be used to create an asset that boosted core revenue streams through increased loyalty.

Forming a partnership with the owners of the much-derided Millennium Dome was both inspired but also very risky. The bet paid off hugely: by the end of 2008, the return on investment was 26:1. More importantly, The O$_2$ has become the world's most popular music venue.

Determined to be different

In 2007 the big six network operators — Vodafone, Orange, T-Mobile, 3, Virgin and O$_2$ — spent a total of £256 million on advertising. It is estimated that over 50% of this was spent on direct advertising, mainly promoting the latest tariff and handset offers.

This was a market driven by the latest deals. Consequently, loyalty was hard to come by. Exacerbating this situation were two other factors. Firstly, the nature of mobile networks is their intangibility. This lack of physical presence made it hard to create brand affinity. Secondly, the most tangible representation of the brand-customer relationship was the payment. As any utility provider is aware, a relationship based on bill payment is not one that engenders loyalty.

To drive allegiance, the brand required a more tangible and visible presence. Yet O$_2$ recognised that brand expression needed to be more than a simple badging exercise as per traditional brand sponsorship. What was needed was a true brand extension, which would enhance the customer experience and provide a rational and emotional reason to stay.

Alongside this condition sat the complex and ever more important issue of convergence between communication, technology, media and content. The convergence trend is perhaps best exemplified in the way music consumption has been transformed in recent years. Strengthening O$_2$ credentials in this arena was therefore a key strategic opportunity.

Risking the odds

Back in 2006, in a prime location on the banks of the Thames, stood a giant empty structure which had been unused since its inglorious incarnation as the Millennium Dome. Even at its peak, the Millennium Dome had never achieved anything close to popularity. Such were the connotations of the Dome that any form of revival seemed pure fantasy. Indeed, demolition seemed a real possibility.

But then along came a visionary partnership between two leading brands: O$_2$ in telecommunications and Anschutz Entertainment Group (AEG) in entertainment. For its part, AEG was looking for a partner with a UK reputation and stature to assist in its vision of creating a concert and entertainment venue not previously seen in Europe. At O$_2$, a core team was convinced this partnership offered an opportunity to deliver a brand extension the like of which had never been seen before.

Unsurprisingly, this optimism was not universally shared. There were grave concerns that the Dome would tarnish O$_2$'s hard-won reputation. The proposal had to go to the company's board of directors before finally being given the green light.

In the end it was the high level of risk that helped clinch the deal. O$_2$ realised that with both partners dependent on each other for success, this was a partnership that could be shaped to deliver beyond traditional expectations. In the three years before the venue was launched, both parties worked closely together. While AEG's expertise lay in the venue's content, O_2 focused on ensuring the design reflected the enhanced customer experience that it sought to deliver.

By the time it was ready to be launched in July 2007, the venue boasted a 22,000-seat arena and a more intimate 2,000-seat concert hall, named 'The IndigO$_2$'. In addition, O_2 designed exclusive customer spaces, including the Blueroom bar and the O_2 Lounge, where access was granted through mobile bar codes. O_2 also created 'O_2 Angels', a team of people trained to greet and direct visitors.

All these contributions were a powerful demonstration of O_2's commitment to its customers at the venue. However, the O_2 team also recognised that for the venue to truly drive loyalty, there was a requirement for a powerful pre-arrival customer benefit.

Creating strong customer bonds

The Priority Ticket offer was thus developed to give O_2 customers a very simple but extremely attractive benefit — the chance to buy concert tickets 48 hours before sale to the general public.

Beyond offering this VIP treatment, it would also create a dialogue with O_2 customers while building a database of those interested in the Priority Ticket offer. Customers could register their music and entertainment preference through the O_2 special phone line (an interactive set of menu options that a caller selected from the phone key pad for more information), or at the Blueroom site online.

Nor did the experience end when customers left the venue, as they could re-enter the Blueroom online after the event and download music, as well as watching exclusive interviews and streamed video.

Creatively turning a negative into a positive

Although now The O_2 is an established part of the London landscape, at the beginning the proposed partnership had been steeped in scepticism and worried about failure. So the creative strategy behind the launch had to fulfil three key criteria:
- Ensure the name stuck and that "The O_2" entered the nation's vocabulary.
- Communicate that this was not a re-badging exercise. O_2 was extending its brand into a new territory with real customer benefits – most importantly, Priority Tickets.
- Above all, create a sense of unassailable confidence that it would succeed.

The launch campaign focused on driving home the association between O_2 and the venue through TV, outdoor and print advertising (Figure 1).

Because multiple messages had to be delivered, the advertising agency VCCP developed a communications plan to run across all media (Figure 2). For example, the outdoor and print campaigns forged a link between the new name and the iconic image of the white tent. The 30-second TV campaign was an opportunity to take the nation on a taster of the varied entertainment on offer at The O_2 and communicate the Priority Ticket message.

A second phase of activity in late 2008 focused purely on driving home the customer benefit of Priority Ticketing through a multi-media campaign (Figure 3).

Figure 1. Launch campaign

Figure 2. Multi-media campaign

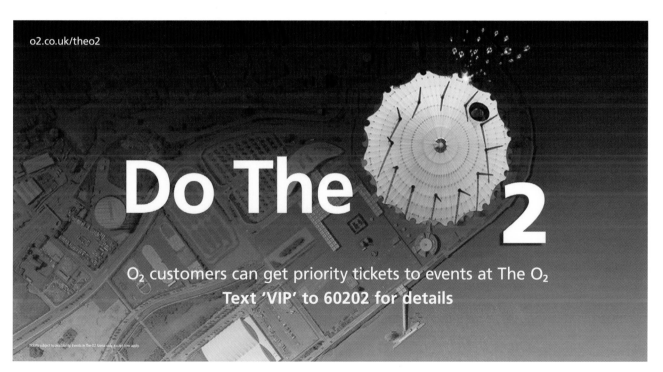

Figure 3. Priority Ticketing campaign

Winning on every front

By any reckoning The O_2 has proved to be a phenomenal success, as the myriad of positive press articles have attested. However, this positive endorsement was never going to be sufficient. For a brand that had, until this point, lived in the ether, here was an opportunity to be touched, played with and talked to.

1. Customer participation

At its most basic level, this was a brand extension that needed to become a successful music venue. By December 2007, just seven months after launch, The O_2 Arena had welcomed a staggering 1.4 million music lovers. The O_2 is now the 'world's most popular venue', selling more tickets that any other venue in the world and outperforming the legendary Madison Square Gardens and the new Wembley Arena. The magazine *Music Week* voted The O_2 the arena of the year in 2008.

2. Customer interaction

The O_2 database was equally successful: by the end of 2008 over one million O_2 customers had signed up for Priority Ticketing. O_2 also sold out its allocation for over 50 pre-sale events, giving in excess of 180,000 priority tickets to O_2 customers.

Over the same time period there were over 100,000 entries for The O_2 Blueroom competitions and 100,000 live music downloads. On average, SMS campaigns received a response rate of 4%, while email campaigns achieved a significant 15% response rate.

In fact, from the launch of The O_2 until the end of 2007 over 900,000 unique visitors spent time on The O_2 section of the Blueroom, which was developed by the agency AIS. There was thus massive uplift in customer engagement with the brand: three months post-launch there was a 263% uplift in pre-pay customers logging their music preferences.

3. Boosting brand perception

There were early indications that this success was having a measurable effect on perceptions of the O_2 brand. Those aware of The O_2 showed significantly more positive attitudes to the brand on nearly all attributes. What's more, as Table 1 shows, the brand attributes most influenced by experience and awareness of The O_2 were strategically relevant.

Brand attributes most impacted by experience and awareness of The O_2 (customer and non-customer)	Average improvement in attribute: non aware-experienced %
Provide a good customer experience	+57%
Have the best range of mobile handsets	+51%
Offer the best range of services for your lifestyle	+50%
Is the leading phone network	+49%
Look after their customers better	+49%
Are networks that have better services than others	+43%
Are brands that are setting the standards for the future	+43%
Appeal to you more than other networks	+41%

Table 1. Impact of The O_2 on brand attributes 2007
Source: Millward Brown

Unprecedented return on investment

In order to assess the impact of The O$_2$ on revenue, an econometric model was developed to look at the impact on customer loyalty. This showed an immediate but lasting impact on churn among the whole customer base. This equated to approximately 10% for post-pay customers and 20% for pre-pay. Without taking into account acquisitions generated, the model calculated a return on investment of 26:1 by the end of 2008.

Perhaps the greatest testament to the success of this brand extension is the roll-out of similar venues in other O$_2$ markets. In September 2008 O$_2$ World opened in Berlin, followed in December 2008 by the opening of The O$_2$ in Dublin.

Waitrose

03

Transforming performance through perceptive brand extension

Snapshot

The food retailer's new 'essential' brand saw Waitrose combine quality and value to deliver dramatic growth despite the recession.

Key insights

- When the recession hit Waitrose realised that having its brand synonymous with quality food and ethical principles could be in danger of driving price-conscious shoppers away.

- Its new value range struck precisely the right note by offering Waitrose quality at affordable prices.

- Outdoor advertising had a key role to play in getting the message to the high street.

Summary

Waitrose is the food retailing arm of the John Lewis Partnership, one of the UK's most successful and trusted companies. But the recession which began in 2009 presented a big challenge for the retailer because its brand was so closely associated with quality food and a strong ethical stance. The risk was that its stores would become an infrequent 'nice to do' visit rather than a vital 'need to do' because consumers were tightening their belts.

However, a new brand — essential Waitrose — found exactly the right tone for an upmarket supermarket's first value-led proposition. In spite of concern that a 'value' range from Waitrose would undermine its premium credentials, a bold marketing initiative, a strong product offering and a stylish brand identity delivered the most impressive results in Waitrose's history.

By the end of 2009 the 'essential' brand accounted for 16% of total sales, with sales of individual products running on average 17% ahead of previous levels. And, at a time when total grocery market growth was slowing, the launch spurred the business as a whole into growth.

Recession begins to bite

At the start of 2008, Waitrose was thriving. Having for many years enjoyed a reputation as Britain's best quality supermarket, it had recently announced ambitions to double the size of the business within ten years. Opening its doors to a broader audience with marketing that proclaimed, 'Everyone deserves quality food', it promised to open up a world in which quality food was the norm and not the exception.

Then, in the autumn of 2008, recession arrived. Overnight, price became a priority. In a mature market, where growth was being driven by inflation rather than volume, retailers could not afford to lose shoppers to competitors. Discount and money-off became the dominant voice of the competition.

Consumers' attitudes changed too. The psychological impact of the recession stretched further than the direct financial impact. While only a minority of shoppers had seen a reduction in their income, almost all felt the need to rein in spending. The spirit of the age made being thrifty a priority and careful spending a must. Waitrose shoppers talked of responding by trying to maintain their premium spend at Waitrose, but switching their non-treats to lower-priced alternatives by shopping around for deals on packaged staples and expanding their repertoire to include more discounters.

This new-found emphasis on thrift posed significant problems for Waitrose. Even when not suffering the effects of a recession, many believed that Waitrose was primarily for special occasions, not every-day shopping. They simply saw Waitrose as beyond their budget.

It was critical, therefore, to find a compelling way of 'marketing' value. But the business could not afford to compete on price alone. Indeed, brand devotees would be rankled if it did. So, a definition of accessible, affordable quality was required — and one that could be populated with a fresh brand which would not damage the 'genius' of Waitrose.

A perfect storm of opportunity

In March 2009 the business launched essential Waitrose: a new brand with 1,400 staples such as meat, tinned tuna, eggs, jam, biscuits, milk and pasta, as well as household cleaning products, and all at affordable prices (Figure 1).

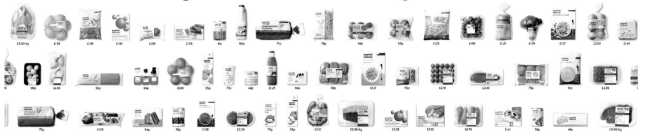

Figure 1. The new range

Given the timing of its launch, it was seen by many as a rapid response to recession. In truth, the idea of a quality-driven 'value' brand had been conceived some time earlier. Its inception was the result of business concern about how accepted Waitrose was for 'everyday shopping'. Tackling this misconception head on had been a live issue for many months previously. As a retailer intent on widening its appeal, Waitrose was aware that it did not have a clearly signposted, 'value-tier' offering. An affordable, accessible brand would be critical if commercial ambitions were to be realised and British shoppers to connect with the belief that: 'Everyone deserves quality food'.

By developing a consistent design for its own-brand goods, it sought to create a new brand offer that would be more easily recognised across the store.

Clearly, the recession injected a sense of urgency into this project. After all, such a brand could now offer recession-influenced shoppers a way of behaving more price-consciously. Business foresight, marketing authorship and recessionary context had thus delivered a perfect storm of opportunity. Nonetheless, the launch of essential Waitrose raised eyebrows across the industry and among consumers — would this work or, instead, be perceived as pretence?

Assessing the risks

This brand launch came with risk attached, as is inevitable with all brand launches. But the risk was made more acute on the basis of first, the recession and secondly, the parent brand's premium association with loyal consumers. Specifically, Waitrose might be seen to be 'chasing the pack' and mirroring the discounter tactics of its rivals but being the last to do so. Its hard-won reputation for food leadership would be hard to regain if it was seen to be throwing it away with a knee-jerk reaction.

Further, research had shown that Waitrose customers liked their stores just as they were. They did not want to see the brand go downmarket or change. But the business realised how imperative a re-orienting of association would be if 'essential' was going to work and attract back lapsed or infrequent shoppers.

There was a risk, too, that introducing a 'value' range could damage Waitrose's impeccable quality record. A brand which only nine months previously had pronounced that it would never sell a 2p sausage could well be seen as compromising in order to compete. Marketing had to reassure people of the quality of the essential range and its commitment to strong ethical principles. This was critical. While the full brand range was competitively priced, pricing was not structured to compete with rivals' more basic economy ranges.

Defining value

Despite these challenges, the competitive context offered the store an opportunity to talk differently about the concept of 'value'. Recession had ushered in wave after wave of price messaging in a marketing environment in which value brands spoke only about price. In contrast, essential Waitrose offered a more holistic definition: not cheap, in the traditional sense, where shoppers assume and accept a level of compromise on quality, or the classic value-for-money trade-off. Rather, Waitrose would present a values-for-money transaction where 'values' stood for affordable, accessible Waitrose.

The business believed that this definition would cut through the marketing clutter. For its broadest customer base, essential would appear not to — because it didn't — compromise. 'Quality' and 'affordability' could — feasibly — co-exist and succeed in recessionary Britain.

By designating the new brand as 'essential', and not 'value' or 'basics', Waitrose ensured that existing customers would feel at ease with the new venture. And, by building stylish quality cues into a packaging design that borrowed from the simple white visual vernacular of 'value', Waitrose ensured that customers understood that this was not the 'dumbing down' of a premium brand.

A simple but elegant debut

The new brand was given a pared-back identity, with product packaging transparent wherever feasible. Design was kept pure and had an elegance to complement the parent brand's upscale association (Figure 2). Sophisticated and simple, essential Waitrose reached out beyond packaging and fixture to feature at natural touchpoints like the checkout as well as within the glossy confines of the magazine *Waitrose Food Illustrated*.

Figure 2. The new design

Effort was taken to cross-promote too, so that shoppers would appreciate that they could purchase from solely within the essential brand when they shopped at Waitrose for their usual products.

In keeping with the 'spare' spirit of this brand, above-the-line advertising was unashamedly straightforward and devoid of creative conceit so as not to obstruct this distinctive definition of value. All communication was underpinned by a simple statement of fact as an end-line: "Quality you'd expect at prices you wouldn't" (Figure 3).

Overall, marketing both within and outside the store, including online, sought to convey a sense of affordability and quality combined to announce the arrival of this universal, inclusive brand. These measures were vital if Waitrose was to compete within the realm of value-led grocery while not reneging on its high-street heritage or status. The desired response was that shopping at Waitrose could, once more, be the main grocery shop.

Making media the message

Media planning was important in 'democratising' the brand. Outdoor media took it out onto the street, appearing in situations where 'everyday' food decisions were made, such as en route to supermarkets, during the commute, on high streets and so on. The new 'essential' brand invited a wider audience to experience Waitrose more often. And, by selecting high profile "impact" sites — backlit, premium-located and grand scale (including Europe's largest poster) — the brand was able to reinforce not just quality cues, but brand stature too.

Importantly, by using a channel rarely used by the grocery category (4% of spend in 2009), essential delivered the cut-through needed to rise above the crowd. Meanwhile, TV gave Waitrose coverage among a core demographic of ABC1 housewives with children and was scheduled to influence people's 'end of week' shop.

Press showcased the new brand through a variety of 'media firsts' and innovative formats. Online investment also enabled this new brand to intercept consumers when they went looking for inspiration for meals.

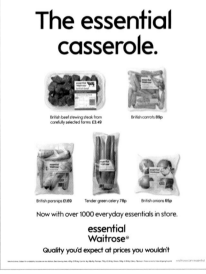

Figure 3. Examples of advertising

Getting the right result

Given the context, the launch of essential Waitrose produced the most impressive results Waitrose had ever seen.

First, it was one of the most talked-about initiatives of the year. *The Guardian* noted that Waitrose had "defied gloomy predictions that it would lose to cheaper rivals as the recession took hold'. *The Grocer* said that "The essentials strategy has clearly worked… consumer response has been overwhelmingly positive", *Just Food* hailed Waitrose as 'The Comeback Kid' and, in December, *Marketing* magazine placed essential Waitrose at No.3 — the highest placed brand — in the Top 10 marketing moments of 2009.

The response from competitors was flattering too. Sainsbury's, for example, produced an identikit campaign for its 'basics' range. When Marks & Spencer retaliated by comparing its own 'value' products with essential Waitrose, it "well and truly backfired', according to *Management Today*.

Awareness of the new brand rose to 83%, while the correlation between ad awareness and trial saw consistent growth for all shopper types.

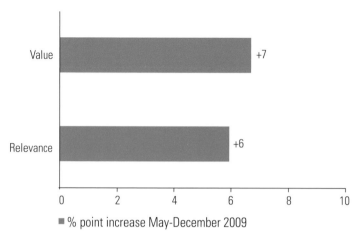

Figure 4

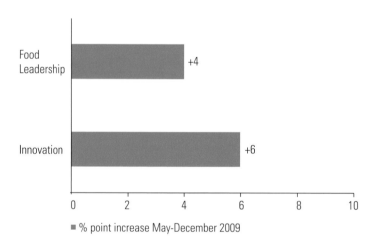

Figure 5

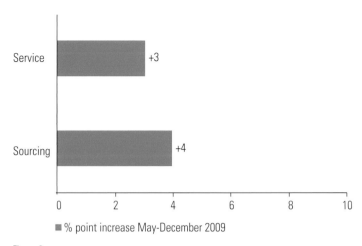

■ % point increase May–December 2009

Figure 6

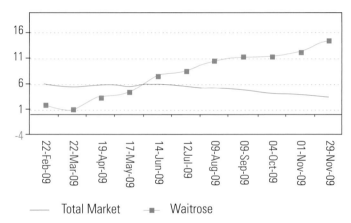

——— Total Market   ·-■-· Waitrose

Figure 7. Waitrose growth has improved after launch of Essentials, whilst total market growth continues to slow down.
Source: TNS

Purchase intention, too, strengthened with recognition of the advertising campaign, with 64% saying they are "more likely to purchase from Waitrose". Levels of brand attribution — which had at times been lower for Waitrose in a category where it was outspent by competitors — were the highest ever seen, with 88% of those who recognised the advertising correctly identifying it as being for Waitrose.

Additionally, brand perceptions improved significantly with 69% of shoppers feeling 'a little or much better about Waitrose'. Value perceptions also increased by 7%. Significantly, at a time when it had never been more threatened, Waitrose gained relevance too, as Figure 4 highlights.

Figure 5 shows that perceptions of food leadership and innovation increased demonstrably. Impact even filtered through to perceptions of service and sourcing, as Figure 6 illustrates. Most significantly, at a time when total grocery market growth was decelerating, the launch of essential drove the whole business into growth, with total sales up 14.6% by the end of November 2009 (Figure 7).

By the end of 2009 the brand accounted for 16% of total sales, with sales of products within the essential range running, on average, 17% ahead of previous levels. And, while some of this sales contribution came from existing shoppers 'trading down', nearly 60% came from new shoppers or from existing shoppers adding essential Waitrose products to their repertoire.

Estimating the return

The launch of essential Waitrose saw the company enjoy its most successful year ever, increasing total sales by 14.6%, or nearly £600 million, and enjoying its best-ever Christmas.

Given that essential was the only initiative to flow through all marketing channels during this phase, it is fair to credit the brand with dramatic commercial effect. Annualized incremental sales of essential lines alone were £80 million, or £60 million after accounting for cannibalization. This equated to a 7% uplift.

Waitrose would expect an uplift of approximately 5% from pricing reductions. Its business could, therefore, credit 2/7 (28.6%) of the £60 million uplift to advertising alone—in other words, £16.8 million. Applying a standard FMCG industry ratio, the business estimated that its long-term gain (£16.8 x 2½) was £42 million.

In respect of payback (applying an industry average profit margin of 32%, which provided an incremental profit of £13.4 million minus the £4.7 million campaign media spend) a net profit of £8.7 million delivered £1.85 for every £ 1 invested. Given the total growth of the business, this figure, more than likely, underestimates the real contribution of essential Waitrose.

Chapter 4
Brand Revitalisation

Peter Kirkby
Vice President,
Global Marketing
Excellence, GSK
Consumer Healthcare

Hindsight is a great thing. As you read the following four case studies some will be wondering: "Shouldn't the problem have been prevented in the first place?". It's a fair question and when you read "product quality had been ignored and advertising had been consistently cut" it's a salutary reminder that you ultimately 'reap what you sow'. However, what's interesting is that three of the four case studies are food-related, playing in categories where consumer expectations have changed considerably, and pretty quickly. Keeping large organisations sufficiently responsive to consumer needs and competitor context is easy to write about, but clearly much harder to do.

What all four case studies have in common is:
1. Recognising there's a problem to fix in the first place. It might sound obvious but, without new management, it can be more seductive to tinker around the edges than really tackle the route cause.
2. Genuinely listening to the consumer, and becoming more externally-focused.
3. A clear sense of where the brand has come from and where it needs to go — compare the different solutions McDonald's and KFC developed in response to the same essential problem.
4. Focusing on the fundamentals in the mix. To quote Hovis "(we needed to) get back to the basics of what had made us so appealing in the first place".

Resist the temptation to read the case studies and think "it wouldn't have happened on my watch". Ask instead: "Are we doing enough to make sure we're not a future revitalisation candidate?". Prevention is better than cure!

McDonald's

04

Learning to love the brand again

Snapshot

How a massive overhaul of every part of the UK business won the brand renewed public affection and led to record-beating sales.

Key insights

- McDonald's embarked on an ambitious revitalisation of the brand following a series of events that had damaged brand perception to improve every aspect of the business.

- Based on substantial investments in research, food was revamped and reinvented, restaurants redesigned and staff morale boosted.

- The result: the UK had its best-ever year of sales growth in 2008 since it first opened its doors in South London in 1974.

Summary

McDonald's is the leading global food service retailer, with more than 32,000 local restaurants serving more than 60 million people in 117 countries each day. More than 75% of McDonald's restaurants worldwide are owned and operated by independent local men and women. In the UK McDonald's faced the challenge of revitalising the brand and the business. It needed to re-connect with its customers, bolstering their trust in the brand and engaging with them on a new level in communications. It recognised that key to achieving this would be a renewed commitment to listening to and understanding its customers, and being open and transparent as a business.

It was a big challenge. In 2005 McDonald's business performance and brand perceptions had reached a plateau. A combination of factors in the brand's recent history had undermined consumer trust. It seemed that the nation's love affair with McDonald's might be over. In response, it re-focused around a clear vision and ambitiously overhauled just about every aspect of the business and the way it presented itself.

By being customer-led over the next three years McDonald's UK made record levels of investment in upgrading the experience for customers in the areas that mattered most to them. This included improving the fundamentals of the business: the food, the restaurants and communications. The business flourished, with eleven consecutive quarters of growth, and its best ever year of sales growth in 2008 since it first opened its doors in south London in 1974.

Taking stock

In 2005 McDonald's business performance and brand perceptions had reached a plateau. A combination of factors in the brand's recent history such as the Mclibel trial, Eric Schlosser's book *Fast Food Nation*, general disquiet about obesity and fast food and the film 'Supersize Me' had undermined consumer trust. It seemed that the nation's love affair with McDonald's might be over.

So the brand had to win back its place in customers' affections by overhauling just about every aspect of the business that could affect its relationship with them, and finding the right way to express itself in communications.

A fresh start

The process of change really started with the appointment of Steve Easterbrook as chief executive in early 2006. He made several new senior appointments, blending fresh thinking with internal promotions to usher in a culture of change.

The business went through a period of rigorous self and customer analysis. Much of the insight boiled down to a simple truth: although lots of consumers still went to McDonald's, they didn't feel as good about it. The brand had to get back to the basics of what had made it so appealing in the first place and re-ignite the passion it had attracted from customers.

Crucial to this would be the definition of a clear vision as the basis for the new brand story. This was defined as the 'progressive burger company':
• Progressive: signifying the commitment to change.
• Burger: because that was the true heart of the brand.

• Company: because McDonald's behaviour as an organisation is important to customers, employees and stakeholders and is the key driver of trust.

This was to become the focus for the business and the brand: addressing core customer concerns to rebuild trust in the brand. This meant acting to fix the fundamentals of the business: the food, the restaurants and how the brand presented itself in communications.

To achieve this, the business was determined to achieve a new depth and breadth of consumer insights to inform and inspire its decision-making. Qualitative projects such as co-creation weekends, spent with groups of consumers, employees and franchisees to help unlock insights into how to build a better McDonald's, and ethnographic research were complemented by a 4,000 sample usage and attitude study and continued use of the brand's established quantitative tracking tools.

Becoming customer-led in every area of the business

Over the next three years McDonald's UK made record levels of investment to upgrade the experience for customers in the areas that mattered most to them: the food for both adults and children and the restaurants.

1. The food

Improving food perceptions was clearly absolutely critical to re-appraisal of the brand.

A grown-up menu for adults

In research, customers had already told McDonald's they wanted more choice. In response, the brand had initiated a programme that made more changes to its menu in three years than it had done in the previous thirty. Innovations across the menu saw the introduction of products such as new chicken recipes, using only 100% chicken breast meat from approved poultry farms.

Now even more choice was added. Bagels and porridge were launched at breakfast and fat, salt and sugar content were reduced. Organic milk and Rainforest Alliance coffee were introduced and a 10-year programme for free-range eggs culminated in their exclusive use throughout the menu.

It was also vital to ensure that customers were provided with options that matched their tastes and wallets. More premium food was launched, both beef (e.g. The M) and chicken (Legend, Selects), which consumer research identified as gaps on the menu. The aim was to offer better products to build better impressions with the public. To give an indication of the scale of the success of some of these recipes, McDonald's UK sold 21 million Chicken Legends in 2008.

Healthier Happy Meals for children

Parents wanted the Happy Meal to remain a treat for their kids — still to include a toy, for example — but were concerned about nutrition. Changes had already been made in 2004, adding choice with fruit bags and carrot sticks, but new moves included adding fibre to buns, serving fries unsalted if parents preferred and introducing semi-skimmed organic milk and fresh orange juice. In addition, the salt, fat and sugar content was managed to ensure that nearly 80% of Happy Meal combinations were not high in fat, salt and sugar as defined by the Food Standards Agency.

Parents also said they wanted help getting their kids to eat more fruit and vegetables, so the advertising approach was evolved to use licensed properties such as Kung Fu Panda to promote the 5-a-day items in a Happy Meal. Today McDonald's is one of the biggest providers of cut fruit to children in the UK. This led to the share of family visits growing vs the market: in 2008, for example, 80% of families visited McDonald's.

2. Makeover for the restaurants

Research showed that customers saw room for improvement in some aspects of the McDonald's experience, so these were addressed with a series of investments.

An inviting new look

The single most visible signal of change to consumers was the store re-imaging programme, which began in 2006 and which completely changed the look and feel of the outlets. Out went the 1980s hangover combination of bright red, yellow and plastic. In came softer greens, purples and wood, more modern and contemporary furniture, materials and seating configurations. McDonald's became as cool a place to hang out as any coffee shop.

By the end of 2008 80% of the high street restaurants had been refurbished, with consumer research showing increased consumer commitment to the brand and rising sales.

Encouraging a new attitude

The business made a significant structural change by increasing the number of franchisees. Entrusting more restaurants to local entrepreneurs was a huge success, based on the simple premise that if it is your own business you tend to run a better restaurant. At the same time, focus on improving operating standards led to cleaner, more efficient and friendlier restaurants, while investment in new kitchen equipment enabled the serving of fresher, hotter food. This was complemented by improved communication to stores. The result was distinctly improved customer satisfaction scores. In addition, extended opening hours to reflect changing lifestyles saw more stores trade for 24 hours at least once a week.

A series of innovative ideas

Other initiatives offered evidence of the brand's progressive ethos.
- McDonald's was the first restaurant chain to launch ethical coffee onto the High Street with Rainforest Alliance coffee, lattes and cappuccinos at sensible prices. In 2008 McDonald's sold 10 million more cups of coffee than in 2007.
- It started using bio-diesel made from its own used cooking oil to power the lorries that deliver to restaurants.
- It became the first chain to introduce free wi-fi across the UK — a move that provided customers with a reason to visit more often.

Rebuilding trust in the brand through communications

These physical changes to the business needed to be matched and amplified by communications that engaged people on a different level, which meant that the brand needed to change its conversation with consumers to regain their confidence. Various beliefs, rumours and 'urban myths' had spread about the brand and had gone largely unchallenged.

These were now attacked head-on, demonstrating a new transparency and determination to set the record straight.

The brand challenged the public to make its own mind up about McDonald's, launching a website called 'Make up your own mind', which invited people to ask any questions they wanted and have them answered honestly. In addition, Steve Easterbrook went head to head with Eric Schlosser, author of *Fast Food Nation*, on Newsnight in May 2006.

This was a big gamble, but it paid off. People saw a different side to McDonald's. And it was highly symbolic internally, giving the confidence boost necessary to drive genuine brand revitalisation. The company now regularly meets with government bodies and non-governmental organisations (NGOs) to provide them with the facts about its food and is a willing participant in debates.

McDonald's also became the first restaurant chain to introduce nutritional labelling onto packaging to help people make the right choices for themselves. Internally, several initiatives aimed at upgrading the employee experience were introduced, including the McJob campaign (see Chapter 9), new crew uniforms and the apprenticeship programme.

These changes were shared with the media in an open and honest manner, which continued to challenge media expectations and force reappraisal. The ratio of positive to negative brand messages improved dramatically. For example, during the third quarter of 2008 68% of messages were positive, compared to only 9% negative, with 23% neutral — a remarkable indication of how far the brand had progressed.

Engaging with advertising

McDonald's had always been committed to using advertising to drive its business, but now was the right time to take the opportunity to use it more pro-actively to manage its brand image and perceptions. The intention was to signal to consumers and stakeholders that the company was talking to them in a new and engaging way to celebrate the truths about, and show pride in, the brand.

A prime opportunity for doing this was the Happy Meal, where the changes in the product offered the ideal platform for re-connection with mothers' heads and hearts, through a combination of emotional storytelling and rational reassurance to shift attitudes and make a statement.

This led to the 'That's What Makes McDonald's' campaign, in which the 'Planting' TV commercial told, charmingly and engagingly, the truth about the core ingredients of a Happy Meal, celebrating the food and connecting it back to its source (Figure 1). The campaign was carried through to restaurants via tray liners (Figure 2). And it was used as a key internal communications tool, signifying the brand's new direction and attitude.

Tracking showed that the campaign was the brand's most successful TV campaign this century, and there were strong signs of positively influencing brand perceptions (and not just among the mothers at whom it was primarily aimed). By the end of 2008 not only had the key messages the brand wanted to communicate been picked up by 'Happy Meal' mums and the general audience of young adults, but the campaign had gone a long way to restore its relationship with the British public. 'Planting' had made them feel better about McDonald's (Figure 3).

In the broader advertising context, it is worth noting that as part of improving communications effectiveness McDonald's conducted a thorough econometric study which helped refine media selection, leading to a 29% improvement in advertising return on investment (ROI) since 2005.

Savouring success

From mid/late 2006, the business saw a marked improvement in sales, 'guest counts' and market share. Customer perceptions of the brand also improved significantly, especially on the 'trust' measure which represented a key objective for the brand.

Figure 1. Stills from the TV campaign

Figure 2. Restaurant tray liner

	HM Mums wv 2	General aud wv 2	Benchmark (McD's avg.)
Reach & Branding			
TV ad recognition	62%	59%	50%
Brand Linkage	56%	56%	62%
Creative resonance	77%	69%	55%
New & relevant news			
McDonald's cares about ingredients in its food	96%	94%	75%
McDonald's makes food good quality ingredients	95%	92%	75%
McDonald's don't use processed food	82	77%	75%
Challenging/motivating			
Challenges me & makes me feel better about McDonald's	49%	40%	27% (mums) 16% (Gen. aud)
Likelihood to visit	50%	49%	30%

Figure 3. Performance summary - Family Trust 2008

Appreciation
&
Branding

Communication

Desired effect

1. Business performance

By the end of 2008 McDonald's in the UK had seen 11 consecutive quarters of growth. For the full year 2008 European sales grew by 8.5%. McDonald's does not publicly disclose sales data by individual market. However, to give an indication of the scale of revitalisation, the UK had its best ever year of sales growth in 2008 since it first opened its doors in South London in 1974.

Market share also grew despite operating in what is recognised as one of the most competitive eating out markets in the world. In the 'informal eating out' sector, McDonald's enjoyed four consecutive quarters of increasing share of market from the last quarter of 2007, outstripping the growth that the sector itself was showing over the same period.

2. Consumer perceptions

Changing perceptions of an established brand is notoriously difficult. However, by the end of 2008, significant improvements had been made in all but one of the 30+ brand metrics that were continuously tracked.

First and foremost, McDonald's revitalisation was achieved by listening to its customers and, as a result, making record levels of investment in the things that matter most to both customers and employees. The restaurant experience was significantly upgraded, openness and transparency had become fundamental to the way the company does business and marketing activities were achieving new levels of effectiveness and relevance.

Hovis

04

Re-establishing an iconic brand

Snapshot

A powerful and consistent marketing campaign brought a languishing brand back to life.

Key insights

- Mounting a well-coordinated, carefully integrated and comprehensive marketing campaign which included product improvement and new packaging quickly transformed the Hovis brand from an also-ran to a share-grabbing star.

- By refreshing the brand's powerful advertising legacy and using an innovative assortment of media channels, the campaign became the most talked-about of the year while also generating huge amounts of additional media coverage.

- Significantly improved consumer perceptions translated into rising sales, share and a healthy return.

Summary

Hovis is a great British brand, owned by Premier Foods. Founded 122 years ago, it was a household name for generations. However, since 2006, Hovis had found itself in serious trouble. Over time product quality had gradually been ignored. Advertising spend had been cut and the packaging had become somewhat tired.

By the end of 2007, Hovis' share was plummeting, exacerbated by the runaway success of rival Warburtons. If the brands continued to diverge at this rate, then there would be a 20% point share gap behind Warburtons by the end of 2008, equivalent to £360 million sales per annum.

A new marketing team arrived and began to develop a coherent marketing strategy, including rethinking the communications and new product development. It had a significant impact on performance by the end of December 2008. A year later, perceptions of the brand had risen dramatically, boosting sales and clawing back market share from its rivals.

Beginning the fight back

By the end of 2007 the 122-year-old Hovis brand was in deep trouble (Figure 1). The prospect of such a sharp decline was not only alarming in itself, but it also had some important side-effects. Firstly, retailers were watching with growing impatience. If this was not addressed soon, distribution might be affected, which would then cause sales to spiral further downwards.

Secondly, morale was low among the 6,500-strong workforce. Finally, the decline of Hovis spelled trouble for its parent, Premier Foods plc. Since Hovis was the company's biggest brand by far, any difficulties affected investor confidence, as summed up by a damaging headline in the *Sunday Times*: 'Is Premier toast?'

Faced with such a set of formidable challenges, in early 2008 Premier Foods appointed a new marketing team led by Jon Goldstone and Julie Leivers. They quickly set about assembling a new roster of agencies: MCBD for advertising, Frank for consumer public relations (PR), Cirkle for trade PR, JKR for packaging, Communicator for online communications and MediaVest for media planning and buying. They then galvanised these agencies into acting as a tight unit working towards a complete relaunch of the brand by September 2008. With the final agencies only put in place in April, this gave the company an extremely ambitious time frame of four-to-five months to turn everything around.

The new team pored over the existing data from Millward Brown to IRI with fresh eyes and also commissioned further research, including qualitative and semiotics. From this, it became clear that consumers were increasingly differentiating between 'good bread' and 'bad bread'. They associated the former group with 'healthy, natural food from real bakers' whereas they characterised the latter group as consisting of 'processed products from mass manufacturers'.

The problem for Hovis was that it was increasingly being relegated to the latter group. This was a travesty, given that Hovis' products actually tended to be more natural and healthier than those of their rivals, as well as the brand's historically strong associations with baking heritage and 'goodness'. So the team decided to move Hovis back into pole position as the leading 'good bread' (natural, healthy tasting bread from real bakers).

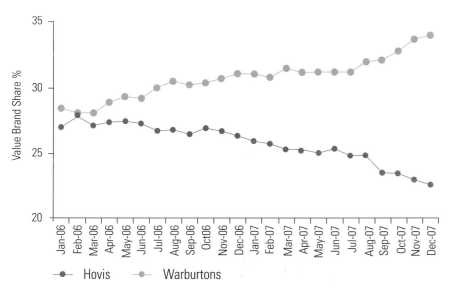

Figure 1

A multi-pronged strategy

There were several critical elements to the turnaround strategy:
1. Improving the product.
2. Revitalising the packaging.
3. Creating outstanding communications.
4. Generating PR and word-of-mouth.

1. Improving the product

The first issue to be tackled was product quality. An intensive programme of testing was put in place, which showed that Hovis came third out of three on all its breads. White, Wholemeal and Best of Both were identified as particular priorities for improvement and new formulations were introduced which promptly beat all their rivals in further testing. The Soft White reformulation was particularly important, as its launch in May 2008 (backed by an outdoor campaign) helped stabilise sales before the main relaunch.

2. Revitalising the packaging

Having improved the product, it needed to be showcased more effectively. Guided by further research, the entire range of 30 SKUs were completely redesigned. They were given a much bolder look, with strong colours, an iconic updating of the logo and confident display of the bread itself. In research, the new design was found to be 'A very strong new pack for Hovis — an excellent expression of the positioning' (Figure 2).

3. Creating outstanding communications

Relaunching the Hovis brand was particularly challenging in that any creative idea would be measured against one of the nation's favourite commercials of all time: the 35-year old commercial 'Boy on bike', which was regularly voted viewers' favourite ad of all time (Figure 3). Here, MCBD

decided that it would be crazy to ignore the legacy of this advertising altogether and so reintroduced the original concept of a boy on a journey, clutching a loaf of bread. But this time the lad found himself running through all the major events of the last century before returning home safely in 2008.

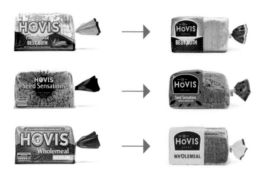

Figure 2. The new packaging

Figure 3. 'Boy on bike' ad

Figure 4.
Press campaign

The moral of the story was that Hovis is 'As good today as it's always been' — which was a perfect encapsulation of the underlying brand strategy. This thought also proved the inspiration for a striking press campaign, where classic Hovis ads of yesteryear were updated to showcase modern products (Figure 4).

4. Generating PR and word-of-mouth

Every opportunity was taken to stoke editorial coverage and word of mouth:
- Journalists were cast as extras to help maximise coverage.
- Employees were also cast to ensure internal support.
- A survey was commissioned to ask consumers which historical events best summed up the British 'spirit' (later used on radio and on TV interviews).
- A 'trailer' was created to be used as a piece of teaser content for the City (and for YouTube, Media Guardian and Brand Republic).
- An interactive educational pack tied into the New Literacy Framework was created.

Maximising the media strategy

TV advertising kicked off the launch because the brand needed to be catapulted back into the nation's hearts and the medium remains unbeatable for engaging people emotionally. However, this was no ordinary TV campaign. Most famously, the launch ad was a media first, running at 122 seconds (one for every year of Hovis' history which itself worked well as a PR story) before cutting down to 90 and 10 seconds. Equally importantly, appropriate programming was chosen for the ads, such as Coronation Street (where ITV took the unprecedented step of cutting the soap by two seconds to accommodate Hovis) and the 'Pride of Britain Awards'.

Online was used to maximize interest, with websites such as MSN and Virgin Media taken over on launch day. Over 300,000 people watched the ad online in the first month alone. A slightly different mix was used during the product communication phase. TV continued to be used as a form of 'air cover' but was also supported with more direct media such as newspaper advertising, door drops, inserts and outdoor sites located near supermarkets.

Once the big brand idea that Hovis was 'As good today as it's always been' was launched, the next step was to provide some specific product evidence. So throughout 2009, a number of hard messages were communicated under the campaign umbrella.

For instance:
- Highlighting the surprising fact that two slices of Best of Both contained as much calcium as a glass of milk.
- Challenging consumers to 'feel healthier or your money back' when switching to Hovis Wholemeal.
- Conveying the news that Hovis white bread had been named Britain's softest, in taste tests.
- Using Seed Sensations poppy seed loaf to raise money for the Royal British Legion on Remembrance Sunday.

Significant consumer impact

The 2008 campaign was the most talked-about of the year: 72% of consumers saw the campaign and millions more saw the media coverage surrounding it, which was worth over £2 million in total.

Thousands more discussed the campaign online. Indeed, a record 180 blogs included conversations about Hovis over the period. Meanwhile, 274,000 people visited the new Hovis website, with almost half (133,000) watching the TV commercial there.

And a further 180,000 people watched the ad on YouTube in the first month alone.

The advertising went on to be named campaign of the year by both *Campaign* magazine, the BBC and the British Television Advertising Awards. It received the same title in three separate polls of the British public conducted by Film4, UTalk and Mintel. Over 1,000 people even went to the trouble of writing to Hovis to congratulate it directly. Significantly, given the wider commercial situation described earlier, the campaign was also welcomed by the City and the trade. In addition, in 2009, another UTalk poll named the 'Poppy/British Legion' ad the best commercial of the year.

The campaign wasn't just appreciated for its entertainment value, though. 86% of viewers took out the main message that Hovis is 'as good today as it's always been' (vs. a norm of 52%). And 65% said that the advertising 'got me thinking differently about Hovis'.

Figure 5 shows how perceptions of Hovis rose dramatically over 2008-9 because of the brand's

revitalisation. Interestingly, perceptions of modern relevance rose significantly as well as perceptions of heritage. These improved brand perceptions were accompanied by improved product impression across the board as brand-specific activity kicked in 2009 (see Figure 6), while consumers increasingly associated Hovis with innovative, differentiated products. As a result, consideration of Hovis rose by 11% points from 2008-9.

More significantly, this translated into actual changed behaviour, with penetration rising from an already high base (72.5% to 74.6%). In addition, as Figures 7 and 8 illustrate, both frequency and number of products bought rose significantly.

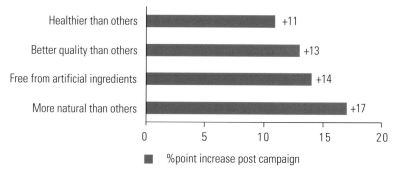

Figure 5

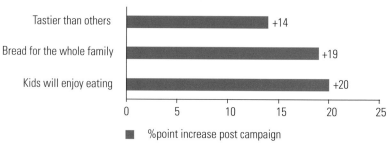

Figure 6

Beating expectations

After two years of more or less continuous decline, Hovis sales started to rise — and kept rising, until the brand was up 14% year-on-year (YOY). In absolute (£sterling) terms, this made Hovis Britain's fastest growing FMCG brand in 2009.

Within this, the format-specific campaigns were particularly successful. For instance the 'Voted Britain's softest' campaign drove Hovis Soft White sales by 36% YOY. Meanwhile, the 'wholemeal challenge' activity grew share of brown bread by 2.3% points and the 'Best of Both with calcium' activity grew its share of the half-and-half category by 4.1% points. On a different note, the 'Poppy' campaign in 2009 raised over £110,000 for the Royal British Legion.

Most importantly of all, overall share rose consistently, so that the 20% point gap predicted never materialised. Instead, Hovis was now only a tantalising 6% points behind Warburtons, and continued to make ground.

With such a dramatic and conspicuous success story, the campaign was also welcomed by the City and the trade. Premier's shares outperformed its fellow British food producers by around 24% in 2009. While this was not all down to the Hovis campaign, the activity did feature prominently in the analysts' reports. Investec, for example, concluded that 'it is clear that the relaunch has been a success in terms of sales and marketing'.

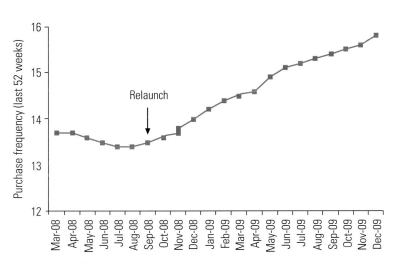

Figure 7. Source: TNS

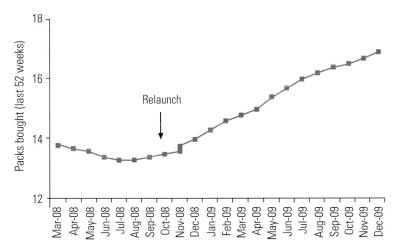

Figure 8. Source: TNS

What about other plausible causes for the brand's success?

- It certainly wasn't about slashing prices. The average price of a Hovis loaf actually rose significantly over the period, because of increases in the cost of raw materials.
- Nor did Hovis raise prices by less than the competition. Warburtons also raised its prices in 2008, meaning that the relative gap between the two brands remained virtually static. However, while perceptions that Hovis was 'worth paying more for' rose by 4% points over the period, Warburtons' score on this measure fell by 4% points — suggesting that the campaign was more successful in justifying the price rise.
- The brand wasn't boosted through the use of promotions. All bread brands (especially Warburtons) increased their use of promotions over 2008-9, due to the recession. However, the analysts at Dresdner Kleinwort noted that Hovis' strong performance wasn't simply being achieved by a ramping up of promotions.
- Nor were there benefits from distribution gains, either for the master brand or the main SKUs.

Robust returns

Finally, while bread sales as a whole rose by about 2% in volume over the period, the share data proves the impact of the campaign on the brand's fortunes. Hovis had originally been projected to hit 17% share by the end of 2008, with further declines in 2009 very likely. By the end of 2009, however, Hovis had actually achieved 26% share — 9% points above this projection.

In a £1.81 billion market, these nine incremental share points were worth £163 million sales per annum. But to calculate the real return on marketing investment (ROMI) the longer-term value of these sales should be factored in. Applying a rough FMCG industry ratio, it is estimated that these effects could have been 2.5 times greater than in 2008, giving a potential total of £407 million.

Applying the company's average gross margin of c.30% would give the company a potential return of £122 million. If the spend of £15 million accounted for at least 12% of the results, the campaign will have easily paid for itself.

All images appearing in this case study are reproduced by permission of Premier Foods.

British Gas

04

Getting back to great

Snapshot

The UK's leading energy supplier turbo-charged its brand performance by going back to customer basics and rising above price-led promotions.

Key insights

- British Gas was determined to revitalise its brand by putting the customer at the heart of its strategy.

- It did this by uncovering valuable customer insights about the relation of people to their homes.

- This formed the basis of a dramatic overhaul of its marketing approach which led to a number of key customer-centric initiatives which, in turn, transformed brand perception and performance.

Summary

British Gas, part of the Centrica Group, provides gas, electricity and home repair services to millions of customers in Scotland, Wales and England. In 1986 the company received the accolade of the 'Brand of Britain' by The Marketing Society. In the years that followed, however, its reputation fell. The erosion of key brand health measures was accompanied by a declining customer base. There was widespread acknowledgement that the company had had its eyes fixed more on the competition that its customers.

In 2008 British Gas set out on a 'journey back to great', beginning with a wholesale re-evaluation of its approach to marketing and putting the customer at the heart of this brand revitalisation. A new organising thought was developed based on the insight: 'Your home is your world. Count on British Gas to look after it'. A number of initiatives, including becoming the principal partner of British swimming and environmental programmes, were developed as part of this revitalisation.

Not only did this lead to the proportion of customers claiming British Gas as their first choice of energy supplier rising to an all-time high, but 2009 saw the first substantial growth in customer numbers in seven years.

Losing sight of the customers

British Gas has been powering Britain for almost 200 years, evolving from the 'Gas, Light and Coke Company' in 1812 to become the leading provider of energy and home services in Britain today. 1986 was a defining year in the company's history, when The Gas Act returned the gas industry to the private sector and British Gas plc was formed.

The iconic 'Tell Sid' campaign, with its strapline: 'If you see Sid, tell him', aimed to persuade the British public to invest in its shares. British Gas was one of the highest spenders on advertising that year and the campaign one of the most successful of all time. The initial public offering (IPO) of 135p per share valued British Gas at £9 billion. The offer was four times oversubscribed and The Marketing Society recognised British Gas as the 'Brand of Britain' in 1986.

In the years following privatisation the energy market was characterised by massive upheaval. When the period of monopoly ended in 1998, consumers were free to choose their gas supplier. Fierce competition followed and new entrants, hungry for their share of the market, were engaged in a race to the bottom.

With its customer base being continually eroded, British Gas played its part in the price wars, seeking to retain customers with promises of cheaper deals and balance its losses with increased product holdings. However, by focusing on differentiation through price, energy brands risked dissolving into homogenous substitutes. Furthermore, with each price rise and fall the energy market became ever more confusing and consumer apathy increasingly turned into anger.

With its eyes firmly fixed on the competition, British Gas lost sight of what the consumer really wanted and failed to define what the brand stood for beyond size, heritage and trust — credentials common across all major players.

While its communications were rationally strong, focusing on expertise, reliability and price, British Gas had failed to connect emotionally with its customers. As a result, customer numbers continued to decline (Figure 1). Although by the end of 2007 it was still market leader, British Gas was far from being the 'Brand of Britain'.

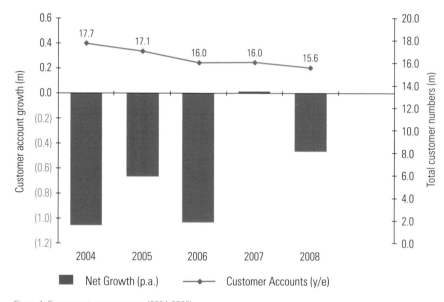

Figure 1. Energy customer accounts (2004-2008)

Rethinking every aspect of the brand

In 2008, British Gas set out with the vision of getting 'back to great'. Measures of 'greatness' were defined as:
- Being first choice energy provider.
- Increasing the key drivers of brand choice ('value' and 'being easy to deal with').
- Arresting the decline in customer numbers.
- Growing market share.

To deliver this, the new marketing team members were united in their belief that British Gas must prove that it stood for more than homogenous energy supply and their conviction that to revitalise the brand the consumer needed to be at its heart. This encompassed a number of key initiatives.

1. Gaining a new view of the customer

Prior to 2008 customer segmentation at British Gas was based on transactional relationships such as energy consumption and product holdings rather than needs.

Placing the consumer at the heart of the British Gas revitalisation required a new segmentation, and one that could facilitate a deeper understanding of customers and prospects. The new segmentation was built by assessing more than 50 consumer behaviours. It was designed so that it could, over time, lead to more targeted investment, efficient and effective new product development and relevant relationship and proposition development.

Critically, the organisation was quick to embrace and activate the segmentation across all areas of the business, supported by engaging internal communications.To ensure the segmentation remained a living tool, an ongoing customer panel was set up reflecting the eight identified segments. This gave consumers a genuine voice at the very top of the organisation, covering everything from airing frustrations about call centres to helping shape British Gas strategy on future energy supplies.

2. Uncovering new consumer insights

British Gas has played an important part in helping people run their homes and home is where the heart is, especially for the British. Eight out of ten consumers agreed that "it is important to me to be able to own my own home", This was consistent across all demographic groups, even the youngest.

After all, home is where you eat, you sleep, you raise a family and you entertain friends. In times of uncertainty (and in 2008 the UK was experiencing the most severe recession since World War II) trends show that people spend even more time at home with their families.

Every year, across the country, millions of customers trusted British Gas enough to invite them into their homes, believing that with British Gas their homes were in good hands. In addition to gas and electricity supply, British Gas offered a wide range of home services including plumbing, drainage, appliance and electrical care. This made it well-positioned to understand what customers needed to help them with the smooth running of their homes, and, by extension, their worlds.

Through this understanding of the role British Gas could play, a new central organising thought was developed, rooted around the insight; 'Your home is your world. Count on British Gas to look after it'. Research endorsed the power of this thought, with 84% of consumers saying they related to it.

3. Developing new propositions

While historically propositions had been developed based on the products British Gas wanted to sell, new propositions were now being developed focusing on the needs of the different customer segments.

- A new 'Energy Smart' proposition — promising 'no more estimated bills'—was developed to meet the needs of the segment of customers who were interested in energy efficiency, placed high value on transparency and were happy transacting online.

- A new 'Call Ahead' proposition, promising that 'British Gas engineers will call ahead to let you know they are on their way', was developed to appeal to the segment of customers who were juggling busy lives, had little time to deal with energy providers and liked using the phone.

- A 'Cheapest Electricity in Britain' proposition was developed to appeal to the segment of customers who sought value, wanted to be rewarded for loyalty and looked for certainty.

While all the propositions had broad appeal across the customer base, the starting point for each stemmed from a rich understanding of how British Gas could most effectively 'look after the world' of one particular segment.

4. Forming new partnerships

New partnerships were developed as part of the British Gas journey to becoming great again. These partnerships demonstrated how a revitalised British Gas was actively 'looking after your world', not just talking about it.

Going swimming

In March 2009 British Gas announced its British swimming sponsorship. Swimming is part of the fabric of British life: 12 million people and 50% of British Gas customers swim every month. British Gas swimming sponsorship supports the national team, as well as grass-roots projects such as Pools4Schools. One in five British children leaves primary school unable to swim the curriculum standard of 25m, often because they don't have access to a pool. Pools4Schools responds to the challenge by using temporary, mobile pools to teach children to swim. The initiative has enabled hundreds of thousands of children to learn this key life skill.

Because families are at the heart of the company's customers, in September 2009 every British Gas customer was given the opportunity to enjoy a free family swim merely by printing off a voucher. The campaign was fronted by Olympic champion Rebecca Adlington. 1,200 pools signed up to the swim and by December 2009 more than 150,000 families had taken part.

Generation Green was a programme established by the company with the aim of creating, rather than inviting, 'green' behavioural change. It is a nationwide schools initiative promoting environmental awareness, incentivising green behaviour and bringing together schools, children, their families and friends.

It was designed to require little effort for teachers to set up and run, but which would deliver significant and long-lasting benefits through a combination of green lesson plans and rewards. Supporting it was a sophisticated communications strategy that sought to recruit schools and engage children before the broadcast advertising began. By the end of 2009 Generation Green had engaged 9,972 UK schools and provided over 514,900 hours of green learning, affecting almost four million children.

5. Creating new advertising

The new consumer insight — 'Your home is your world. Count on British Gas to look after it' was brought to life by an engaging creative vehicle that placed customers at the heart of the brand. The campaign was launched in March 2009 and featured people's homes on individual planets being cared for by British Gas. The strapline 'British Gas. Looking after your world' articulated the brand essence.

The creative work (Figures 2 through 5) had a more modern and future-facing feel than previous British Gas campaigns, and while familiar images such as the British Gas van still featured, new assets such as animation, voice-over and music signalled revitalisation. The 'Planet Home' creative approach enabled a wide range of propositions, including price, to be communicated in a consistent and compelling way.

Figure 2. Example of creative work

Figure 3. Example of creative work

Figure 4. Example of creative work

Figure 5. Example of creative work

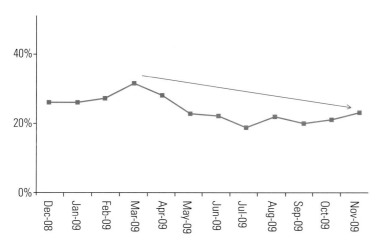

Base: Dec 2008-Nov 2009 Monthly trends
All (1027-1042); British Gas customers: (339-377); Competitor customers (651-700)

—■— Competitor Customers

Figure 6. The proportion of competitor customers claiming they would never use British Gas is down significantly

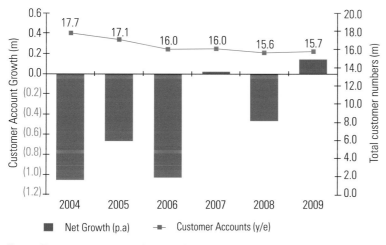

■ Net Growth (p.a)   —■— Customer Accounts (y/e)

Figure 7. Energy customer accounts (2004-2009)

Steering the brand back on course

Although it was only the start of a long journey, the new marketing vision and strategy, developed with CHI & Partners and Carat, had a dramatic effect in a short time. For example, the proportion of customers claiming British Gas was their 'first-choice energy provider' was at an all-time high at 64% by November 2009, while the proportion of competitors' customers claiming they would never use British Gas declined significantly from March 2009 to the end of November (Figure 6).

The proportion of customers believing British Gas to be more expensive than other energy providers was at a record low and the key brand drivers of 'value', and 'easy to deal with' all showed significant gains.

The Planet Home campaign exceeded all targets, with cut-through with branding and affinity scores all showing significant gains. In terms of business effect, it was more successful than any previous campaign in driving sales.

Econometric modelling, independently assessed by Billetts, showed that, based on acquisition and retention the campaign returned £3 (net present value) for every £1 invested. Perhaps the clearest evidence of brand revitalisation is that in 2009 British Gas substantially grew customer numbers and expanded market share (Figure 7). This has continued in 2010, with customer numbers growing by 500,000.

All images appearing in this case study are reproduced by permission of British Gas.

KFC

04

Finger lickin' good

Snapshot

A powerful combination of product development and inspired marketing that was true to the brand restored KFC's fortunes on the high street.

Key insights

- A fresh business strategy, rigorously implemented through all aspects of marketing, transformed the KFC brand from sharp decline to category-beating growth.

- The strategy was based on the courageous decision to buck the trend among fast food outlets to talk about their 'healthy' options and instead stress the great product taste.

- This was accompanied by cleverly-timed new product development to reach both key target audiences of young people and families at the same time.

Summary

KFC Corporation, based in Louisville, Kentucky, is the world's most popular chicken restaurant chain. It operates more than 5,200 restaurants in the US and over 15,000 around the world. It is part of Yum Brands!, which had revenues of just under $11 billion in 2009. KFC reached Britain in 1965 (before either McDonald's or Burger King). It now has over 700 stores.

But by 2005 KFC had lost its way, with a lacklustre reputation on the high street and slumping sales. So in-depth research was carried out to find a way to revitalise the brand's fortunes. A new strategy based on taste not only set the brand apart from its competitors but it brought back both families and young people. A cycle of new product development carried out over the year also increased both frequency of visits and expenditure.

By April of 2006 the brand grew steadily for the first time in three years, peaking at 30% year-on-year (YOY) growth. Communication boosted the brand's popularity to the point that the average spend rose by over 60p per ticket throughout the year.

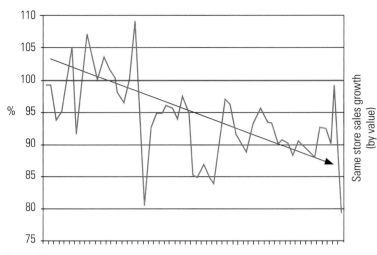

Figure 1. 2005 sales
Source: KFC

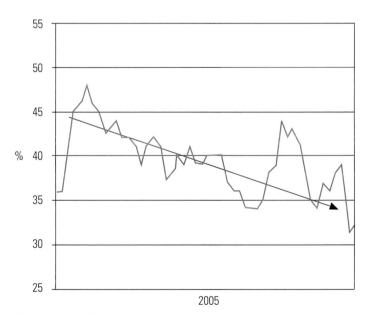

Market defined as all QSR users

Figure 2. 2005 Market penetration
Source: Conquest, Quantitative (BIT)

Headed in the wrong direction

By the end of 2005, KFC was in trouble. It had become a dinosaur on the high street. The brand remained as famous as ever, but now felt out of date and favour. KFC no longer seemed to have a role for consumers in modern Britain. Sales were in freefall, suffering ongoing and serious decline. Market penetration was also falling (as well as average ticket value). This poor performance was a result of a number of challenges facing both the category and the brand itself (Figures 1 and 2).

1. Category challenges

The nation's attitudes to food changed significantly over 2005. The 'health agenda' that had been brewing for a few years, reached critical mass. Jamie Oliver launched 'school dinners' (See Chapter 10) and Gillian McKeith became a household name among a host of food and diet-related programming. As a result, quick-service restaurant (QSR) brands became public enemy number one. This, combined with the relentless coverage and hype about obesity in the media, had a significant impact on consumers' dietary aspirations. For example, according to a 2006 study by TNS and the Food Standards Agency (FSA), by the end of 2005 67% of people believed they should eat fewer fatty foods, 64% fewer sugary foods and 58% less salt.

Moreover, new competitors were challenging the category, offering healthier alternatives. Service stations, supermarkets, chemists and coffee shops were all selling ready-to-eat food — significantly fragmenting the market. Branded sandwiches such as Subway and Prêt-a-Manger were stealing market share from KFC as they increased their number of stores and gained market penetration. McDonald's and Burger King followed suit by attempting to become health-focused in response to public pressure.

2. Brand challenges

There was an abyss between how the brand projected itself and customers' experiences. Recent advertising had given the brand a much-needed injection of credibility, youth and energy. However, while the advertising portrayed this appealing and sexy image, the reality was tired stores and underwhelming products.

The other challenge was new product development (NPD), an important element in this market. There were two key audiences for these quick-service restaurants: 'families' and 'teens and young adults'. These groups accounted for 89% of KFC's sales.

In 2005 KFC's NPD was aimed at the youth market, with snacking items developed to increase their frequency of visits. The problem was that KFC then became the place for snacks (with low ticket prices and margins), not a meal destination. Attempts were also made to create healthier food with a range of non-fried chicken, salads and a response to new competitors with sub sandwiches. As well as confusing consumers about what the brand stood for, these innovations were either failing or cannibalising regular sales.

Meanwhile, families were leaving the brand. Despite eating more meals together they weren't choosing KFC (an FSA food trends study in 2006 showed 57% of people ate one meal a day with all family members compared to 52% in 2004) and sales among families were suffering accordingly. Families did not feel the brand was for them any more — an image reinforced by poor service and stores frequented by 'youths'. This was particularly damaging for sales because families' average spend was almost three times that of young adults.

Learning from in-depth research

A new direction was badly needed. In the face of media pressure for healthy living and against fast food, what would motivate people to return to KFC? An in-depth qualitative study was launched to improve the understanding of consumer attitudes and inform brand repositioning.

- **Fast food tastes good.** The obesity debate gave consumers a new awareness that 'fast food was not healthy'. However, this didn't mean total abstinence from their favourite food. While still seeking 'better for you' cues, they didn't want fast food to be 'good for you'. Consumers choose fast food because it tastes good, not because it's healthy. As one said, "You've decided to go to McDonald's. Why would you buy chopped-up apple?"

- **KFC tastes especially good.** There's something especially compelling about the taste of KFC: "You can't make it yourself and competitors can't get close". KFC's singular taste unified all consumers. Once the desire for KFC lodged in consumers' minds, there was nothing else that would satisfy the urge. The thought of the taste quickly turned to a craving that had to be satisfied.

- **What the KFC taste means to each audience.** For families, KFC's strength was the product itself. The media's food obsession had made parents particularly aware of the authenticity of their food (in light of bad publicity surrounding products like Turkey Twizzlers). As well as seeking an economic way to feed hungry mouths, they wanted the reassurance of 'real food'. KFC was the only high street fast food outlet that served freshly-prepared whole chicken, not reformed or reconstituted chicken products. This authenticity was seen to be a crucial benefit.

Teens and youths also craved the taste of KFC. They were seen as impulsive eaters who ate whenever they were hungry. They followed their cravings and weren't brand loyal, but constantly looking for variation and new tastes. Although their mealtimes were less formally defined than families, they were frequent purchasers of meals on the go. If they got the urge for KFC, they followed it.

Devising a ground-breaking new strategy

The brand platform chosen for all communications was 'That chicken urge can only be satisfied with the irresistible, indescribable taste of KFC'. This was indeed a radical step — doing the exact opposite of competitors and in the face of popularly-accepted consumer trends. While competitors attempted to embrace healthy eating trends, KFC repositioned itself around the fact that its product tasted delicious (Figure 3).

In other words, KFC became proud of its chicken again, reminding people about the heart of its brand and simultaneously connecting with what consumers sought from the fast food market.

The big challenge, however, was to take a single brand message and make it compelling for both audiences. So all marketing activities proudly put food at their heart. The brand's endline was changed to become: 'You've got great taste.'

Families were identified as the primary audience for reviving the brand, with mothers as the key decision-makers at dinner, deciding whether to take the night off or treat the family. Products, messages and media were all aimed at them. Youths became the secondary target, with separate products and communications developed specifically for them.

Nor was there any repeat of the previous mistakes where NPD sought to introduce healthy salads or 'sub' sandwiches. The year was instead divided into eight promotional periods in each of which one family and one youth product were promoted (Figure 4). As well as generating news, these products also encouraged current consumers to increase both

Figure 3. KFC brand identity

PERIOD	1	2	3	4	5	6	7	8
FAMILIES	Family Feast	Free Ice Cream	Mum's Night Off	Deluxe Boneless Box	Favourites Bucket	Family Feast	Zinger Chicken	Boneless Box
YOUTHS	Zinger Tower Burger	2 Piece Chicken Meal	Wicked Meal	Toasted Twister and Salsa	Blazin' Hot Mini Fillet	Fully Loaded Box Meal	Zinger Mix & Match	Buffalo Toasted Twister

Figure 4. Promotional calendar 2006

their frequency and ticket price per visit, with new 'layers' of products avoiding cannibalisation of existing products.

Four new meals were introduced which either made mothers' lives easier, or offered greater variety or better quality for the family. For younger consumers there were five new products offering variations of taste. The introduction of individual box meals also raised spend among this value-conscious group.

New products were not only rigorously tested in both qualitative and quantitative research, but were also trialled in test regions supported by above-the-line and in-store communications. Only after a sufficiently good test performance were they added to the national calendar.

Selling the great taste

Given the strategy of constantly giving both targets new reasons to buy KFC, the challenge was to support all promotions with communications without significantly increasing the media budget.

1. Advertising

Advertising followed the NPD strategy by using media to ensure each group was targeted as effectively as possible. In all channels the core message was irresistible taste.

- To target mothers, prime-time TV was used in the run-up to the evening meal. Commercials used insightful truths about everyday family life to illustrate the relevance of new products and KFC began to feel like a mainstream, accessible, family brand again.

- The youth target was more likely to be out and about. Above-the-line spend was transferred from TV to posters within close proximity of stores. The product was made the hero of the ads, with appealing food photography in order to spark that unique KFC craving.

2. In-store communications

All messages were also carried through to the in-store environment which simplified the customer's journey to purchase and reinforced new purchase behaviour. There was a distinct synergy of communications.

3. Other channels

In order to inform customers about provenance and nutritional details, a number of actions were taken. For example, the website was updated to contain all such information, and in-store leaflets about the food's sourcing were produced. This was to provide reassurance, not to claim the food was 'healthy'.

4. In-store experience

The new pride and energy in the brand was also reflected in the stores and customer experience. Staff training was focused on teamwork and education in new products. In addition, 30% of the estate was refurbished, with a tangible impact on sales.

Revolutionising brand performance

The results were dramatic. KFC demonstrated immediate growth as the new marketing plan was implemented.

- Sales rapidly improved. By April the brand was experiencing sustained growth for the first time since 2003, peaking at 30% year-on-year growth. Despite losses in the first quarter the year ended in significant growth (Figure 5).

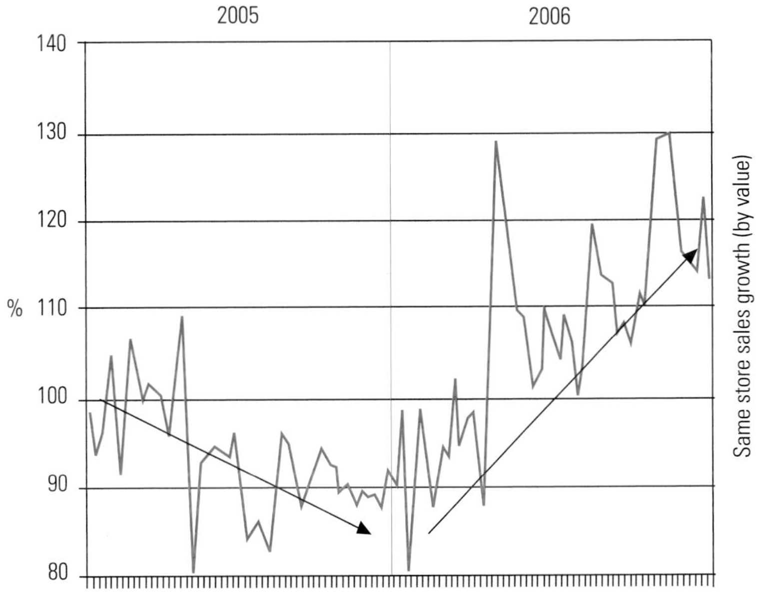

- The brand's increased penetration was a key factor behind the sales growth: shifting from a low of 31% in December 2005 to 49% a year later. This would be a significant change in fortunes for any brand, but was unprecedented, given the adverse factors this category had faced.

- Ticket price, which had been in continued decline, also rose steadily, partly as a consequence of the increased number of family meals but also because the brand was now able to sell products at a price premium based on the new positioning of superior taste. The average spend rose by over 60p per ticket over 2006.

Standing out from the competitive crowd

While other fast food brands continued to lose share of total eating occasions. KFC defied this trend, demonstrating continued growth at the expense of its competitors such as McDonald's and Burger King. Perceptions of the KFC brand increased compared with its two major competitors. This measure combined perceptions of 'value', 'experience' and 'food' for each brand. KFC went from being considered the same or worse than these competitors to being superior in every area. Significantly, KFC's food was its leading brand strength.

As well as a superior image, KFC also found a new salience among consumers. While awareness of its competitors declined, KFC reached an all-time high level of brand awareness. The communications strategy was clearly reaping its rewards.

However, KFC didn't simply 'purchase' these improvements. The brand's advertising spend increased only marginally between 2005-6, while it continued to be consistently outspent by McDonald's. KFC's proud new tone of voice was reflected in

Figure 5. Sales growth
Source: Conquest, Quantitative (BIT)

consumer attitudes. While other brands were losing their fans, KFC retained its popularity. By the third quarter of 2006, the gap between KFC and McDonald's was at an all-time low (Figure 6).

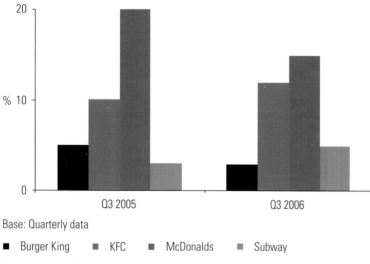

Base: Quarterly data

■ Burger King   ■ KFC   ■ McDonalds   ■ Subway

Figure 6. Favorite QSR overall
Source: Conquest, Quantitative (BIT)

The greatest success was among the new core target audience. KFC's penetration and frequency among families improved radically, restoring KFC's penetration to over 50% (a 20% change). This clearly demonstrated the fundamental role the marketing strategy played in the brand's revival.

Chapter 5
Sustaining the
Brand Promise

Chris MacLeod
Director of Group
Marketing,
Transport for London

'Brand' must be one of the most overused terms in marketing, alongside the word 'marketing' itself. But once the brand positionings have been developed, the charts written and the big presentations made, the talking has to give way to the real world work of delivering and sustaining the brand promise. And the results of what this can achieve are perfectly demonstrated in the three case studies in this chapter.

Starting first with Marks & Spencer (M&S), I can remember a time when M&S prided itself on not advertising. But a new management team recognised that customers were increasingly out of touch with the affordable quality the brand offered. New advertising and more relevant products helped restore its 'promise'. But marketing is a lot easier when the economy is on the up; the strength of M&S was to stick with its positioning when things got tougher.

Turning to Virgin Atlantic, we find another case where the marketers have stuck with a long-term positioning and also maintained a commitment to high profile, differentiated advertising. Virgin has always been known as a bit of a rebel —but the challenge with such a positioning is how to maintain it over time.

Its solution was to keep doing things that bit differently and to maintain the distinctive brand 'voice' of its founder.

Finally, we have Audi. There is something of Apple about the way Audi has developed in recent years, with a major commitment to design and a totally integrated product experience. Strong advertising has again played an important role. And every stage of the customer journey is strongly branded and distinctive, adding up to a highly differentiated brand and impressive growth in recent years in a demanding and competitive sector.

So what are the lessons from these impressive brand operators?

A commitment to a strongly differentiated positioning and a willingness to support this with distinctive advertising. Strong product and service integration through the marketing mix. Consistency. Nothing too unusual there; but perhaps the most important requirements of all are bravery and a preparedness to stick to what you believe in and deliver it. It's easier said than done.

Audi

05

Vorsprung durch Technik Marketing

Snapshot

A consistently high standard of car marketing has turned
Audi into an iconic, best-selling brand in the UK.

Key insights

- Audi has championed integrated, consistent, innovative and creatively ground-breaking marketing for over 25 years with the famous strapline *Vorsprung durch Technik*.

- This has helped make the brand the modern icon of the prestige car sector with an enviable competitive advantage.

- The power of the UK's approach to marketing is evidenced by the fact that sales in this market have out-performed those of Spain, France, Germany and Italy.

Marketing has played an instrumental role in Audi's inexorable rise from being a niche brand to challenging for the lead in the prestige car sector. It is proof that consistent needn't mean conservative, and that creative can also mean effective. For 25 years, Audi's distinctive approach has continued to challenge the boundaries of convention in marketing and the car industry alike. It has become synonymous with one of the most memorable straplines in advertising: *Vorsprung durch Technik*.

Summary

Audi has manufactured cars since 1909 in Ingolstadt, Germany and is the major premium brand within the Volkswagen (VW) Group. In the UK, Audi has now become firmly established as a leading force within the prestige car sector, famed for its engineering and admired for its commercial success.

Pushing boundaries

Vorsprung durch Technik has not just been Audi's brand message, but has also underpinned the philosophy for its behaviour. Audi has always been innovative in the way it reaches its customers, pushing the boundaries of convention, expectation and technological possibility and proving the brand's progressive credentials rather than just claiming them. However, this has never been about novelty for its own sake. Innovation has also allowed the brand to communicate in new and more relevant ways with the audience.

1. Launch of a new channel

- As car news became part of entertainment culture, in 1999 Audi created the Audi TV Channel. This was the first branded TV channel. It created a singular platform for prospective customers to engage with the brand at their own leisure within the context of TV entertainment and without the pressure of a showroom. In 2009 the channel moved from Sky to an on-demand model as it continued to evolve.

2. Imaginative content creation

- Since 1994 Audi has been a magazine publisher, producing a high-quality monthly magazine.
- In 2003, Audi created an edition of *GQ* magazine. The 'Power Edition' featured modern icons of power, including the Audi RS6.
- For the launch of the new TT, Audi offered contemporary versions of classic music tracks, with its 'TT Remastered' campaign.

3. Generating brand buzz

- To launch the A6, Audi partnered with the *New Scientist* for a competition, giving away a trip to space.

- 2003's A8 campaign involved the biggest-ever single burst of outdoor activity with the wrapping of 80 landmark buildings with giant posters.

4. Going interactive

- Interactive TV has been exploited for a number of TV campaigns, giving viewers a chance to access more content and register interest.
- Audi was the first car brand to move online, winning awards for its creativity as early as 1996. Audi.co.uk functions as a virtual dealership, enabling customers to research and configure the perfect Audi.

Consistent integration

Integration has been a key tenet of Audi's communication. Creative ideas are executed across every relevant channel, allowing consumers to have a seamless experience with the brand across the many touch-points they may experience in purchasing a car.

Integration has a multiplying effect for creative ideas. As the communications have been integrated across more channels, the marketing spend per acquisition has reduced, proving the power of integrated creativity.

Creative excellence

Since 1982 Audi has set the standard for great car advertising. It has used communications as a potent tool to create a distinctive identity for the brand. Audi's witty, intelligent but understated tone of voice has earned it a place in the British public's hearts and minds, and its advertisements get more than their fair share of attention.

Figure 1. Clip from R8 advertising

Figure 2. Clip from R8 advertising

"Any motor advertising that breaks the mould of the traditional car commercial, with its laboured shots of leather interiors, alloy wheels and sleek bodywork, is to be welcomed. Clearly a supporter of this philosophy, Audi has made a point of applying creative thinking in the development, not only to its cars but also to its marketing."
Source: Superbrands Volume VI

The brand has perpetually infiltrated popular culture and been a genuine talking point. Award-winning campaigns that exemplify this have included Villa, Number One, Wakeboarder and R8 Construction, which had the tagline: 'The slowest car we've ever built' (Figures 1 and 2).

Building close customer relationships

Customer retention is crucial in the automotive sector for long-term growth. Customer communications can build a sense of loyalty, and ultimately drive repurchase. Audi has developed an architecture of customer communications with a focus of fostering much tighter relationships with the brand: the Audi Customer Journey. This maps the ownership cycle and optimises communications within this.

Using all direct media channels (direct mail, e-mail, outbound telephone etc.), the tone and focus of each communication is varied to reflect the requirements at each ownership stage.

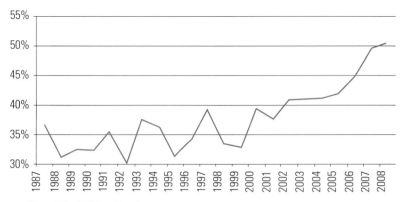

Figure 3. Audi UK brand loyalty

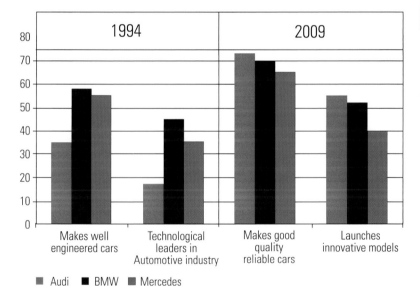

Figure 4. Brand image shifts over time

Audi has also built a predictive marketing database that understands the lifestage of each customer (Table 1). This ensures direct communications are timely and well targeted. The impact of this initiative has been marked: Audi's loyalty rate has increased rapidly since 1987 (Figure 3).

Table 1

Ownership stage	Focus
Post-vehicle handover	Celebration/reinforcing decision
Early ownership	Getting to know your car
Mid-ownership	Getting to know the Audi range
Late ownership	Keeping your Audi in perfect condition
Retention/repurchase	Choosing your next Audi

Excelling at distribution

In 1982 Audis were distributed from the corner of VW showrooms nationally. A key part of the brand's success has been to build a network of dedicated Audi Centres as tangible local flagships for the brand. These have allowed the brand to build local relationships with customers and offer integrated purchase and service experiences. The network has also helped galvanise the sales force. Most recently, the Audi West London Centre opened in 2009, including two floors committed to Audi's brand heritage of *Vorsprung durch Technik*.

Developing a modern iconic brand

By 2010 the Audi brand was the modern icon of the prestige car sector. This is the consequence of years of single-minded brand-building. From once having been the outsider, then becoming a quality contender, Audi has set the agenda in the prestige sector. Audi's reputation among car buyers for 'engineering excellence' and 'innovation' has now overtaken BMW and Mercedes (Figure 4). Further evidence of the impact of marketing has been its rise in the car buyers' consciousness, with brand awareness more than doubling. The Audi brand's success has not been limited to shifts in brand image measures alone. It is now a brand with genuine momentum and advocacy among buyers of prestige cars, with the highest levels of advocacy, preference and buzz among this audience. Most crucially, Audi has become the most desirable and considered brand among the car-buying audience.

The numbers say it all

The ultimate measure of marketing success is the brand's commercial success. Sales have increased radically over the last 25 years. Volume sales have increased by 452% and value sales by 1,325%. No other car brand has grown its share of the market at this rate, let alone managed to compete genuinely with the most established prestige brands.

Volume sales increased from under 20,000 in 1982 to over 100,000 in 2008 (Figure 5), while value sales have increased steadily since 1987 (Figure 6). Even before volume sales began to rise significantly, the brand was able to command an increasing premium per car as its reputation improved.

Audi's market share has also grown consistently since the late 1980s, from 1.18% in 1982 to 4.73% in 2008 (Figure 7). The emergence of Audi's brand is evidenced by the brands from which it has stolen market share. In 1987 the brands Audi buyers were most likely to switch from were Vauxhall and Ford. By 2008 these were BMW and Mercedes.

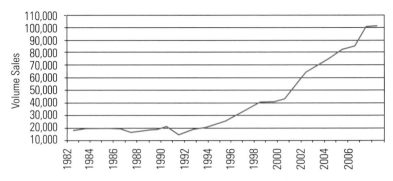

Figure 5. Audi UK volume sales

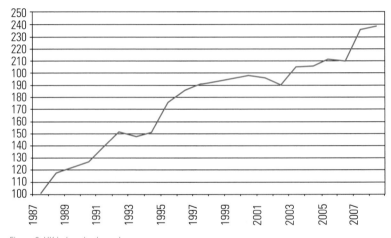

Figure 6. UK indexed value sales

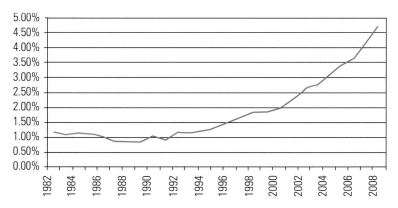

Figure 7. Audi UK market share

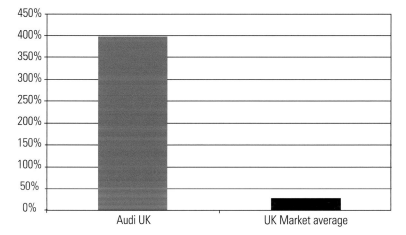

Figure 8. Relative UK performance versus UK car market 1982-2008

Moreover, since it began to compete actively in the prestige sector in the mid-90s, Audi's share of this sector has grown from 24% to 33% and it continues to rise at the expense of its direct competitors: Mercedes has declined and BMW has stagnated.

While Audi's commercial success in the UK has been impressive in its own right. The impact that its marketing approach has made is highlighted when measured against Audi sales in other European markets, with Audi UK sales significantly outperforming its European counterparts.

The performance of the Audi brand in other European markets (Spain, France, Germany and Italy) is the most solid control for highlighting the impact of marketing. The cars they sell are identical to the UK and have similar market dynamics, competitors and economies. The only independent variable in the UK has been the marketing approach, and the brand in the UK has far outgrown the European markets.

Since the inception of *Vorsprung durch Technik*, well over a million Audis have been sold in the UK, with the millionth reached in 2007. This feat would have taken until 2024 at the rate of Audi's old competitive approach.

All images appearing in this case study are reproduced by permission of Audi.

Marks & Spencer

05

Quality worth paying more for

Snapshot

The determination of Marks & Spencer to hold fast to its message of quality through both the good and bad times reinforced the brand's premium positioning and its profitability.

Key insights

- Despite the recession Marks & Spencer (M&S) held its nerve by maintaining its premium pricing and continuing to invest in brand-building advertising.

- Refusing to lower prices meant the retailer didn't suffer the fate of companies which cut pricing in the bad times and then struggled to raise them again.

- Outstanding communications, including iconic advertising, were an important part of its strategy.

Summary

M&S is one of the UK's leading retailers, selling clothing, food and homeware. In what have been troubled times for the UK high street, the retailer took what appeared to many in the media to be two foolhardy decisions. First, it was determined to maintain its price premium when competitors were slashing their prices to the bone to survive. Secondly, it decided to continue to invest in brand-building advertising to justify that premium.

Even though newspapers were full of stories of falling sales and declining share prices and consumer confidence plummeted, measures of M&S's 'brand momentum' remained consistently positive — despite premium pricing in a discounting world — and were shown to be directly influenced and maintained by advertising.

As 2009 progressed, so M&S's sales performance and share price began steadily to improve. It was able to resist the margin-pinching 'race to the bottom' in which many of its competitors were engaged and which they would find very hard to reverse once the recovery set in. By the last quarter of 2009, M&S had achieved its strongest performance for two years, with shares outperforming the DJ Stoxx European Retail Index by 46%.

The good times, the bad times

In the years prior to the recession, when M&S was faced with a takeover bid by Sir Philip Green, it invested heavily and consistently in advertising that was universally acknowledged to have increased footfall, sold products and benefited the brand by raising measured scores on such dimensions as 'quality', 'trust', 'understanding' and 'worth paying more for'. This, in turn, boosted the share price.

As the dark clouds of recession loomed, things got tough on the high street. It was, without doubt, the worst recession in living memory. As a consequence, consumer confidence plummeted by an unprecedented forty percentage points. Some of the biggest names in retail crashed out of business. Only four or five years ago, for example, it would have been hard to imagine the high street without Woolworths. But it happened.

Perhaps unsurprisingly, more or less the whole of the industry went into a discounting frenzy. And Britain's biggest retailer, Tesco, became Britain's biggest discounter. But every cloud has a silver lining:the Primarks of this world, whose business models were built around absolute bargain-basement prices, did very nicely for themselves. But everyone else was hurting.

Standing firm

One retailer that did not cut its prices as deeply as the rest, and that did not abandon its commitment to brand-building, was M&S. This was despite the fact that keeping a steady nerve when all around were panicking was hard and, at times, painful. In consequence, stories abounded about the 'troubles' and 'difficulties' suffered by the brand. In January 2008, when £5 billion was wiped off of the share prices of high street stores, the media were quick to pin the blame on M&S, which had just reported a 2.2% fall in sales.

"Credit crunch wipes a third off of M&S profits" said one headline. *Troubled High Street Giant M&S to cut jobs"* said another; *"M&S sales likely to fall again,"* said yet another. The negative press coverage was creating a vicious circle. But M&S still did not rush to join the price-cutters. Chairman Sir Stuart Rose announced that he was confident that a strong brand left M&S "well positioned to compete by improving our operational delivery and continuing to focus on quality, value and choice. "And communications were central to the job of turning the vicious circle around.

In February 2009, *Marketing Week* published the results of a survey, carried out by Brandhouse/The Centre for Brand Analysis in 2008 at the nadir of the recession, into the emotional appeal of a hundred of Britain's leading brands as judged by consumers. The only retailer to feature in the Top 10 was M&S, which came seventh. This is despite the fact that M&S's prices consistently indexed at +8, versus Tesco's -11 and Asda's -22.

Meanwhile, in sharp contrast to this precipitous drop in consumer confidence overall, attitudes to M&S as measured in terms of brand momentum were far less volatile, and never strayed into negative figures, not even at the very worst of times.

Consumers, it seemed, continued to feel good about the M&S brand despite the best efforts of the media doom-mongers and the appeal of price-slashing rival retailers. Gradually, the drop in M&S's sales and profits began to slow down, so that by April 2009 the year-on-year drop for the quarter was just 4.2%. Investors who, acting on the strength of media reports, had been expecting a continued downward spiral, were taken by surprise. The result was that the share price jumped by 12% overnight.

One of the strongest influencing factors driving this strong brand momentum was consistent advertising. Even throughout the worst of the recession, M&S advertising explicitly focused on building the brand's quality perception, rather than 'selling off the family silver' for short-term gain by just plugging the latest low prices.

Consistency of communications

The overarching communications strategy was based around the idea that M&S provides 'quality worth paying more for': you pay a bit more but get a lot more back. This brand campaign ran across all parts of the business celebrating the brand's long-term commitment to quality. The activity also coincided with M&S's 125th anniversary. This enabled it to assert its stability and heritage in a time when big names were disappearing from the high street. The retailer was able to show how the brand had been there for people through the decades. The TV spot told stories that illustrated the lengths M&S has gone to bring the best quality products to the high street for the past 125 years.(Figures 1 through 10 show some of the TV stills from the M&S 125 years campaign. Figures 11 through 17 show a selection of outdoor ads from the M&S 125 years campaign).

The TV campaign was supported by national poster and press to provide a sense of scale and stature and featured 'hero' products such as Oakham chicken, the iconic chocolate pudding, lingerie and tailoring.

Figures 1-10. Stills from the 125th anniversary TV campaign

Figures 11-17. The 125th anniversary poster campaign

The brand idea also ran across the Plan A activity to show how committed the retailer was to becoming more sustainable and which helped to reinforce M&S's quality credentials (see Chapter 11). Stories included Fairtrade cotton, sustainable fishing suppliers and traceable meat (Figures 18 and 19).

The quality message was also reinforced in promotional activity: namely 'Dine in for £10'. This reframed the competitive positioning strategy to challenge restaurants directly because compared with a meal out, £10 for three courses plus wine represented fantastic value for money. Despite being a promotional mechanic, this actually raised quality perceptions and positioned the food as worth paying more for, not only among core customers but crucially among occasional food customers too, helping drive footfall and basket size.

Finally, even the M&S Christmas campaign reflected the changing mood of the UK consumer. Rather than celebrate with the opulence of previous years, it focused on the integral role M&S has played in the nation's Christmas for so many years. (Figures 20 through 28 show M&S Christmas TV stills).

Taking the long view

For a premium-priced high street brand to ride out of such a deep recession so well and to be in the position it is now in is a remarkable thing. But the longer-term achievements of consistent, long-term brand-building in both good times and bad are even more important. Econometric modelling has shown that the long-term payback of consistent brand investment are, on average, four times greater than the short-term profit boost generated by cutting it.

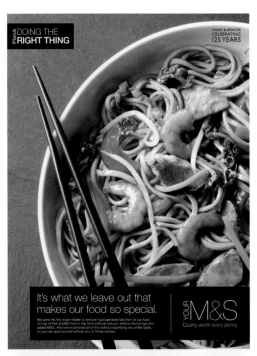

Figures 18-19. Press campaign

Figures 20-28. Stills from the Christmas TV campaign

In contrast to many of its rivals, M&S continued to build its brand equity, continued to maintain its price premium and to justify it through advertising, and refused to damage its reputation for quality in pursuit of short-term gain, even when its profits and share price were falling. Nor did it educate or condition its shoppers to trade down to 'bargain basement' goods where once they would have been prepared to pay a bit more for quality.

It took time for this strategy to begin to pay off, and it took nerve. But, by the start of the last quarter of 2009, it began to pay off, with the *Wall Street Journal*, on 30th September, reporting how, after being "hit hard in the recession, losing ground to cheaper rivals like Primark in clothes and supermarkets in food", M&S had begun to turn its fortunes around, announcing its best financial performance for two years.

The result was a gradual growth in share price over 2009. By the end of the year M&S was outperforming the DJ Stoxx European Retail Index by 46%.

Virgin Atlantic 05

Still pioneering after all these years

Snapshot

Virgin Atlantic's distinctive brand voice has seen the once-maverick challenger brand become one of the UK's favourite airlines.

Key insights

- A distinctive brand attitude and tone of voice has provided consistency for Virgin Atlantic while at the same time offered the brand the flexibility to behave in a dynamic, multi-faceted way.

- The sassy Still Red Hot advertising to celebrate its 25th anniversary was one of the most talked-about campaigns of 2009.

- This approach to communications has consistently fulfilled the three core objectives of keeping the brand top of mind, delivering 'Virginness' and giving people a reason to choose the airline over competitors.

Summary

Virgin Atlantic is one of the UK's major airlines, owned 51% by Richard Branson's Virgin Group and 49% by Singapore Airlines. In 2009 Virgin Atlantic celebrated its 25th anniversary with the multi-award winning Still Red Hot campaign. In an industry struggling to ride out a worldwide global recession, this campaign was dubbed by Richard Branson the best Virgin Atlantic ad ever made.

From a marketing perspective, it marked an important milestone for the brand, not only celebrating 25 years in the business, but almost two decades of consistently disruptive communications. The consistency in Virgin Atlantic communications has come through the cultivation of an inimitable brand voice and iconic visual identity. It is this that has acted as the golden thread uniting communications.

This approach has kept the brand in the public consciousness, imbued it with 'Virginness' and helped raise it to its status today as one of the UK's favourite airlines.

The birth of a true challenger brand

In 2009 Virgin Atlantic celebrated its 25th anniversary in the midst of the global recession with the multi-award winning Still Red Hot campaign. Said by founder Richard Branson to be the best Virgin Atlantic ad ever made, it rapidly acquired iconic status.

From a marketing perspective, it was an important milestone for the brand: not only celebrating 25 years in the business, but almost two decades of consistently disruptive communications. Rather than straight-jacket such an entrepreneurial brand with a rigid communications idea, the consistency in Virgin Atlantic communications came from the cultivation of a distinctive brand voice and stylish visual identity. Whether launching a new route in the network, communicating the onboard experience or taking tactical advantage of a gaff by long-term rival British Airways (BA), this distinctive Virgin Atlantic attitude was fundamental to the communications strategy.

Marketing is only one of many disciplines to have played a part in Virgin Atlantic's success. But marketing has been crucial to the growth of the business and key to helping the brand claim its rightful place as one of the UK's favourite brands.

It all began when Richard Branson launched Virgin Atlantic with a single leased aircraft making its inaugural flight from London Gatwick to Newark Liberty on June 22nd 1984. At the time, the idea that a brand best known for launching Culture Club and the Sex Pistols could be extended to encompass an international airline seemed hardly credible. Against

Stills from TV advertising

Terence Stamp 1993

Helen Mirren TV 1994

Grim Reaper 1997

Iggy Pop 2001

all the odds and to the surprise of many commentators, Branson turned a profit in his first year of operation. With dedication, often in the face of adversity, Virgin Atlantic continued to expand over the next decade.

RKCR and Manning Gottlieb OMD started working with Virgin Atlantic in 1994, just as the economy was sliding into recession and the airline was posting its first operating loss since launch. In partnership the three organisations developed a communications strategy that helped secure the future of the airline.

Giving voice to a maverick personality

With a route network less than a twentieth the size of BA, Virgin Atlantic was never going to be able to provide a credible alternative for all journeys. But where there was a comparable offer it was critical that Virgin Atlantic emerge as the preferred brand for both business and leisure travellers.

To this end three communications objectives were developed:
1. Keep the brand in the public consciousness so it would be thought of alongside BA (and therefore get on the consideration list).
2. Communicate the unique attitude that defines the Virgin Atlantic brand i.e. 'Virginness'.
3. Give people, whether flying Upper Class, Premium Economy or Economy, reasons to choose Virgin Atlantic over competitors.

Rather than impose a rigid campaign vehicle on such an innovative and dynamic brand, a distinctive brand voice and iconic look were adopted to act as the golden thread of consistency. This enabled effortless stretch across the wide variety of messages for each cabin, audience, route and channel as well as the ability to respond with ease to tactical opportunities.

Print ads

BA don't give a shiatsu 1993

A chauffeur at both ends 1995

Fly the flag 2005

Make it swanky 2009

The brand voice was modelled on the personality of Virgin's founder Richard Branson. If the Virgin Atlantic brand can be said to have attitude, that attitude was his — maverick, challenging, witty and innovative. For nearly 20 years this brand voice has remained consistently fresh and innovative, helping Virgin Atlantic communications rise above and stand out from the competition.

The Still Red Hot 25th anniversary campaign was the very epitome of this attitude and further leveraged the style and glamour long associated with the brand (Figure 1).

Figure 1. The Still Red Hot 25th anniversary campaign 2009

Figure 2. The 'Can't Get it Up' blimp 1999

Launching the Still Red Hot campaign with 90-second TV spots gave the brand the stature and scale needed to assert the brand's confidence at a time of economic uncertainty. This was complemented by premium outdoor sites and press titles to deliver the product superiority story. Tried and tested response-driving in the press and on the radio acted as the bedrock to the campaign, ensuring goodwill translated into sales.

Outsmarting the opposition

The Virgin Atlantic attitude was reflected as much in media strategy as creative execution. With a budget less than a third the size of BA, being seen in the company of the big established players was critical to conveying a sense of scale. Occupying environments best known for premium brands added a sense of sophistication and style. Media firsts, such as front-page colour strips in the early nineties and being the first commercial brand to run podcasts, helped reinforce the innovative nature of the brand.

Capitalising on tactical opportunities also added to the brand's dynamism and challenger status. For example:
- Placing the Upper Class Suite (new flatbeds) outside the BA lounge in Heathrow's Terminal 4.
- Flying a BA 'Can't Get it Up' blimp above the London Eye (Figure 2).
- Proactively recruiting BA business flyers during BA strikes.

Surpassing expectations

There is a wealth of evidence to demonstrate the effectiveness of Virgin Atlantic communications since 1993. But given the sheer volume of data, turning it into a comprehensive summary is problematic. This is further complicated by the inconsistencies in sources and measures over such a long period.

Despite this difficulty, results from a variety of sources have been gathered to illustrate the effect of communications against each of the three communications objectives. Particular focus is given to the Still Red Hot campaign.

Meeting objective 1: Keeping the brand in the public consciousness

To secure a brand in people's thoughts, particularly when a budget is dwarfed by that of the competitors, highly visible communications are needed — campaigns that get talked about. Stunts such as the blimp over the London Eye are examples of activity that generated significant public relations (PR) value in relation to cost.

Tracking evidence over the last 17 years shows Virgin Atlantic communications consistently achieved high levels of cut-through which translated into spontaneous awareness. For example, the first Helen Mirren 'Legs' execution in 1994 still achieved 73% spontaneous recall 12 months after airing. There was one occasion when both BA and Virgin Atlantic were targeting the same audience with a similar message about flatbeds. Branded recognition per 100 television rating points (TVRs) for Virgin Atlantic's ad 'Beauty Sleep' was more than double that of BA.

The recent Still Red Hot campaign caused just the splash intended and made sure the headlines were all Virgin Atlantic's (and for the right reasons) during the crucial January 2009 business period. There was a great deal of positive coverage on the TV in particular, including a feature on the BBC 6 o'clock news, the Chris Moyles show on Radio 1, the Alan Titchmarsh show and Loose Women. Brand buzz increased 11% points in the first two weeks of the campaign.

Looking at the full 17 year period, Virgin Atlantic closed the gap with BA in top-of-mind awareness from 54% Virgin Atlantic versus 87% BA in 1993 to 74% Virgin Atlantic vs 73% BA in 2009 (Figure 3). Communications does not claim sole responsibility for this but there is no doubt it has played a key role.

Meeting objective 2: Delivering 'Virginness'

'Virginness' is defined by the following six attributes: stylish, helpful, up-to-date, dynamic, innovative, fun. Each of these attributes has been shown to correlate with brand preference and is therefore key to ensuring the efficacy of communications.

Since 1993 all six attributes increased significantly relative to BA. Tracking evidence shows this can be attributed directly to communications, with individual campaigns generating significant increases in each of these brand scores (Figure 4).

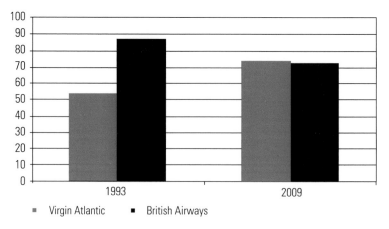

Figure 3. Spontaneous brand awareness of Virgin Atlantic vs BA 1993-2009
Sources: 1993 Brand Asset Valuator (spontaneous brand awareness among travellers); 2009 Hall & Partners Tracking, June (spontaneous brand consideration among first / business class long haul passengers)

The Still Red Hot campaign enhanced Virginness even more (which in turn correlates with brand preference).

Meeting objective 3: Giving people reasons to choose Virgin Atlantic

This objective can be measured through increased brand preference over time, corresponding with communications. Between 1993 and 2006 brand preference for Virgin Atlantic relative to BA increased from 49 to 73. This means by 2005 Virgin Atlantic had gained significant ground but still lagged behind its rival.

Tracking evidence from Virgin Atlantic campaigns pointed to significant increases in brand preference after each burst of advertising from 1996-2006. The fact that 54% of people said they would consider Virgin Atlantic in the future, yet only 28% had actually flown with the airline, showed preference had not been solely driven by the onboard experience.

Still Red Hot had a direct impact on preference for the brand among all audiences, finally pushing Virgin Atlantic ahead of BA on the measure for all three traveller groups (Table 1). These unprecedented levels of brand preference coincided with record sales for Virgin Atlantic in a market severely depressed by the global recession. On the 27th January 2009 all records were broken for revenue and bookings on the Virgin Atlantic website. In addition, UK bookings were up 28% year-on-year (YOY) and revenue was up 2.3% YOY, while bookings coming via pay-per-click tripled in the last week of January.

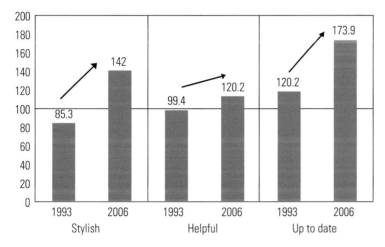

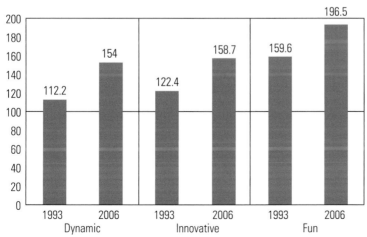

Figure 4. Strengthening of "Virginness" for Virgin Atlantic relative to British Aways between 1993 and 2006 (Brand Asset Valuator 1993-2006)

Solid returns

In May 2009 Virgin published a £68 million profit and a bonus handout for all employees just one day after BA publicly admitted to a £401 million operating loss.

Table 1. Brand preference for Virgin Atlantic and BA-Jan/Feb 09 vs 08
Source: Hall & Partners Brand Tracking

	January 2008(%)	January 2009(%)
First/business travellers		
Virgin	47	64
BA	63	63
Premium economy travellers		
Virgin	55	72
BA	61	64
Economy travellers		
Virgin	24	47
BA	35	38

Despite the compelling evidence that communications for Virgin Atlantic have been successful at meeting the three key objectives, with such a complex market and so many factors influencing sales, econometric modelling is the only way to isolate and quantify the impact of communications.

The latest Virgin Atlantic econometric models built by BrandScience cover the period from March 2007 to February 2009. While not necessarily representative of the full 17-year case history it is an indicator of the level of return that has been delivered. It is estimated that a total of 184,865 bookings were generated over this time with the following breakdown by cabin class:
• 125,583 in Economy
• 19,862 in Premium Economy
• 39,420 in Upper Class

This equates to a total of £213.64 million in incremental revenue. Based on a total investment in marketing communications of £20.77 million over this same period there was a revenue return of £10.28 for every £1 invested in communications between March 2007 and February 2009.

Looking at the Still Red Hot campaign in isolation, the return on investment was even higher at around £19 revenue for every £1 spent.

There can thus be little doubt that the communications has not only made the sense of 'Virginness' surrounding the brand ever stronger, but it has delivered substantial benefits to the company's performance.

All images appearing in this case study are reproduced by permission of Virgin Atlantic.

Chapter 6
Marketing
Communications

Amanda Mackenzie
Chief Marketing and
Communications Officer
Aviva plc

If you can think back 20 years to when the choice of media was TV, press or posters, what defined a brilliant idea then is what still defines a brilliant idea today. Only the variables have become greater and so have the chances of possibly diluting the effects through making too many choices. All the more satisfying, then, that these cases have navigated this complex world and not let it steer them off course.

I recall meeting with 10 media analysts who could not believe that TV was still so powerful for mass market audiences. You would think no one watched the TV anymore, and yet, here we are, with some quite huge shifts in behaviours and great payback from people doing precisely that.

Thinkbox had the extraordinary role of reminding the marketing and advertising community that TV was alive and well. It did this admirably with case histories of advertisers in an innovative and textbook approach .

In true Mars style, Pedigree showed how it can boil a brand down to its essence which perfectly matches the product and its relationship with its consumer (or in this case, purchaser), execute brilliantly and see the results follow—and raise money for a good cause.

For Dulux, the idea of 'Colour me beautiful' is just as big even if the 'Dulux paint dog' isn't centre stage. It realised that it risked being eaten by both ends of the market and so turned to consumer insight from which to develop an expert and yet accessible positioning.

Not only did rugby club Harlequins achieve superb results from a very small budget coordinated magnificently but it has been part of the huge popularisation of rugby.

And, finally, Sainsbury's, which has proved over the years so adept at using insight about what is happening right now and making it relevant and compelling for a supermarket customer.

These case studies demonstrate vividly how marketing can drive profitable growth. We as an industry should always remember the power of a simple, brilliantly-articulated idea stemming from a very clear business issue.

Dulux

06

Colour me beautiful

Snapshot

A brand in danger of losing its way gave itself a makeover and brought a healthy glow to its performance.

Key insights

- Dulux had to reposition itself to find a new place in a market where middle-of-the road brands were being fatally squeezed and where it was seen as a masculine brand in a market with women as the main shoppers.

- The key insight into its consumers was that they didn't want paint — they wanted help with matching colours.

- By mounting a campaign which emphasised the role of colours and how they worked together through Dulux, it became the aspiring decorator's brand of choice.

Summary

ICI Paints produces some of the world's top paint and decorative product brands. The company was bought in 2008 by AkzoNobel, one of the world's foremost industrial companies. The combined business is the leading global coatings manufacturer and the number one in decorative paints and performance coatings, as well as being a major worldwide supplier of specialty chemicals.

Dulux is one of the most famous brands in the UK. However, in 2005 the brand was in an uncomfortable position: it found itself positioned as a masculine brand in a decorative paint market driven by women. Worse, it was being squeezed in terms of pricing from the own-brands at one end and the premium paints at the other.

The company decided it had to overhaul its marketing. Research had uncovered a valuable insight: people needed help not just choosing colours but matching them. The resulting campaign enabled Dulux to remain number one despite a fierce onslaught from retailer brands, sustain a price premium in a volume/value war that had pushed prices down and grow share in a declining market.

Fighting the battle on two fronts

Dulux is one of the UK's most famous brands, with almost universal awareness and a proud heritage. When people see an Old English sheepdog, they are more likely to think paint than farming. Over the years, however, and because of its long heritage in the UK market, consumers had come to perceive Dulux as a somewhat traditional and staid brand.

So, while the name was universally known, the onslaught of upmarket property design TV shows such as Grand Designs and Property Ladder saw the brand looking more like a do-it-yourself (DIY) brand than a home improvement brand. The brand also had something of a masculine image in a market for decorative paint now driven by women. In 1996, men and women accounted for equal shares of the paint market. By 2005, women were the main shoppers, accounting for 150 million litres and men for only 81.4 million litres. So the 'handyman' image was a big problem.

The other challenge was price. As in many markets, the risk of switching to a retailer brand was now negligible — people wouldn't think twice about buying Tesco wine and now they didn't think twice about buying B&Q paint. They were more than good enough and much cheaper. For instance, 2.5 litres of coloured emulsion from B&Q would cost £6 less than the equivalent paint from Dulux.

The company had been addressing this issue by marketing its technical expertise to create any colour the consumer desired with the strapline: 'You find the colour, we'll match it'. The goal was to fend off the own-label onslaught by creating unique products that were not comparable (once a consumer had decided on a colour, then near-enough was not good enough).

But the retailer competitors were upping their game here too, so creating a new approach was critical.

At the other end of the spectrum, premium brands such as Farrow & Ball and Fired Earth set the pace in terms of aesthetic perceptions. Although these brands had a very small share of the market they were style leaders and had a disproportionate share of voice in the influential interiors magazines.

While the brand was still robust, it had experienced sizeable share erosion between 1999 and 2002. The company could see the clouds on the horizon, facing the classic marketing dilemma of holding the middle ground in the face of erosion from price players at one end and quality players at the other. The clearest indicator of Dulux's problems could be seen in the discrepancy between high brand preference scores in brand tracking (nine out of 10 people claimed to 'insist on' or 'prefer' Dulux) and the comparatively low market share of around 35%.

Marketing's big challenge was to address these looming issues and create a new, valuable connection with customers to justify Dulux's role as a leader. The first step would have to be a true understanding of its rapidly changing audience.

Getting under the skin of would-be interior designers

Visiting people's homes and watching them go through the decorating process proved to be enlightening. Everywhere the company's researchers went, they saw evidence of just how highly stimulated people had been by the media's encouragement for people to keep on improving their homes. Homes were the new fashion, and people's interest in decorating them creatively was higher than ever. It was hardly surprising: they were exposed to a huge number of home decor TV shows and magazines (which, if put together at the time, would have had a total media value of about £1 billion annually) that provided stimulation and inspiration for them to keep their homes looking great.

Unfortunately, people's enthusiasm often had pretty appalling consequences, as those lucky enough to view the lady in Kingston who had painted a mural of Stonehenge at dawn on her son's bedroom wall can testify. The problem, it was felt, was that makeover and property shows had made interior design seem desirable and extremely easy, but the reality was that aspects of it, such as designing a successful colour scheme, were actually really tough and not enjoyed at all.

In going back to the data evidence which hadn't seemed relevant until now was found to back this up: over 40% of people claimed to be dissatisfied with their hard work once they had finished decorating.

The roller coaster ride of decorating

Mapping the journey from deciding to give a room a fresh new look to enjoying the finished result showed that it was without doubt fraught. In the beginning aspiring decorators had great hopes and excitement as they decided to embark on a new look. But they began to plunge down when they entered store and were bewildered by choice and struck by the expense. Then came the hard part of actually putting paint on the walls before — if they were lucky — rising high again on the joy of a great result. The problem was that Dulux appeared in this ride just as things started to turn unpleasant as they tried to work out what to buy.

The company had a hunch that true brand success would lie in the 'fun' bit — the planning and dreaming. It needed to win the war before people got as far as the store. But what role could Dulux play here? While choosing colour for a room had many enjoyable stages (e.g. getting inspiration and shopping around), the narrowing-down stage was much more difficult. This was the point at which consumers move from a general colour to an exact shade.

Consumers said that they found visualising a particular colour in a room difficult and imagining a colour scheme of more than one colour even harder. At this point, lack of confidence and indecision often led to non-purchase, delayed purchase or compromise. This high level of unhappiness with the decorating process suggested there was a huge unmet need. People needed help — colour help (Figure 1).

In addition to the strong brand and consumer rationale for championing colour, the company's portfolio analysis work led it to conclude that it should push coloured emulsion aggressively, given its healthy profitability and future growth potential.

So here was a problem Dulux could solve. It could help people bridge the gap between desire and expertise. At the start of 2006 Dulux would move from being a paint company to a 'colour help' company. Consumers would decide on Dulux shades before they got to the store and thus the brand could earn their loyalty before the actual point of sale.

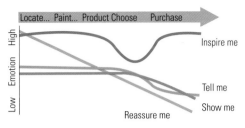

Most shopper segments clearly find this a difficult process

Finding the specific product and choosing being the toughest stages

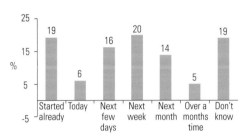

Of those that bought nothing 24% had put the job off and hence can be assumed lost to the task

Figure 1. Ease of shop

Helping customers become colour experts

In order to help people with colour, marketing's role would have to be to change behaviour and not just perception. Part of this would include encouraging the creation of service and product initiatives to develop helpful colour tools for people — tools that could translate preference into purchase by guiding people through the process of choosing their perfect colour scheme and, in doing so, guide them to choose Dulux.

The first tool was a colour scheming system that rolled out in DIY stores in 2006. This system organised the entire Dulux Colour range into a coordinated system that was easy for the consumer to use. Horizontally, the colours were organised into

moods: rich, fresh, warm and calm. Any colours then chosen from one of these rows would go together.

The second was a website designed to inspire and guide consumers through their colour decisions, dulux.co.uk. It was interactive to allow users to experiment in private and ultimately feel like masters of the art of colour combining, The website helped consumers visualise and experiment with colour schemes by letting them paint virtual rooms through a tool called 'Mouse Painter'.

Finding the perfect match

It enabled them to create their own virtual moodboards just like professional interior designers did. It suggested colours that would go with other shades in toning, harmonising and contrasting colour schemes. Having found the colours that they wanted, visitors could then go on and order colour swatches and calculate the amount of paint required for their own rooms.

In order to demonstrate the brand's expertise in colour through communications, it was crucial to go beyond merely telling people how these new tools could help them choose a colour to paint their walls. This expertise and colour help had to be category-redefining and convey a sense of gravitas. The company could see an opportunity to communicate with people about the multi-dimensional relationships between colours, thereby reflecting the consumer truth: the real difficulty wasn't choosing one colour, but putting two or more colours together. In order to achieve this level of gravitas necessary, traditional paint language had to be banished from the vocabulary.

The language had to be that of colour, not paint. This led to a groundbreaking idea: Dulux are experts in helping you with colour chemistry. Colours are like people: they have personalities. Some go together and some don't. This was then summed up by the endline: 'We know the colours that go'.

Human relationships were used to represent great colour schemes and show the chemistry that exists between people. This idea of colour chemistry and the 'We know the colours that go' campaign became one of the most successful in Dulux history, infiltrating nearly every single part of the business: from Dulux employee business cards, to business-to-business communications and to the more traditional means of consumer communications (Figures 2 and 3).

It appeared on TV as sponsorship for the hit US TV series Ugly Betty, print and online media. The idea also appeared on Dulux's colour cards, in press advertising, PR, advertorials, banner ads, and on the Dulux website. It even influenced the training of Dulux staff to become experts in colour chemistry themselves.

Achieving significant success

The launch of the Colour Expert marketing activity saw market share increase at its peak in 2006, by 2.5%. This was worth an extra £19m in sales every year (Figure 4).

This growth was despite the fact that the whole market was, up until the end of 2006, declining by 2%.

Making the Colour Mixing range the focal point of the brand led to a continuing increase in both value and volume growth of this range (Figures 5 and 6).

Figures 2 and 3.
Examples of ad campaign

JAN 98-DEC 99	JAN 99-DEC 00	JAN 00-DEC 01	JAN 01-DEC 02	JAN 03-DEC 03	JAN 04-DEC 04	JAN 05-DEC 05	JAN 06-DEC 06	JAN 07-DEC 07
12.7	13.1	14.7	15.2	15	14.4	13.9	13.9	13.5
14	15.5	17.3	19.2	18	14.9	14.2	12.8	13
32.4	30.6	33.2	32.9	33.1	31.8	31.8	30.7	31.2
40.9	40.8	34.8	32.7	33.9	38.9	40.1	42.6	42.3

☐ Dulux ☐ Own Label ☐ Crown ☐ Others

Figure 4, Value brand share of total paint multiples
Source: GFK

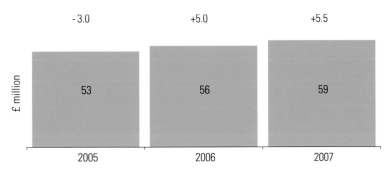

Figure 5. Value growth of colour mixing range
Source: GFK

The marketing activity also had a positive effect on the brand's ability to maintain a price premium in a market that was having its pricing squeezed. In addition, brand consideration enjoyed a notable increase from 59% to 70% — which paralleled the communications.

The online campaign achieved a click-through rate of up to 16% and of those that saw the ads online, 79% were positively motivated by it. Site traffic itself was up during the campaign period by 80%, with an average time of 14 minutes on the site and 9% conversion to action (Figure 7).

In 2006 the brand was regarded as a traditional, somewhat old-fashioned paint brand. By the end of 2007 the brand had emerged even more strongly and as one based on helping people find, choose and put colours together.

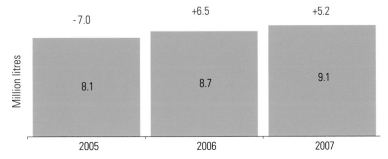

Figure 6. Volume growth of colour mixing range
Source: GFK

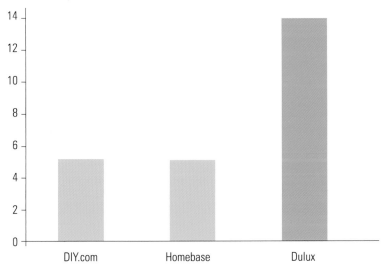

Figure 7. Average minutes per visitor
Source: Comscorce June 2007

All images appearing in this case study are reproduced by permission of AkzoNobel.

Sainsbury's

06

Feed your family for a fiver

Snapshot

Sainsbury's convincingly persuaded customers it was responding to the credit crunch by adapting an existing successful campaign for more straitened times.

Key insights

- Sainsbury's took its highly successful brand idea of 'Try something new today' and fine-tuned it for the tough economic climate by creating a memorable and effective new campaign: 'Feed your family for a fiver'.

- This played a significant part in showing customers that it was responsive to their changing needs in tough times.

- The campaign led to strong sales uplifts and a transformation in the perception of the brand as value for money.

Summary

Sainsbury's is the UK's longest-standing major food retailing chain, having opened its first store in 1869. It now serves over 18.5 million customers a week and enjoys a market share of around 16 per cent. Its large stores offer around 30,000 products, including non-food products and services in many of its stores. Its TU clothing range has one million transactions per week. An internet-based home delivery shopping service is also available to nearly 90 per cent of UK households.

Since 2005 the 'Try something new today' strapline had been a vital component of Sainsbury's success. It worked by giving people simple food ideas and so earning a little extra spend from them every time they shopped. 2008 was supposed to be a year to build on 'Try's' success.

But in early 2008 the credit crunch began to bite and shopping habits began to change dramatically. Encouraging people to spend more was no longer such a good idea. The resulting shift to focusing on just how shopping at Sainsbury's could offer both quality and value through 'Feed your family for a fiver' was a resounding success, delivering £540 million in incremental sales revenues by the end of 2009.

No resting on past laurels

The strapline of 'Try something new today' had been at the heart of Sainsbury's success since 2005. It had been created to help earn a little extra spend from customers whenever they shopped. If each of Sainsbury's 14 million weekly shoppers spent an extra £1.14 every time they shopped, then Sainsbury's would achieve its business goal of £2.5 billion additional sales over three years. And it worked: by January 2008 the £2.5 billion goal had been achieved ahead of schedule.

But the year ahead looked like it was going to play out quite differently to the previous three. Northern Rock had collapsed. The phrase 'credit crunch' had entered the language. Food inflation was rampant. Shopping budgets were being cut and shoppers were looking for ways to save money.

It was clear that 2008 was going to be a tough year for retail in general and for Sainsbury's in particular. 'Try' was a brand idea that had been created under different circumstances, when people had money in their pockets and were happy to spend the odd extra pound on something they may not have tried before. 'Try' had driven sales by inspiring existing customers to spend a little more. Could it still work when what was needed was to help existing customers spend less? It was clear that 'Try' would need to adapt to changing circumstances.

By 2007 every metric showed the brand to be in excellent health. Figure 1 shows that Sainsbury's was by then the most desirable mainstream supermarket in which to shop (when you exclude the two major rational drivers of store choice — location and price). But the brand did have one remaining problem, which didn't hold it back in the good times, but which was likely to prove a greater problem in a downturn: poor price perception.

While prices were now in line with the competition according to the industry price index, the perception that Sainsbury's was more expensive than its rivals was proving hard to shift. Supermarket price perceptions tend to remain remarkably static due to a strict pecking order in customers' minds, from Marks & Spencer down to the discounters.

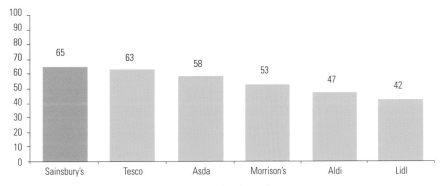

Figure 1. "Would shop there if location/price wasn't an issue..."

From past experience the company knew that tactical communications (i.e. communicating prices and deals) was a relatively weak force in shifting price perceptions and that communications would be needed at the brand level.

Getting to grips with harder times

It was imperative to begin to understand how the economic downturn would begin to change shopping behaviours.

Tightening belts

In research, shoppers said that they were reviewing shopping decisions in a number of ways:
- Cutting budgets.
- Trying 'cheaper' stores.
- Buying more on promotion.
- Trading down from premium to standard to value ranges.
- Cutting out discretionary spend.
- Switching from branded products to own-label products.
- Cutting back on convenience foods.

Quantitative studies confirmed the company's biggest fear: in one survey 13% claimed they were likely to change their store and 25% claimed they were beginning to cherry-pick offers from other stores. These changes to shopping behaviour would require the retailer to employ a number of marketing tactics (e.g. lowering more prices, increasing amounts bought from deals, pushing own-brand).

But the headline conclusion was clear: the company would need to demonstrate to any existing shoppers thinking about shopping elsewhere that Sainsbury's could cut the cost of their family shop. But discounting created two problems: it would cost a huge amount to implement and might go unnoticed without communications to reinforce the shift. This had traditionally been a problem as pure price messages tended not to stick to a brand better known for quality messages.

So the company set itself two communications objectives:
1. Show that Sainsbury's food is not only great quality but also great value.
2. Inspire people to 'Try something new' to help reduce their shopping bill.

Simple food ideas were likely to be the key to success as they had always been the most powerful component of 'Try'. And it was important to continue inspiring people to try simple food ideas but now to make low price a fundamental component of those food ideas.

Providing inspiration at the right price

More research was needed to understand how cooking habits were changing and what kind of food ideas might work in the new economic climate. What is a constant theme still applied: people were in a rut with their cooking and welcome food ideas to help them out of it. The credit crunch was a powerful force but wasn't strong enough to reduce the power of this never-ending need.

One change that was noticed was that people were getting a little less experimental with their cooking. They seemed to respond better to ideas which were twists on old favourites (things they knew their kids would definitely like) rather than some of the more unusual ideas that Sainsbury's had been offering so far.

But the most revealing aspect of this research was discovering that while people tended to know exactly what they spent on their big food shop, they were often rather inaccurate about what they spent on any individual home-cooked meal. When people were asked how much they spent on an average weekday family meal, after some initial head-scratching they tended to guess at between £6 and £12. The gap between what people guessed they spent (£6-12) and what the retailer knew they could spend on the ingredients at Sainsbury's (£4-5) opened up a fantastic opportunity for the new communications to exploit this gap between the perception and reality of Sainsbury's value.

The result was a simple, memorable idea: 'Feed your family for a fiver'. This led to the creation of 30 family meals with Sainsbury's products based on strict rules:
- All meals would cost under £5.
- All ingredients would be at their standard everyday low prices and not on promotion.
- Meals would need to be substantial enough for a hungry family of four.
- Meals would need to centre around a good portion of protein.
- Meals would need to include a range of items from 'Sainsbury's basics' to 'Taste the difference' to show that Sainsbury's offers value across the store.
- Meals would need a 'twist' to maintain the inspiration expected of 'Try's' food ideas.

Cross-channel communication

'Feed your family for a fiver' was a fully integrated campaign from sofa to store that, since its launch in March 2008, received two major periods of advertising support (March-October 2008 and June-July 2009), with lower level support at other times (January-February 2009). The elements included:
1. Internal communications. The idea was launched first to Sainsbury's 150,000 colleagues via internal communications. A competition for colleagues to submit their own 'Fiver' ideas was run and free samples were distributed.
2. Free tip cards in store. As with all 'Try' communications, 'tip cards' showing products and cooking instructions were displayed in store (Figure 2, overleaf).
3. In-store point-of-sale (POS). POS was used to theme the store and help shoppers locate ingredients.
4. Magazine advertising. Weekly press advertising featured the meal ideas, with some executions featuring five meal ideas to help shoppers plan a week's meals.
5. Television advertising. Four 30" TV executions were created, each featuring Jamie Oliver challenging a shopper with the idea that he could help them feed their family for a fiver at Sainsbury's ('Meatballs' 'Bacon pasta', 'Salmon fishcakes', 'Lamb burgers').

As seen on TV

FEED YOUR FAMILY FOR A FIVER

Meatballs 'n' more

Jamie xx

Sainsbury's
Try something new today

500g Sainsbury's coarse cut mince £1.55

Loose onion 13p

Loose garlic bulb 35p

500g basics spaghetti 23p

2 x 400g tins of chopped tomatoes 88p

907g frozen garden peas £1.62

Items from your store cupboard: dried oregano, olive oil, salt and pepper

Figure 2. Tip card

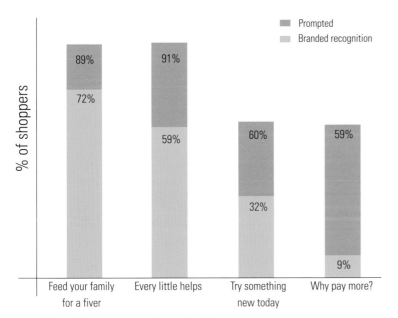

Figure 3. Recognition of supermarket slogans (Aug '09)
Source: IPSOS MORI Brand and Communications Tracker

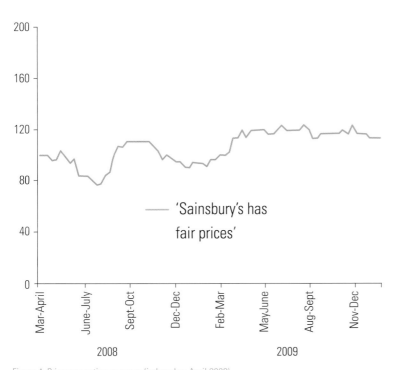

Figure 4. Price perception measure (indexed vs April 2008)

The taste of success

The results surpassed expectations.

1. Instant buzz

Tracking and qualitative research showed high levels of buzz the instant the campaign launched, with the idea being spontaneously and accurately played back by respondents, many of whom were clearly beginning to reassess their views of Sainsbury's prices as a result.

2. TV breakthrough

Recognition of the TV executions in the campaign were among the highest ever seen for the company's advertising, with the execution for 'Lamb burgers' achieving the best recognition score for any Jamie Oliver TV ad tracked so far.

3. Memorable advertising

The 'Feed your family for a fiver' element proved to be exceptionally memorable in the advertising, with spontaneous recall hitting 47% at the height of the TV support behind the campaign.

In addition, prompted recognition of the slogan 'Feed your family for a fiver' built rapidly, and by August 2009 this stood at 89%, virtually identical to that of Tesco's 'Every Little Helps' at 91% — a slogan 15 years older and with an advertising spend advantage to the tune of hundreds of millions of pounds (£340 million in advertising support from 2005-2009 alone). And 'Fiver's' branded recognition of 72% was by this time well in excess of the 59% achieved by 'Every Little Helps' (Figure 3).

4. Significant shifts in perceptions

Brand image tracking showed perceptions of Sainsbury's having 'fair prices' improving significantly during the campaign period. The image shifts were both greater than ever seen before on this measure but also greater than that for any other brand measure (Figure 4). At the same time, there were dramatic downward shifts in perceptions that prices at Sainsbury's were 'quite a bit higher' than other supermarkets over the campaign period. Finally, there were a number of notable correlations between the Fiver idea and key brand measures such as 'has fair prices' (a key objective since this is a measure that impacts overall sales), 'heard good things about' and 'would recommend to others'.

5. Working its magic on sales figures

All ingredients featured in the meal ideas saw strong sales uplifts, whether featured in advertising or only on tip cards, with especially high uplifts for the key 'protein' at the heart of each meal as shown in Table 1.

Table 1

Meatballs idea: **Beef mince +20%, 'Basics' spaghetti +70%**

Bacon pasta idea: **'Basics' penne +240%, 'Taste the Difference' bacon +13%**

Salmon fishcakes idea: **'Basics' salmon fillets +500%**

Lamb burger idea: **Lamb mince +50%**

Sausages and roasted vegetables idea: **'Butcher's Choice' sausages +100%, sweet potatoes +380%**

Chicken and couscous idea: **'Freedom Food' chicken +100%, couscous +46%**

Pork burgers idea: **'Freedom Food' pork mince +71%**

Remarkable return on investment

The OHAL's econometric model showed that the £6.9 million campaign delivered £203 million in sales and a profit of £31.6 million. Rather pleasingly, this equates to a return on investment of just under a Fiver: £4.60.

In October 2009 Sainsbury's was voted 'Supermarket of the year' at the Retail Industry Awards. The strength of the business and the agility shown in adapting the brand to the economic climate was cited as the primary reason for this accolade.

All images appearing in this case study are reproduced by permission of Sainsbury's.

Pedigree

06

Making the brand a dog's best friend

Snapshot

A thoughtful and heart-warming campaign put Pedigree at the forefront of helping homeless dogs.

Key insights

- Love of dogs is at the heart of the Pedigree brand so it had to be integral to its marketing strategy.

- The resulting corporate social responsibility (CSR) campaign which focused on helping homeless dogs was a perfect fit for the brand's promise.

- Not only did it help dogs find homes, but it brought consumer attention to the problem and had huge impact on brand perception.

Summary

Pedigree is part of global food manufacturer Mars. In the UK, it wanted to demonstrate that love of dogs is at the heart of the brand by backing up its beliefs with action. In January 2008 it launched a major CSR initiative as a key part of its marketing, 'The Pedigree Adoption Drive', to help charities re-home over 100,000 dogs found abandoned each year in the UK.

The campaign encouraged responsible dog ownership and also raised awareness of dogs in need of a loving home. Furthermore, a donation for every Pedigree product sold during the campaign went to rescue charities to help them continue their great work.

The multi-channel campaign included a six-part TV series with ITV. Dog lovers responded enthusiastically, with almost £500,000 raised for homeless dogs. The brand benefited as well: sales increased, while there was a eight-point increase in those who believed that Pedigree had the well-being of dogs at its heart.

Bringing the heart of the brand to life

Pedigree has always believed that dogs make our lives better. In 2005 it made that belief tangible by launching a manifesto campaign to convey its core promise — that everything it does is for love of dogs, and that every dog deserves to be fed well and have a loving home.

If dog love was the core of the brand, than caring for dogs had to be at the core of the marketing activity. CSR would not simply be an add-on but would complete the brand promise to consumers, the wider public and staff.

What's at stake

The scale of the problem is daunting. Every year more than 100,000 dogs are found stray or abandoned in the UK which puts immense strain on rescue centres. These charities receive no government funding, relying entirely on charitable donations to keep doing their vital work and depending on volunteers giving their time.

It costs a huge amount of money every year to provide and maintain the level of veterinary care, food and shelter these dogs need. For example, it costs more than £10 million every year to run Battersea Dogs and Cats Home, one of the largest shelters in the UK. In 2007 Battersea cared for 9,262 dogs and 3,069 cats. And Battersea is just one among many shelters in the UK.

In 2008 Pedigree launched The Pedigree Adoption Drive to support the charities that care for dogs. The company decided to create a fund to offer financial assistance to shelters. 1p from every Pedigree product sold over a three-month period would be put into a dedicated fund for charities and shelters with projects that helped abandoned dogs.

Applications to the fund were to be considered by the trustees of The Kennel Club Charitable Trust, along with a representative from Pedigree, Suzy Roffey and Clarissa Baldwin, the chairman of the Association of Dogs & Cats Homes. This board would operate as an impartial expert body familiar with the needs and requirements of rescue centres.

By working with The Kennel Club the company ensured that 100% of the funds donated reached charities, as the Trust's administration costs were funded by The Kennel Club. Each grant would also be followed up by a case study to guarantee that 100% of the funds helped homeless dogs directly.

The campaign also aimed to inspire Pedigree consumers, retailers and the wider dog-loving public to help this worthy cause by raising awareness of the situation of homeless dogs in this country and then giving people a variety of ways to help. This could range from simply buying Pedigree products through to visiting a rescue centre to checking their suitability for adopting a dog.

Calling all dog lovers

The campaign had two core aims:

1. Educate:

- Make people aware of the situation of homeless dogs in the UK and show them how essential the work of dog re-homing centres is.

2. Inspire:

- Pedigree consumers, staff and the greater dog-loving British public to help homeless dogs by showing them how easy it is to make a difference, from buying Pedigree, and/or volunteering at a centre, to going all the way and adopting a dog.

The resulting campaign was integrated across a number of channels.

Digital

To achieve its aims Pedigree focused on the key audience: dog lovers. The website would be crucial to the campaign because it would be the primary source of in-depth information about the Pedigree Adoption Drive and would also include information about responsible dog ownership and how and where to adopt dogs. The website would also feature the stories of the homeless dogs featured in the advertising.

People could sign up to receive regular updates about the adoption drive and further information about adopting dogs. There was also an area for charities to apply for grants. Traffic was driven to the site through advertising and public relations (PR), sending out targeted emails and sponsoring takeovers of the Yahoo home page. The results exceeded expectations:

- In the first quarter of 2008 the website had 150,000 visits and 760,000 page views.
- 62% of these visits were direct, not from searching: i.e. consumers typing in www.pedigreeadoptiondrive.com.
- People viewed on average 5.07 pages per visit and spent an average two minutes 42 seconds on the site.
- In the first week of the campaign the Pedigree Adoption Drive site was channelling more than 50% of the traffic of all Pedigree sites combined.

Above-the-line advertising

The company decided to use only real homeless dogs and their stories to tell the adoption drive story. Each of the 12 dogs featured in the campaign was a homeless dog from Battersea (Figure 1) and every one of them was then adopted. Being able to tell real stories about real dogs added honesty, credibility and strength to the campaign, which was created with TBWA London with the TV produced by Juice Creative.

Isaac (Figure 2) was the hero of the TV work. After being adopted he began training as a mountain rescue dog, which was a great example of the potential every homeless dog has. The national TV campaign featuring Isaac and other dogs was voiced by the actor Neil Morrissey, chosen as spokesman because he had a shelter dog, Tiggy.

Advertising-funded programming

One of the central aims of the Pedigree Adoption Drive was to increase awareness of the great work done by charities 'behind the scenes' helping abandoned dogs. Through the media agency Mediacom, Pedigree contacted ITV with an idea for a TV show showing the work of the people who saved abandoned dogs and the charities that homed them. Mediacom and ITV went on to develop Dog Rescue, a series with six-30 minute shows, with branded sponsorship bumpers created by TBWA.

The show was seen by 9.6 million individuals across the series. On average, 15% more viewers joined the show whenever it was aired, gathering real momentum. Those who had seen the show identified more strongly with Pedigree (10% more identification with the brand) and felt the brand was meaningfully differentiated (+11% 'the brand fits with my pet's needs').

PR coverage

The company received a staggering amount of PR coverage for the adoption drive campaign. Managed by Jackie Cooper PR, the main event of the campaign was the 'big walk' through Battersea. The spokesman Neil Morrisey and his adopted dog Tiggy joined hundreds of local residents, Battersea volunteers and Pedigree staff for a walk through Battersea park to raise the profile of the campaign.

Neil and Tiggy featured on BBC News 24 and also appeared on Loose Women and This Morning talking about the Pedigree Adoption Drive. The story ran in the *Daily Mail* among other leading publications and also appeared on many blog sites. For example, there were:
- 218 pieces of branded coverage.
- Campaign MBR: 7.49 million.
- Campaign reach: 180 million branded media impressions.
- Campaign cost per impact: 0.04 p.
- Campaign return on investment : 25:1.

On-pack and in-store

In-store support for the campaign was crucial, given that donations were generated from every Pedigree pack purchased. There was information about the adoption drive on the pack along with branded food donation points at point-of-sale (POS).

Figure 1. The campaign

Pick me

I'm Isaac. I was left to fend for myself on the streets of London when I was just 3 months old. Luckily Battersea Dogs & Cats Home rescued me. I can't wait to share my love with a family. I'm an active dog and like to be busy, I want to follow you around, play by your feet and be your loyal friend.

Every Pedigree pack sold helps a homeless dog

The Pedigree® Adoption Drive™
because every dog deserves a loving home
www.pedigreeadoptiondrive.com

Pedigree
We're for dogs

Figure 2. Isaac

Donated food was given to rescue centres local to the store. These arrangements were made between the individual supermarket managers and their local charities. Pedigree supplied them with the POS materials and received excellent feedback from the charities who were delighted to create relationships with the local retailers.

There was wholehearted support from the major supermarkets, including Morrison's and Asda. Specialist pet food retailers got fully behind the campaign as well: staff at some stores even wore branded shirts during the campaign. This level of staff engagement among retailers was a valuable asset.

A good result for dogs

The campaign had a huge impact on the fortunes of homeless dogs, not only by raising money for the charities that look after them, but by helping to increase awareness of the problem through the campaign messages. It reached millions of people around the UK. The results speak for themselves:

- £489,000 donated to help homeless dogs.
- The company received over 160 requests for grants from charities around the country, over 150 of which were granted. Many of these were small organisations, so the grants were of huge value to them.
- An estimated 43 million people encountered the campaign.

Sales uplift

The campaign contributed strongly to a year-on-year value sales increase of 6% over 2007-8, with a clear increase in incremental sales over the period of the campaign compared to 2007 (Figure 3).

Boosting the brand attributes

The campaign also had a very positive impact on perceptions of the brand. The IPSOS/MORI Brand Equity Tracker showed phenomenal results when comparing the fourth quarter of 2007 with the first quarter of 2008. Each of the following scores shifted significantly in measurement:

- Motivation increased from 50 to 61. 'This brand fits with my needs and my pet's needs, it is relevant to me'.
- Trust 74 to 80. 'I have confidence in this brand and I trust it'.
- Identification 54 to 63. 'I have something in common with this brand. If this brand were a person I would like them'.
- Quality 67 to 74. 'This is a brand that stands for quality'.
- Dog well-being 58-66. 'This brand has dog well-being in its heart'.

This was the ideal CSR campaign for Pedigree. It enhanced the brand, grew the business and helped vulnerable dogs. The company continued the campaign in 2009, this time donating 2p from the profits of every product

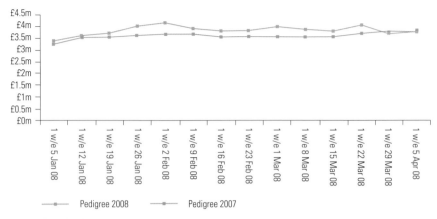

Figure 3. Total brand sales results

Thinkbox

06

Reviving the fortunes of TV as an advertising medium

Snapshot

Thinkbox changed perceptions of the TV advertising medium by persuading a particularly cynical industry audience about its value.

Key insights

- Thinkbox, with the support of the TV companies, revitalised 'brand TV' and increased its share of an extremely challenging advertising market.

- A three-year campaign saw TV well on the road back to its rightful position in the hierarchy of display media.

- Success came from repositioning the medium by vigorously addressing the misperceptions surrounding it, proving it works and generally championing it.

Summary

Thinkbox is the marketing body for commercial TV in the UK in all its forms. Its shareholders are Channel 4, Five, GMTV, ITV, Sky Media and Turner Media Innovations. They together represent over 90% of commercial TV advertising revenue through their owned and partner TV channels.

When it was launched in February 2005, it had three main objectives:
- To produce a fundamental re-evaluation of television as a commercial medium.
- To achieve recognition that TV advertising is vital and has a strong future.
- To protect TV revenue.

By the end of 2006 aggressive targeting of the TV budget by 'rival' media in combination with no unified voice for TV had led to progressive decline in its share of display advertising to an all time low of 39.7% (22% of total advertising). Stories of 'the death of TV' were rife and a piece of quantitative tracking research revealed that it was held in low esteem by large sections of the industry.

During a three-year programme of communications and research focused around the four broad strategic pillars of: EffecTVness, Leadership, Education and Inspiration, Thinkbox, in partnership with the TV companies, not only transformed industry perceptions of TV as a medium but grew TV's share of revenue.

Facing the facts

Although it might seem counter-intuitive to regard commercial TV advertising as a brand, it certainly has all the characteristics of one since it occupies an emotional space in people's minds and has a very specific set of brand associations. That's why Thinkbox was launched in February 2005 as a joint marketing initiative for commercial TV (Figure 1). By this time, other media trade bodies had already been going for some years: the Newspaper Society since 1923, the Radio Advertising Bureau since 1992 and even the Internet Advertising Bureau (IAB) — representing the 'new' medium of the internet — since 1997.

Given TV's historical status (though not revenue dominance; print was and still is the biggest advertising sector), it was widely regarded as the medium from which share could and should be stolen. Aggressive targeting of the TV budget by 'rival' media in combination with no unified voice for TV led to a progressive decline in its share of display advertising to an all-time low of 39.7% (22% of total advertising) in 2006.

That same year Thinkbox commissioned some quantitative tracking research to look at industry attitudes to TV. This made for grim reading. Perceptions of TV were low, scoring particularly poorly for targeting, innovation, interactivity and value for money. Media agency staff gave the most negative responses of all (Figure 2).

One cause of the negativity was due to what the organisation came to term the 'internet fundamentalists'. These were an extremely vocal and very influential minority among the online community who wished TV dead and who appeared to be controlling the journalistic narrative. Almost every week there would be a story about the death of TV. The only two areas of comfort for the TV industry were advertisers and viewers.

Advertisers, while being excited by what the web offered their businesses, still appreciated TV advertising as a very significant business driver. Viewers, far from abandoning TV, made it clear that it was alive and well by watching more and more commercial TV as every month went past.

Figure 1

(%)	Total	Advertiser	Advertising Agency	Media Agency
	n=280	n=93	n=93	n=94
Is engaging to audiences	61	67	58	59
Is the home of great brand advertising	61	61	⑦⑦	㊻
As a medium is relevant to today's advertising market	60	65	⑦④	㊶
Offers effective sponsorship options	50	53	㊿	㉛
Is an accountable medium	40	45	49	㉕
Offers a variety of uses	37	38	31	41
Currently has good quality programming	29	㊺	33	⑨
Offers innovative ways of marketing a brand or product	27	20	22	27
Is particularly good as an interactive medium for advertising	25	㉟	28	⑪
Is great for reaching niche targets	23	20	22	27
Is an ideal medium for tactical ad campaigns	23	24	22	㉔
TV campaigns offer good value for money	19	21	㉛	7

Q6: 5 point scale of agreement on statements about TV as advertising medium
Base: All respondents (n=280)

◯ = significantly different @ 95% to total

Figure 2. TV industry perceptions. TV as advertising medium agreement (strongly agree/tend to agree)

Understanding the challenges

There were a number of specific challenges identified:
- Without expensive econometric modelling, many advertisers found it very difficult to isolate TV's exact effect. There was a lack of credible, industry research to prove categorically TV's effectiveness to company chief executives and finance directors.
- There were surprising levels of ignorance on basic TV facts: viewing, consumer behaviour and the impact of new technologies, even among people whose job it was to know them.
- Excitement about the transforming power of technology had been appropriated by the online industry. Technology was largely regarded as a threat to TV.
- Planners in media agencies had fallen out of love with TV since they felt that it wasn't an area where they could publicly demonstrate their insight and innovation and win an award. All the exciting planning opportunities seemed to be in other media.
- Other than a flurry of excitement around the major TV award ceremonies, the received wisdom was that TV ads weren't as good as they used to be. Clients were rarely celebrated and credited with the important role they played in developing breakthrough creativity.

Defining the audiences

With limited resources it was vital for Thinkbox to prioritise its diverse audiences. The selected groupings were:
- Advertisers (because they ultimately decide how much the overall marketing budget is) jointly with media planners in media agencies (because they recommend how that budget should be allocated by broad channel).
- Those people who were the major influencers on the primary two audiences (journalists, creative agencies, analysts, bloggers, etc).
- The rest of the media and communications industry.

Setting the strategy

Thinkbox developed four key strategic pillars to help inform the programme of activity.

1. EffecTVness.
- Focus on effectiveness as the fundamental underpinning of the entire programme: why TV works, how well it works, why it will continue to work.

2. Lead. Don't follow.
- Behave like a brand leader: position TV as the catalyst for (and therefore ally to) all other media. Stress TV *and*, not TV *or*.
- Lead by example and use TV to promote TV.
- Lead the debate, particularly on topical issues.

3. Education, education, education
- Ensure the facts about TV are known and understood.
- Correct misperceptions and challenge myths whenever they appear.

- Influence the influencers who can do the education job for TV.

4. Be inspired and inspiring

- Share and celebrate best practice work in terms of creativity, planning and effectiveness.
- Focus on the exciting possibilities of new technology and demonstrate how it will benefit advertisers.
- By defining television as the content, not the technology, create an exciting narrative for the future of TV.
- Be evangelists for TV.

This was an immensely varied and intense three-year programme. The main highlights which took place within the context of the four strategic pillars included:

1. EffecTVness

A series of significant research studies on effectiveness were commissioned, launched to the media, shared at events, put on the website in 'nickable' form and then taken on the presentation trail. Key initiatives included:

- The Payback study. This was a major econometric study done by PricewaterhouseCoopers on the long-term effectiveness of different media which revealed that TV delivers the best return on investment, at £4.5 million for every £1 million investment.
- TV and response. This analysis looked at the impact of television on web and other short-term response channels.
- TV and online. Collaboration with the IAB showed that using TV and online is significantly more effective for advertisers than using either alone.
- MeTV. This research examined the potential effectiveness of emerging opportunities within online TV.

- TV sponsorship. Pioneering research revealed how and why sponsorship works and how its impact can be best measured.
- Headline sponsorship of the IPA Effectiveness Awards. This is independent, rigorous proof of the effectiveness of TV and produces a raft of excellent case studies which can then be filmed and distributed.
- Finally, there was a successful trade advertising campaign highlighting the medium's effectiveness (Figures 3 and 4).

Figure 3. Trade campaign

Figure 4. Trade campaign

2. Lead. Don't follow.

- The adoption of brand leader behaviour meant taking a confident approach to its relationship with other media, initiating collaborative research projects (TV and online: better together, with the IAB) and, even when provoked, not denigrate other media. Multi-media campaigns were championed with TV at their heart to drive other media.
- Lead by example. This led to the first TV ad for TV advertising which ran in May and December 2009. It achieved 325 million impacts on TV, 80,000 hits on YouTube and increased traffic to the website more than fourfold. The Sun called it: "The ad everyone's talking about."
- Commitment to televisual communications.
- Lead the debate on topical issues with blogs, Twitter, event topics, regular column in *Media Week*, articles and thought pieces.

3. Education, education, education

- There was a zero tolerance approach to myths and inaccuracies in media, with all factual errors immediately responded to and corrected.
- The set-up of a compelling website. The aim was to make it a one-stop shop window for TV information. Initiatives of note include: the hugely popular 'nickables' section, the interactive cost calculator, the technology glossary and the case history library (Figure 5).
- Strive to simplify and clarify complex issues. For example, '7 Killer Facts about TV', FAQs (Frequently Asked Questions) and FUCs (Frequently Uttered Codswallop).
- Presentations. In spite of limited resources, Thinkbox's presentation strike rate over the period was a presentation to an agency or advertiser every other working day. The company spoke at every conference it could.

Figure 5. Website

- Publishing information. BARB viewing data and advertising spend data is published on the website once a month. There is also an annual report 'A year in TV' which is an invaluable resource to the industry (Figure 6). In addition, in 2008 a major supplement on the future of TV was published in *The Guardian*.
- Free training. In 2008 a free 'Introduction to TV' training course was established for entrants to the industry and in 2009 an additional 'Introduction to TV technology' course was introduced.

4. Be inspired and inspiring

- The 'Thinkboxes' in association with *Campaign* and *Marketing*. These were the first monthly awards for TV advertising and were launched in 2008 to reinforce the business-transforming power of fantastic TV creativity and celebrate the clients and agencies that created it. Each month the Creative Academy votes to decide the winning ad from a shortlist, showcased in *Campaign*. The winner is announced in *Marketing* with the client featured.
- The Thinkbox TV Planning Awards in association with *Campaign* and *Media Week*. These were launched in 2007 and have become one of the significant events in the media awards calendar.
- Sponsorship and partnership programmes. Partnerships were formed with key industry organisations to provide a platform for inspiration of audiences about TV creativity and effectiveness.
- Major events programme. This ranged from the very large such as the Thinkbox Experience in 2007 and Televisionaries in 2008 to the more modest, such as a regular programme of events at the Soho Hotel and other regional venues, to the extremely modest, such as the 27 in-house events held in 2009. Live web-streaming was introduced in 2008

to broaden the audience, while whole classes of advertising courses at university watched the live stream.
- New language. This included the development of new language and enthusiasm for the way advances in TV technology were discussed: e.g. "3rd Age of TV", "Liberating TV technology". Technological innovation was used as the hook to excite people's interest.
- Web content to inspire. This included a specially-developed interactive emulator, TV ad galleries, ads of the week and a TVIQ competition each Christmas.

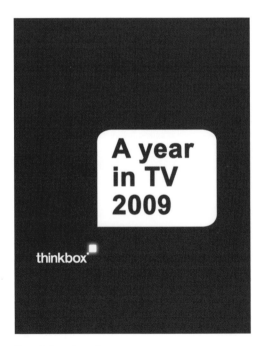

Figure 6. Annual report

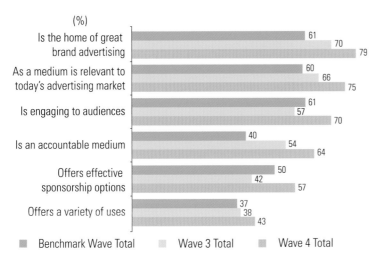

(%)

Figure 7. Advertiser and agency perceptions of TV...
TV as advertising medium agreement (strongly/tend to) over time
Source: SPA

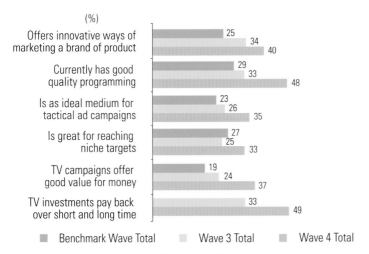

(%)

Figure 8. ...have improved during Thinkbox's brief life
TV as advertising medium agreement (strongly/tend to) over time
Source: SPA

TV transformed

All these efforts paid off handsomely.

1. Perceptions of TV

- This improved with each wave of tracker research (Figures 7 and 8).
- December 2009's tracker revealed the marked difference in attitudes to TV of those who were aware of Thinkbox compared to those who weren't. (Figure 9 overleaf)
- 2010 began with a report from Deloitte predicting that, despite the increasing popularity of on-demand TV, linear broadcast TV is "likely to remain dominant not just in 2010 but for many years to come".
- In its last-ever edition, *Media Week* in 2009 reviewed the performance of all the trade bodies, awarding Thinkbox the only 'A grade' for the job it had done in transforming perceptions of its medium.
- In 2008 Thinkbox gained enough public relations coverage to fill three complete editions of *Media Week* and in 2009, enough for six editions.
- Accolades continued to come from the industry, such as this one from the head of media investment at a top three advertiser: "My perception is that Thinkbox is doing an excellent job and I think you'll find that that is the opinion of most of the market. "

2. TV revenue

The ultimate proof of whether 'Brand TV' was on its way to full recovery could be expressed in the advertising revenue that TV earned. Two important issues must be born in mind to see the commercial results in context:

- The cataclysmic global recession which started to impact on the media landscape in 2008.
- The rapid growth of internet media. Headlines appeared mid-2009 declaring that online revenues, including classified, search and email marketing, had overtaken TV revenues. Whether this was true or not — or whether it was even a fair comparison — is a matter of debate. However, internet revenue growth was not at the expense of TV. Indeed, one could argue that TV's recovery was all the more remarkable alongside such a buoyant sector as all online media.

TV's performance relative to other display media is the most meaningful indicator of success.TV's share of advertising grew from its low of 39.68% in 2006 to 42.23% in 2008, the last year for which there are official figures. However, cautious estimates for 2009 suggested that TV had yet again improved its relative performance in this most cataclysmic year, when brand advertising investment had been so severely squeezed. According to Thinkbox's shareholders, TV's net spot and sponsorship revenue declined by less than 10% within a market that had declined by 13% overall.

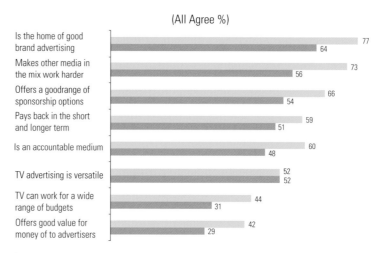

(All Agree %)

Is the home of good brand advertising — 77 / 64
Makes other media in the mix work harder — 73 / 56
Offers a goodrange of sponsorship options — 66 / 54
Pays back in the short and longer term — 59 / 51
Is an accountable medium — 60 / 48
TV advertising is versatile — 52 / 52
TV can work for a wide range of budgets — 44 / 31
Offers good value for money of to advertisers — 42 / 29

Q7. Using a 5 point scale where 1 means 'strongly disagree' and 5 means 'strongly agree' please tell me to what extent you agree or disagree with each phrase as a description of TV.
Base: Thinkbox NOT aware n=254, Thinkboxaware n=160

◼ Thinkbox NOT aware   ▪ Thinkbox aware

Figure 9. Attitudes towards TV
Source: Holden Pearmain

Harlequins

06

Big brand thinking on a shoestring

Snapshot

Despite a tight budget a clever marketing campaign attracted a sell-out crowd for a Harlequins match that has turned into a brand in its own right.

Key insights

- Harlequins Football Club wanted to attract an audience that extended above and beyond regular rugby fans to create a branded event — The Big Game 2 — that would become a regular spot in the annual events calendar.

- The imaginative multi-media campaign punched far above its weight, with outdoor advertising, national and local media, extensive public relations (PR), sponsorship, player appearances, social networking, e-CRM, digital affiliates, radio and experiential marketing.

- More than 76,000 people filled Twickenham on the day of the match, breaking the record for a standard club fixture.

Summary

The Harlequin Football Club was founded in 1866 (although the first recorded game was not until 1867) as Hampstead Football Club and renamed in 1870. The club has won the Rugby Football Union Club knockout competition on two occasions: The John Player Cup in 1988 and Pilkington Cup in 1991. It was also the first British side to win the European Shield in 2001, going on to win the renamed Parker Pen Challenge Cup again in 2004.

Rugby clubs are not known for big marketing budgets or indeed big brand thinking when it comes to marketing. The Big Game 2 was an attempt to fill Twickenham Stadium with 82,000 people for Harlequins vs. Wasps on December 27th 2009. That was a 600% increase on Harlequins' normal match-day attendance.

With just £120,000 to spend during a six month build-up, the club had to be creative to reach out to a non-traditional rugby audience by offering a branded package devised by Bamboo Marketing Communications that offered great entertainment, even better value and, hopefully, a first-class game of rugby. The result broke records for a standard club fixture and became a regular spot in the annual events calendar.

Ambitious goals

There were a number of objectives the club was keen to achieve by launching the campaign for The Big Game 2 (TBG2).

- It wanted to establish a new date in the Christmas sporting calendar and extend the reach of rugby in general by marketing this fixture as the perfect alternative Christmas entertainment option.
- In particular, it hoped to introduce a new audience to Harlequins in the hope it would widen its casual supporter base. This would transform the match from being just another Guinness Premiership pool match to a first-class day of family entertainment that would gain a place in people's Christmas holiday plans.

The campaign had to generate ticket sales far in excess of usual club attendance of 13,000. Its goal was to achieve a 78,000 capacity sell-out (actual capacity is 82,000, but, because of sponsors and box holders, only 78,000 could be sold.). To do that, it had to make the limited budget of £120,000 work

as hard as possible through contra-deals, careful media planning, player appearances and third party negotiation.

A core set of creative elements was developed for use in a rolling campaign from July to December 2009, each focusing on different 'reasons to go':

- Establishing recognition of the brand The Big Game 2 for future years so that it would be strong enough to stand apart from the core Quins brand.
- A contest featuring two opposing top international players (Nick Evans and Serge Betson), appealing to all rugby fans regardless of club affiliation.
- Stressing the value: a top game at Twickenham from only £10 for adults and £5 for children (Figure 1, 2 and 3).
- A great day's family entertainment even for those who were not regular rugby followers.

Figure 1, 2 and 3. Examples of posters and leaflets

A multi-layered strategy

This was followed by a multi-media campaign targeting a wide south east England audience, including all rugby fans, all sports fans and, crucially, casual or non-supporter friends and families planning alternative Christmas entertainment. A high-profile PR campaign was mounted offering unique access to the team with player front-cover shots and editorial content and sent to a wide variety of national and local press.

There were also roadside six and 48-sheet posters (Figure 4), while the autumn international Rugby Football Union (RFU) shuttle bus carried advertising and cross-track posters were placed in major south and west London stations. The club negotiated the appearance of three X Factor finalists keen to sing in front of what would be such a large audience (Figure 5). This alone extended the reach even further. Studio interviews by players and access to the X Factor secured a one-week on-air Capital Radio listener competition to meet X Factor contestants backstage.

There were sponsorship and player appearances at over 40 London and local events. For instance, Danny Care and Ugo Monye switched on Kingston Christmas lights which gained exposure to over 55,000 people, in addition to Radio Jackie pre-publicity (Figure 6) and live interviews and local press interviews.

The Harlequin Honeys embarked on a six-month flyer campaign at relevant London and local events, bars, pubs and restaurants, including heavyweight presence at the autumn internationals. There were digital online partnerships with organisations such as Visit London, *Evening Standard*, SKY, RFU, Kempton Park, Virgin Active, RFU Supporters Club, Kew Gardens and Richmond Council, along with inclusion in their newsletters in return for low-value competitions.

Figure 4. Example of a poster

A constant stream of behind-the-scenes content featuring players was built up to feed onto Facebook fan pages and Twitter. There was also an ongoing e-shot campaign. Finally, photo shoots of various celebrities wearing the charity match-day shirt were organised which gave access to non-traditional rugby media. For example, Monye and David Strettle dressed in rugby kit with Caprice modelling her new range of lingerie with the theme: "You show me your kit and I'll show you mine"

A clever mix of media

Outdoor

The principal aim was to spend as little as possible on conventional paid-for media. Where the club did need to spend money, the chosen media had to deliver impact and longevity. Outdoor was chosen as the primary vehicle to generate awareness in the two months prior to the event. Research showed that outdoor indexed well against the club's core ABC1 family audience who are socially active, use public transport to get to and from work and spend a high proportion of their time out of the home.

Transport media (train stations) were used for their high dwell time, with 48-sheet and six-sheets selected to target ABC1 homes and key arterial travel routes. The CENSYS planning tool was used to map sites to homes and locations such as train stations, schools and offices, thereby minimising wastage and ensuring that the campaign had as great an impact as possible in the key engagement period of November to December. By booking when it did, the club's two-week week campaign stayed up in many cases for over two months.

Figure 5 X Factor finalists

Figure 6. Radio Jackie pre-publicity

Figure 7. Lifestyle magazines

Figure 8. The big day

Newspapers

The main focus was on PR exclusives, with paid-for space in the *Evening Standard*.

Local magazines

Through negotiated ad spend/ PR contra-deals the club reached a combined circulation of 750,000 lifestyle magazines, delivered to ABC1 households in south and west London (Figure 7).

Buses

Advertising was placed on 15 RFU shuttle bus sides which then serviced normal routes on non-match days. These buses were parked in a line facing the 82,000 people exiting Twickenham Stadium during the autumn internationals.

Enjoying a big win

At 3.30pm on December 27th 76,716 people walked into Twickenham Stadium and sat down to be entertained by a giant sea eagle delivering the match ball, three X Factor finalists singing the Harlequins' club song, an Abba tribute band, opera singers and finally, as the teams took to the field, spectacular pyrotechnics launched from the stadium roof. This attendance broke the record for a standard club pool fixture. It also met the key objective of building a brand, complimentary to Harlequins but able to stand alone (Figure 8).

A big pat on the back

The achievement drew praise from many within the rugby community and one of the most respected commentators in the sport, Stephen Jones of *The Sunday Times*, wrote: "*The extraordinary success of Big Game 1 and Big Game 2 has changed the face of professional rugby in England completely. When more than 70,000 go along to watch a regular-season club match, albeit between deadly rivals such as Harlequins and Wasps, then everything we knew about rugby's appeal has to be rewritten. Other clubs will be anxiously searching for their own equivalent games and pressure on clubs to upgrade their capacities will be enormous.*

The courage and vision of Harlequins and the strategies of their marketing agency, Bamboo Marketing Communications, for the Big Games has reaped an incredible reward and has drawn thousands of new faces into rugby's orbit. And re-affirmed rugby's claim to be the best day out in sport."

And in his *Sunday Telegraph* column, Paul Ackford wrote: "*You know when an event is taking off when it comes with its own shorthand — TBG2. The Big Game: 2 for the uninitiated, and where were you hiding while the spectacle was marketed?"*

Chris Foy in *The Daily Mail* wrote: "*A vibrant atmosphere here at HQ as Big Game 2 passed off as a triumph of ambition and marketing."*

This game was not intended to be a major revenue generator and the intangible rewards of building a wider regular club supporter base and the re-building of Quins' brand equity following a difficult summer were impossible to quantify. But the game still generated a respectable profit on a marketing investment of £120,000.

All images appearing in this case study are reproduced by permission of Harlequins.

Chapter 7
Creating Loyal Relationships

Mark Thomson
Media Director,
Royal Mail

Modern marketing has created the promiscuous consumer. The rise of social media is hastening the transition from push to pull. So creating loyalty in an era of ephemera is among this industry's hardest challenges.

Making customers more loyal is about defining your market, differentiating yourself from the competition, and ultimately communicating and reinforcing the brand proposition to your target audience. By giving consumers something a little bit special, you are much more likely to provoke engagement, repeat purchase and a greater degree of brand loyalty.

The case studies in this chapter give ample ammunition for companies seeking to boost loyalty. Take the Walkers 'Do us a flavour' campaign. It's a classic example of a market leader devising an ingenious way of widening the gap over its rivals, by engaging with domestic grocery gatekeepers and snacking workers with what was, in truth, a fun and simple idea.

More Th>n's excellent work, meanwhile, shows another way of engendering loyalty: get personal. By sending letters to their customers with details of dedicated 'account managers', the insurer strengthened the link between corporation and consumer in a commoditised sector.

Technology — whether driving mass production or mass discussion and comparison — is driving exponential growth in competition across all industries. Marketers must be savvy and nimble enough to grasp the advice offered in the following pages, and use it to forge their own path to growing loyalty in a transient market by delivering creative, targeted and integrated campaigns.

More Th>n

07

Profiting from a more personal service

Snapshot

More Th>n enjoyed a resurgence in loyalty when it offered customers their own personal contact manager.

Key insights

- In a commoditised market More Th>n decided to buck the industry trend by putting a personalised service at the heart of its customer relationship management as a source of competitive edge.

- Once a pilot programme proved the worth of creating customer managers, the programme was rolled out across the company and saw satisfaction, retention and cross-selling rates rise markedly.

- It had the added benefit of enhancing staff motivation by empowering front-line employees to take ownership of customer relationships.

Summary

More Th>n is the direct arm of RSA, one of the world's leading insurance groups. It launched in June 2001, offering financial services via the internet and telephone. It provides over two million customers with access to an extensive product range including home, motor, pet and travel insurance.

The company wanted a customer relationship programme that would maintain a two-way dialogue with its customers. The result was an initiative which offered every one of them the opportunity to have a personal contact manager within the customer service team who could deal with their queries and requirements. Each manager would have a direct line and personal email address which they supplied to their customer contacts.

It proved to be a huge challenge and demanded great commitment from stakeholders across the business. But the effort paid off in full: a pilot programme delivered double-figure improvements in retention rates and led to the programme becoming part of the core offering in the marketing mix to key segments. Rising retention rates and sales, as well as a boost in staff motivation, have reflected its continuing success.

A cluttered and commoditised market

Over the last few years the insurance market has become hugely competitive, with consumers able to choose between nearly 400 providers and an explosion of the aggregators. This has led to heightened promiscuity among customers who are savvy enough to know they get the cheapest deals by moving policy every year.

Because there is a perception of very limited product differentiation and with low customer engagement (even during the purchase process) price often dictates who people insure with. That's why the sector spends over £200 million a year on media, battling it out to create switchers in order to acquire new customers. It then relies on retention and cross-selling to drive profitability.

From its very conception in 2001 the More Th>n brand set out to give a better offering in the insurance market (Figure 1). The development of a 'price plus' strategy had seen it grow into one of the top providers in the country. However, in a market that adapts very quickly, it couldn't afford to be complacent. So it had to be continuously striving to keep ahead of the pack by creating new sources of competitive advantage based on its brand philosophy that 'We do more'.

MORE TH>N®
WE DO MORE

Figure 1

A framework for encouraging dialogue

The company's qualitative research had given it two very powerful insights:

- Customers hated 'call-centres'. A quarter of respondents found dealing with people in call centres one of the most infuriating aspects of their day-to-day lives. Long waiting times, slow callbacks and the frustration of having to repeat their problem to numerous call handlers who were based in foreign countries were often cited by consumers as reasons why they disliked dealing with large organisations in this way.
- They wanted to be treated differently as existing customers. Many of them mentioned their annoyance that they didn't feel they benefited or were rewarded for their custom, often feeling that new sales were given priority over servicing existing customers. Some canny individuals would even resort to calling sales lines to be transferred to customer services as they knew it would be quicker.

The company decided to tackle these insights head on. It developed a pioneering and ambitious new customer service initiative whereby every customer would have the opportunity to have a named contact within the customer service team who could deal with their queries and requirements. This would encourage a two-way dialogue with customers, with an emphasis on service and satisfaction to increase profitability, rather than purely pushing products outwards.

The key objectives were:
- To create competitive advantage by building a strong service ethos in an otherwise commoditised market.
- To increase customer satisfaction and thus loyalty.
- To increase value by customer.
- To increase motivation levels among sates staff.

Making the commitment

The programme began with a pilot scheme at the end of 2006/beginning of 2007, where 60,000 motor and home insurance customers were contacted by email and offered a personal named contact in More Th>n, known as their 'personal customer manager' (PCM). It was so successful that the programme was eventually rolled out to the entire customer base.

But the scale of the task was huge and demanded great commitment from stakeholders across the business because:
- PCM's needed to be selected, trained and monitored.
- The company had to undertake the biggest single communication campaign since brand launch.
- It had to re-engineer its customer communications plan and service delivery model to incorporate one-to-one interaction with the PCM.

The PCMs were specially selected to be able to handle customer enquiries on the full range of More Th>n products and services. Customers could contact their PCM via a direct telephone line or email with any insurance query from a simple policy change to checking on the progress of a claim.

Each PCM was empowered to build personal customer relationships through this new contact approach. Where a PCM was personally unable to handle a particular issue — for example, an accounting error — they would still 'own' that customer experience from beginning to end to ensure timely and appropriate resolution for the customer and provide regular communications.

In providing this closer, more personal, relationship More Th>n found that customers were more likely to purchase additional services as well as increasing the likelihood of them remaining with More Th>n across each renewal cycle.

Covering every base

A key consideration for the company was its ability to deliver this initiative without affecting either the profitability of its products or the premium paid by the customer. So the goal was to make this a no-cost option while still meeting the brand promise — and to do so without any negative impact on service delivery to other areas of the business.

An audit of UK call centre capabilities was carried out, followed by the creation of teams of high-performing consultants who could become PCMs. Workshops were run with the teams to explain the strategy and further training was provided so that they were fully committed to their roles and responsibilities.

It was notable that motivation levels within these teams increased dramatically as a sense of ownership of the customers developed. This resulted in a pronounced reduction in sickness and absenteeism and saw sales success by individuals increase. It also created a new performance level with the customer services teams which other employees could aspire to achieve.

The key element was that customers always had a contact they could approach directly. So the company emailed or wrote to customers to notify them of any changes to the person responsible for their account.

Since generating sales was integral to the programme, the company designed the marketing communications to come from the PCM personally wherever possible. This included news on the latest offers and product enhancements, to softer messages such as a card at Christmas or the offer a free winter health check for their car.

A more than positive outcome

Measurability was a critical factor. The company needed to prove to its sponsors within the business that this new approach would have a positive impact on the bottom line. All customer activity was thus tracked in two groups: customers who had opted in to the service either actively or through automatic allocation, and those who hadn't.

The results showed a significant uplift in renewal rates among those registered for the service indexed against those who had not, as Table 1 shows. It also proved that cross-selling was at much higher levels through the PCM relationships than those with the control group (Table 2). These were primary objectives for the scheme, adding millions to the balance sheet in premium income.

Table 1 Renewal rate comparison

	Motor renewal rate	Home renewal rate
Index	120%	105%

Table 2 Cross-sell rate comparison

Segment	Cross-sell rate
Registered for the PCM service	6.85%
Not registered for PCM service	4.07%
Index	168%

The analysis also revealed that the service had a positive effect on mid-term cancellation rates. For these purposes this was defined as a cancellation that took place more than 15 days before or after the renewal date. Table 3 compares cancellation rates between those customers who had registered for the service and those who had not.

Table 3 Mid-term cancellation comparison

Segment	Mid-term cancellation rate
Registered for PCM service	0.14%
Not registered for PCM service	0.55%
Index	393%

Strengthening the customer bonds

Research following the pilot also showed that users of the PCM service were significantly more likely to say that the initiative had raised their opinion of More Th>n's customer service in general. They were also significantly more likely to be completely satisfied with More Th>n's customer service.

Other key findings from the research included:
- 57% of the pilot customers researched said that having a PCM would make them more likely to take out other More Th>n policies.
- 71% said they were now more likely to recommend More Th>n than before.
- 61% said that having a PCM would encourage them to remain as a More Th>n customer for longer.
- 65% said they would use the service again.

An added bonus was that the introduction of the PCM service brought More Th>n unprecedented amounts of media coverage in consumer titles and the national press. While it is very difficult to quantify the value of this, positive endorsement in influential media delivered great benefit in terms of new business generation, customer retention rates and staff satisfaction.

Continually refining the offer

PCM has now became a core part of the offering in More Th>n's value-based segmentation programme. The segmentation model was built on a multitude of variables and was able to classify groups by their value based on their likelihood of buying other products as well as their premium, claims and loyalty ratings.

Findings from research found that the company's most profitable segments ('prudent and proud' and 'discerning discoverers') were also the very same people who placed an increased importance in customer service relationships. Because of this, the company could prioritise the automatic allocation of PCMs to these two segments while less valuable and price-focused segments could be offered the service on an opt-in basis. This enabled the company to be operationally adept with its resources to ensure those that benefited from the service were those that offered most commercial return to More Th>n.

In 2008 in the biggest single campaign since the launch of the brand, over 1.3 million More Th>n customers were mailed or emailed to invite them to register for a PCM (Figure 2). Customers who were mailed could complete and return a coupon to register for the service or, like email customers, could choose to register themselves for the service online using a dedicated page on the More Th>n website.

The customers were then allocated to their named contact and a letter or email sent from the personal customer manager introducing themselves and providing their direct contact details.

After launching to existing customers, More Th>n then placed the PCM service at the heart of it's 'MORE is…' brand campaign by advertising the service to new customers on television, within mailing packs, online and in fulfilment literature (Figure 3).

Figure 2. Invitation letter

Going the extra mile

One of More Th>n's customers wanted to give his wife a Christmas to remember with a brand new car. The only problem was that he needed an insurance certificate to drive it off the forecourt at a time of year when everything slowed down.

His personal customer manager liaised with the office nearest to the customer's home and arranged for the documentation to be printed locally. The manager then sent the customer a route planner to show him the way to the office. The Tuesday after Christmas, the company received a phone call saying thank-you from his grateful wife. They subsequently took out home, pet and travel insurance with the company.

The company's decision to concentrate on offering customers a highly-improved value proposition thus not only paid off in higher levels of customer satisfaction and ultimately the bottom line, but it also motivated front-line staff by empowering them to take greater ownership of and accountability for their customers.

Figure 3. A still from the brand TV campaign

All images appearing in this case study are reproduced by permission of More Th>n.

UPS

07

Helping customers with a helpful widget

Snapshot

By creating an appealing desktop gadget to help its time-pressurised customers UPS successfully attracted new users.

Key insights

- UPS needed to grow and improve retention of existing customers while encouraging lapsed and new users to embrace UPS and its products and services.

- The solution had to differentiate the UPS brand among a crowd of competitors.

- The solution was UPS Widget, a desktop gadget personified by a spirited character whose sole aim was to be a hardworking helper. By December 2008 almost 180,000 had been downloaded.

Summary

UPS is a global company with one of the most recognized and admired brands in the world. With sales of almost $50 billion, it manages shipping and logistics services in over 200 countries and territories.

As the market leader in the US, it decided a few years ago to gain a stronger foothold in other regions such as Europe and Asia, where it ranked third and fourth respectively. It also wanted to understand in more depth its target audience — shipping managers — in order to overcome their inertia about changing suppliers and find a way to get their attention

The resulting solution involved a clever desktop gadget, the UPS Widget, which offered busy shipping managers a simple way to track their shipments at a time when downloadable gadgets were still relatively rare. This helpful gadget was launched with a range of promotional activity in three European markets in September 2007, followed by further campaigns. By December 2008 homepage traffic exceeded 18 million visits, while almost 180,000 widgets had been downloaded.

Going for growth

US market leader UPS wanted to gain a stronger foothold in other global regions such as Europe and Asia, where the brand ranked third and fourth respectively against its competitors. One of the challenges in these markets was to help customers see the benefits of using UPS since, traditionally, companies did not switch suppliers because the effort to change was perceived as greater than the difference it would make. Moreover, the services which UPS wanted decision-makers to consider were not top of mind.

In October 2006 extensive research was conducted among shipping managers. It revealed that they were highly stressed, time-poor and always searching for ways to work more productively. In addition, they wanted to be seen as competent and on top of things when their co-workers demanded delivery status. Shipping managers felt accountable from the moment a package leaves the business. So UPS marketing had to engage the audience on two levels: confirm that UPS could be a trusted ally and partner and act essentially as an extension of their business from within and a business that offered a range of relevant services that would build efficiencies into their day-to-day shipping/logistics efforts.

It was clear that advertising alone would not make them think differently about UPS. The campaign could not simply say that UPS provided useful and innovative solutions. The solution needed to demonstrate this commitment.

Welcome to Widget

The company decided to create a desktop application in the guise of a lovable, hardworking helper named UPS Widget. Widget enabled UPS to claim the ad-free space where the audience spent most of their working day — in front of their computer. The Widget's primary feature was a simplified means of tracking shipments. It offered a distinct brand service by giving customers access to package tracking without having to go to UPS.com, as well as links to other UPS services, direct from their desktop.

Development began in 2006 when downloadable gadgets were not yet ubiquitous, so the notion of providing such innovative technology simply and easily for use by the company's three target audiences of front-desk staff, shipping managers and small business owners was a fresh and exciting prospect.

Making life easier

There were a number of advantages this application offered:
- It integrated the company's own XML tracking functionality and other UPS services directly from users' desktops.
- Users could access news feeds from the integrated RSS reader.
- It also featured a direct messaging channel to users' desktops using a robust and integrated content management system (CMS). This was developed to facilitate rich communication with end users, including direct mail, surveys and news. In addition, it offered a customisable RSS feed.
- Widget enabled a greater level of transparency within the shipping process and as a result empowered its audience by providing information which helped reassure shipping managers and, in turn, their co-workers across the business.
- Finally, Widget, as the UPS hardworking helper, was charming, resonating with customer audiences at all levels.

Launching Widget into the market

In the first phase the print and out-of-home media built awareness of the Widget while online advertising drove people to download the application. Relationship marketing activity engaged existing customers with direct marketing (DM), including email and newsletters and the offer of a Widget stress toy. Widget was brought to life and promoted through a 360-degree campaign aimed at the target audiences' working life and daily commute (Figures 1 and 2).

The role of the creative strategy was to intrigue front-office staff and shipping managers about the company's worldwide express services and ultimately drive them to the microsite to download the Widget. The UPS Widget became the catalyst for an end-to-end marketing effort across six regions that encompassed search engine marketing, online media, the Widget microsite, customer relationship marketing (CRM), including email, landing pages and content served through the Widget CMS, along with out-of-home and print. There was also a robust optimisation plan developed to ensure that all media was meeting the end users' needs.

The key performance indicators (KPIs) were designed to meet the ambitious goals:
- Build awareness of Widget and the UPS brand by encouraging consumer site visits.
- Motivate/excite prospects to learn about UPS products and services.
- Drive downloads and installations.
- Grow and retain UPS business among existing users.
- Encourage lapsed and/or new users to use UPS.
- Make the cost per download as efficient as possible.
- Insure quality users moved to the site.
- Introduce a new DM/CRM messaging channel to promote added value services to customers.
- Create a new and differentiating reason to communicate with customers.

Activities were measured using a combination of Atlas, WebTrends and the Widget CMS.

Figure 1. The Widget campaign

Figure 2. The Widget campaign

Surpassing expectations

The Widget began a dialogue with customers in a more powerful way than advertising alone. It extended the brand, showcased the company's commitment to innovation through relevant technologies and, most importantly, emphasised its passion for partnership.

In August 2008 over 55,000 Widgets were downloaded, with 900,000 interactions and 2.2 million microsite visits, which, in turn, led to over 20,000 referrals to UPS.com revenue-generating activities. Internally, Widget generated a positive reaction throughout the organisation. Externally, there was plenty of buzz surrounding the launch of the Widget, leading to hundreds of blog comments, the formation of social networking groups and Widget Flickr images.

The activity didn't stop there, however. In preparation for the May – July 2008 campaign the microsite was updated with the creation of an overlay page which offered users three ways in to the content. This was very well-received. The Widget technology was also updated to streamline the download and installation by removing the need for a .zip file, making it a more intuitive and easier experience.

The results were exceptional:
- Downloads exceeded the plan by 259.9%.
- Installations exceeded the plan by 147.7%.
- Engaging and task-specific online media were optimised throughout the campaign wave.
- Visits to the home page were 176.3% above plan.
- The number entering the site was 112.5% above plan.

The September – December 2008 promotional wave included the roll-out to three additional markets: Italy, Poland and the Czech Republic.

Better and better

Further enhancements were made to the microsite content to create a richer experience and increase the time people spent on the site. This included:
- New Web shows.
- Thumbnails to encourage Web show viewings.
- Tool tips and 'highlights' to landing-page objects.
- An updated laptop application to drive downloads and demonstrations.
- An additional landing page to drive more users to the microsite to learn more and download the application.

The metrics as of December 2008 showed home page traffic exceeding 18,000,000 visits, with 179,972 downloads, 300,201 demo views and 107,452 Web show views stemming from the September – December 2008 campaign alone.

The UPS Widget campaign was thus a step change for the shipping sector. Driven by consumer insight, UPS radically revamped its targeting and developed a tool that could help its customers do their jobs better. Making Widget the hero of the marketing created a communications tool which encouraged them to use UPS every day.

Walkers

07

Asking consumers to 'Do us a flavour'

Snapshot

Walkers renewed flagging interest in new flavours by ripping up its brand development rule book and getting consumers deeply involved in product development.

Key insights

- Walkers decided to shake up the increasingly sluggish reception to new flavours by turning its traditional approach to new flavour development on its head.

- Its new strategy of user-generated flavours was based on inviting consumers to come up with new flavour ideas and then get the nation to vote on the winner, bringing brand engagement to new levels.

- To ensure widespread participation and debate the campaign ran across more consumer touchpoints than ever before.

Summary

Walkers is the UK's favourite crisps brand and Britain's largest crisp manufacturer, with 16 ranges of crisps and snacks including Walkers Sensations, Doritos and Quavers. It was bought by PepsiCo in 1989.

In 2008/09, Walkers tore up its rule book and launched a radical new campaign to breathe new life into the way the company developed and talked about its flavours by inviting consumers to come up with new flavours. It was a risk, it was a headache, and it was a spectacular success. The business had truly never seen anything like 'Do us a flavour'.

Over the campaign period, the 'Do us a flavour' idea outperformed category year-on-year sales growth by 68%. Walkers also achieved its highest value market share for three years. It attracted a deep level of consumer interaction with the brand, with over a million flavour suggestions. Even more significantly, it showed how a marketing idea could affect every aspect of the business.

Getting flavour back on the map

In 2007, Walkers and its agencies came up with an idea that bent the rules of 'business as usual'.

It came in direct response to a critical business issue: delivering great flavours to tantalise the nation's taste buds had been a fundamental part of the Walkers success story, but in recent times the traditional go-to-market model for launching great tasting flavour news had become less effective. Year on year, flavour news just wasn't selling the way it used to (Figure 1).

The objective was to turn around this decline in sales impact with an idea that could make Walkers' flavour news irresistible once again. After all, when it comes to crisps, flavour is the single most important attribute that drives perceptions of taste, and taste is the key driver of sales (Figure 2).

But if recent efforts at flavour-focused communication had failed to excite the public's imagination, it was clear that Walkers needed to look at a new approach—a fresh way to breathe life into flavour news. The brand team and its agencies found it by shedding any preconceptions about how far the business could be taken outside of its traditional marketing model.

The big idea took shape amid a spirit of having nothing off-limits, and was built on two basic consumer truths:
- Everyone has got a point of view about what would make a great crisps flavour.
- People are passionate about their favourite flavour.

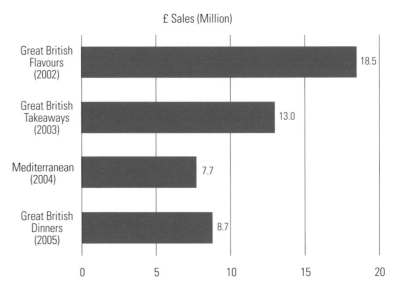

£ Sales (Million)

Figure 1. Source: IRI 6 month post launch

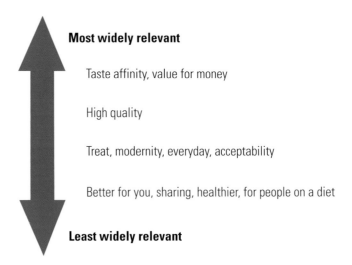

Figure 2. Taste drives crisp catagory purchasing

The idea was simple yet audacious. The company would open up Walkers' brand, product development and decision-making by asking the nation to 'Do Us a Flavour' and get them to create the next great Walkers flavour (Figure 3).

The campaign would work across three phases.
1. The nation was invited to send in their flavour suggestions.
2. An expert panel selected six flavour finalists which Walkers would actually produce and launch.
3. The nation would then vote to decide the eventual winner and new addition to the Walkers range. In a revolutionary promotional model, the winner would be offered a £50,000 prize along with 1% of all future sales of their flavour.

It was an idea which would shatter industry conventions, and stretch the parameters of what was thought possible for the business to deliver.

No more business as usual

To make it happen would involve re-writing every rule in the book:
- Developing a new flavour takes a long time (26 weeks, give or take). This idea meant that research and development (R&D) would need to master six new irresistible flavours in just six weeks. And they weren't the normal kind of flavours: Chilli & Chocolate, Cajun Squirrel, Onion Bhaji, Crispy Duck and Hoisin and Fish and Chips (Figure 4 overleaf).
- Designing and producing new packaging takes a minimum of two and a half months. It would now have to be done in just six weeks.
- The production line can handle a maximum of four new flavours at any one time. It would now have to produce six.
- Retailers are reluctant to list any more than one or two new flavours at a time. Walkers would have to get them excited enough to carry all six (even in the smallest corner shops).
- The standard promotional slot is four weeks. To work in the way it was intended, Do Us A Flavour would need to maintain consumer engagement over a whole year.

Figure 3

Figure 4

Figure 5

This would be a daunting challenge. It was critically important that the marketing team and its agencies had a full and proper understanding of how far it was possible to stretch the business through every step of the process. And it was just as important that the other parts of the company, including R&D, the sales team and people on the factory floor, had the full picture of what the campaign was trying to do and why. Success would depend on this synergy of marketing with the business's other capabilities.

Covering all the media bases

The media strategy also threw up complex challenges for the marketing team and their agencies, as it aimed to engage consumers across more touchpoints than ever before. The media principle was to 'fuel flavour debate'— get the nation talking about the competition to make participation and enthusiasm spread.

Phase 1 involved a 360-degree plan to drive people to the walkers.co.uk website to submit their suggestions. Jointly-viewed TV airtime and rich media in online community sites stimulated people to invent and discuss their flavour ideas with one another. Walkers also launched its first WAP site and increased its e-customer relationship management fanbase to more than 600,000 consumers. Radio DJs hosted 'flavour sports day' promotions. The 'Flavour Army' took flavour fun to the streets, to events and onto Facebook.

The media plan in phase 3 set out to recreate the feel of a general election. This, after all, was an issue of national importance, in which every responsible citizen should take a side. The aim was not only to get consumers to vote, but to be vocal about which flavours they loved (as well as those which they didn't). Rich online and mobile advertising for each flavour encouraged people to vote to keep their favourite. Finalists collected 'grass roots' support through online communities, including individual campaign pages on Facebook. Tying 'the election' together, the 'campaign trail' was filmed and broadcast in a behind-the-scenes documentary series with Yahoo TV: 'Do Us a Flavour News'.

Finally, after weeks of frantic campaigning and voting, there was a winner. The nation chose Builders' Breakfast to be the next new Walkers flavour (Figure 5). News of the result was splashed all over the national press and, of course, was broken in 'Do Us a Flavour News'.

Winning in every way

'Do us a flavour' idea engaged the public for almost a year and the campaign enjoyed exceptional results:
* Over one million flavour suggestions were received — 1,213,853 to be exact — three times the original forecast.
* Over a million votes were cast by the time the winner was announced on May 6th 2009.
* There were 4.3 million visits to walkers.co.uk with four-to-nine minutes spent on site.
* Over 700 pieces of public relations (PR) coverage worth an estimated at £6.5 million were generated.
* The company attracted 27,000 fans to Facebook as well as 820,000 video views on the website, Yahoo and other sites.

Not only did the campaign change behaviour, but more importantly, brand perceptions and the business were changed:
* The brand saw increases in advertising recall across all media (+7% on average), and positive image shifts, not just on flavour associations but also innovation (+14%), and popularity (+15%).

- The campaign drove +4.4 brand penetration, especially among younger, more upmarket buyers (so important to a brand's future).
- It also significantly increased the average number of flavours among core Walkers buyers (from 2.9 to 4.8).
- Over the campaign period, the crisps and snacks category grew +8.7% in sales value year-on-year (YOY). The 'Do us a flavour' idea outperformed this by a considerable margin, delivering a +14.7% YOY sales value uplift. Walkers also achieved its highest value market share for three years.

Beyond the numbers, 'Do us a flavour' brought out the best in hundreds of Walkers employees across the whole organisation.

Chapter 8
Global Branding

Dan Cobley
Director,
North and Central
Europe Marketing,
Google

Global branding? Yes or no? This is one of the most agonising questions to face many marketers with an international remit. In this increasingly global world the potential benefits are clear. But what about the costs? And the risks? Are consumers really so different across markets? How will the transition be managed? Can the benefits really be realised?

These three case studies provide some powerful lessons on the benefits of moving to a global brand platform and how to get there. Moreover, they demonstrate how marketing can lead the whole business to transform and align behind a strong global brand. The key insights I took from the cases, which resonate with my experience working on global branding at Walkers/Frito Lay, include:

- Any strong brand, global or otherwise, needs to be built out of a clear and differentiated positioning, and there is no substitute for quality consumer research in developing this (all cases).
- At the core, consumers across the world are more similar than they are different (Dulux), but it can be important to recognise local variations: for example in marketing maturity or payment methods (ebookers).

- A clear mandate from the very top of an organisation is a key success factor (Aviva).
- The majority of the benefits from global alignment come from common positioning, then from a common visual identity, and finally an aligned brand name (Dulux).
- The transition needs to be managed carefully, and there is no single right way – a big bang or phased approach can be made to work (Aviva).
- A really successful global brand aligns not just your product or service, but everything you do and stand for as a company (ebookers, Aviva).

While these three companies faced somewhat different challenges and each approached them in their unique way, one thing they all share is that marketing played a pivotal role in transforming the whole organisation and extraordinary business results soon followed. Congratulations to all three marketing teams. The rest of us should read, learn, be inspired and strive to have a similar impact on our own organisations.

Aviva   08

Creating a new global brand in a 300-year old market

Snapshot

Aviva successfully managed a massively complex crossborder rebranding programme to fulfil its ambitious vision of strengthening its bond with customers.

Key insights

- Aviva's ambitious new vision for the business based on stronger customer relationships demanded comprehensive rebranding in all its markets — including three of the strongest country brands — to one common positioning.

- Changing the brand in the UK, Ireland and Poland was a huge logistical challenge and involved a team of 700 people working in tandem to deliver on time and to budget.

- An ambitious integrated marketing communications campaign in the UK rebranding Norwich Union as Aviva boosted awareness levels well beyond original targets.

Summary

Aviva is the world's fifth-largest insurance group and the largest insurance services provider in the UK. Its main activities are long-term savings, fund management and general insurance. The brand has existed since 2002 following research conducted by CGNU (itself the result of the merger in 2000 of CGU and Norwich Union) which showed that none of the existing legacy brands had the potential to grow into a single brand that could be used globally. However, it did not extend the Aviva brand to its existing market leading businesses: Norwich Union in the UK, Hibernian in Ireland and Commercial Union in Poland.

This changed with the arrival in 2007 of a new chief executive who spearheaded a strategy that would be built on the effective leverage of a single global brand. In 2008 the company took the brave decision to become Aviva everywhere. While it was aware of the huge challenges, it was imperative in order to deliver its new company vision of 'One Aviva, twice the value'.

The brand migration project was incredibly complex. Despite the many different strands to be woven together it was successfully delivered on time and under budget. In the UK, a fully integrated marketing communications campaign managed the tricky transition from Norwich Union to Aviva.

Figure 1

A unifying vision

Aviva's history stretches back 300 years to when it started selling protection against highway robbery. By the start of the new millennium the business had a global presence and was made up of over fifty brands. In 2002 it began trading under the name Aviva and the businesses in 21 markets began to adopt the Aviva name and visual identity, although a common brand positioning had not yet been established.

The existing brands in the UK, Ireland and Poland were local market leaders (Norwich Union, Hibernian and Commercial Union respectively). It was therefore decided that in these three markets the legacy names should be retained as the company was wary at the time of moving away from such strong brand assets.

However, while these three companies were Aviva's strongest revenue contributors, with about 40% of the total, the strategy of keeping these brands intact would prevent continuing momentum and, more importantly, lack emotional credibility among key audiences such as investors.

In April 2007, new Aviva chief executive Andrew Moss announced a new vision for the business: 'One Aviva. Twice the value'. A key tenet of executing this new vision was to adopt the Aviva name in all the markets, so that customers would identify it by one name around the world (Figure 1). This was partly a specific earnings target— to double earnings per share by 2012— and partly a statement of intent: to harness the power of its global size and stature through the effective leverage of a single global organisation based around the benefits of a strong global brand:

- Stronger innovation: the opportunity to refresh the global proposition and achieve more business with more customers as a consequence of global strength.
- Stronger synergies: operational efficiencies that would improve performance would be created.
- Stronger marketing: there would be spending efficiencies and opportunities for global deals (e.g. sponsorship) if operating as a global brand.
- Global talent: the opportunity to create a single employee proposition and a culture where all employees were part of the same culture would work in favour of the business when attracting the best talent.
- Stronger share price: resulting from all the above effects.

Identifying the risks

Moving to one brand was an exciting opportunity to unite all the businesses and to create massive efficiencies throughout the group. However, in the short term, migrating to Aviva in the UK, Ireland and Poland was going to be a big risk for a number of significant reasons.

As Peter Walshe, global account director of Millward Brown said in the *Independent* on the 23rd of April in 2008, "'The opportunity to create one brand from several has potential, if Aviva can establish the name as clear, modern and, above all, standing for something.... The downside is that Aviva doesn't currently stand for much among many of the company's key audiences; it certainly means little to the consumer. The rebranding runs the risk of throwing away all the heritage, trust and prestige built up over such a long period."

But the real potential for commercial exposure in the UK in particular ran deeper than this:
- Firstly, Norwich Union was Aviva's most significant and successful business. It was an icon of UK plc,

with more than 20 million customer relationships. It was also a core pillar of the fabric of the community, and not just in Norwich, where it is the largest single employer, since it had a strong presence in York and Perth as well. There was thus a real danger of social and reputational damage affecting 15,000 UK employees, their families and their networks.

- Secondly, the Norwich Union brand had exceptional awareness and consideration scores by any category's standards, let alone financial services. In this sector, where differentiation in a traditional marketing sense is very hard to come by, these measures are more than usually important and any drop-off in awareness could lead to a rapid and calamitous fall in consideration, with very negative commercial implications.

To put this into perspective, if the campaign was unable to build awareness and consideration of the Aviva brand up to previous Norwich Union levels during the necessary time frame, a drop in sales volumes and customer retention would be inevitable.

Finding the way forward

This demanded two essential ingredients: a strong team to oversee the migration in the different markets (see 'Getting the right people together') and a powerful, integrated marketing communications campaign in the UK.

Figure 2. Rebranding in the UK

Figure 3. Rebranding in Poland

Getting the right people together

Although the project had an impact on every person who worked for Aviva in some way, the core team members who worked on the migration programme were the central programme office and the programme managers and their teams in the migrating business units. Over 700 people were directly involved with the brand change across the three markets.

A central programme office had been established at Aviva Group Centre in London shortly after Aviva's new company vision had been announced. This team was the fulcrum of the migration and was responsible for liaising with teams from within all the business unit offices. The members were recruited by the group marketing function for their broad range of skills and their proven history of programme management, including meticulous attention to detail.

The team was also selected because of the members' ability to liaise with stakeholders at all levels of the business, as they would be acting as a direct link from, for example, a facilities team member changing a sign on a wall up to the group executive committee. While individual business units were responsible for migration of their businesses, the central team monitored their operational readiness. This included testing and confirming delivery of the programme from a central perspective and managing any risks and issues through the central programme governance.

Balancing the central/local equation

Working with the local marketing teams, the central programme office helped recruit the programme managers to head the local teams in each of the migrating businesses. This ensured appropriate resources would be allocated and that the team selected would be able to meet the diverse requirements of the role. Local programme managers, the business unit leaders, were accountable for the end-to-end delivery of the project in line with agreed timelines and budgets approved by the Aviva board. They were charged with ensuring that the necessary resources and business priorities were placed on the programme, that project governance was followed robustly and any necessary remedial actions were quickly identified.

There were four programme managers at business unit level — one each for the UK general insurance and life businesses, plus Poland and Ireland. The programme managers reported directly into the business unit sponsor leaders (i.e. local marketing directors) but, as they were specifically responsible for the programme, they also managed and motivated multiple teams across IT, operational services, facilities, human resources (HR) and marketing.

The central and local market programme teams agreed that the timings of the three migrations would be staggered to limit risk to the business and also so that learnings could be shared among the teams across migrating businesses. The way in which the brands migrated would also vary to reflect local requirements. The UK would conduct a 'big bang' transition, moving straight from Norwich Union to Aviva on the 1st of June 2009 (Figure 2), although advertising to tell people about the change of name began December 2008.

A two-phased approach was chosen in Ireland: the business would be fully rebranded to Hibernian Aviva in January 2009 and then after another year a full rebranding to Aviva. In Poland the business opted for a three-stage migration: first to Commercial Union Aviva, then Aviva Commercial Union on the 1st of June 2009 and finally to Aviva by June 2010 (Figure 3).

Aiming high in the UK

In line with the need to rebuild spontaneous awareness levels with the change from Norwich Union to Aviva in the UK tough campaign targets were set:
- 20% spontaneous brand awareness by 31st April 2009.
- 25% spontaneous brand awareness by 1st of June 2009 (official switch to Aviva).
- 52% spontaneous brand awareness by 31st December 2009 (legacy position).

To achieve this would be as much about how smart the company was in getting attention as the amount spent. So, as well as rebuilding spontaneous awareness and consideration, it needed to aim for tangible improvements in brand strength over time. The migration offered the company the opportunity to create a truly differentiated brand compared to the main competition.

For example, Norwich Union's brand image had not always exerted a commercially positive influence. Its heritage and strength — which acted as assets in the long-term savings market (pensions and life assurance) — were brakes to progress in the more dynamic categories like direct insurance because they meant 'old-fashioned', 'inflexible' and 'expensive'.

The company commissioned extensive research among customers, intermediaries, investors, staff and other influencer audiences in ten markets — from China to Poland, Turkey to Canada — to scope out the boundaries of a successful differentiating positioning in the financial services sector.

This research pointed to a universal desire for individual recognition and for an explicit combination of expertise and empathy that could contrast with the apparently self-serving nature of the industry and the comparatively low levels of customer service and focus.

An ambitious approach

The UK strategy needed to deliver three key elements:
- Firstly, an unambiguous message signalling the brand change and helping customers to retain the new information front of mind.
- Secondly, it needed to create a sense of newness and difference from the financial services norm.
- Thirdly, it had to present credible customer benefits to the audience.

So the emphasis was put on the forward-facing objectives (global growth opportunities) behind the rebrand as well as the local re-positioning and differentiation opportunities, and to position the change of name as fundamental to those objectives: a herald of the new brand promise and a demonstration of the brand's commitment to differentiation and customer care.

Aviva differentiated itself by using its name change (from Norwich Union to Aviva) to introduce a new customer promise (*'No one recognises you like Aviva'*), thus demonstrating its commitment to behaving differently from the rest of the category while also creating fame for the new brand to drive all-important awareness levels to previous Norwich Union levels.

In the first of three phases, starting in December 2008, TV, print, outdoor and digital advertising trumpeted the forthcoming name change using selected celebrities, place names and events where the adoption of a new name had been crucial to their subsequent success (Richard Starkey to Ringo Starr, Peak XV to Mt. Everest): 'Sometimes a change of name is more than just a change of name. Sometimes it's a chance to show the world, who you've always wanted to be' (Figures 4 and 5).

In Phase 2, which preceded the actual re-brand date of June 1st, brand advertising ran featuring Aviva customers expressing how they wished to be treated, and hated being treated, by financial services companies. Each commercial expressed the brand's desire to build the new Aviva around its customers: 'This is not business as usual. This is a company being built around you'.

In both cases the use of celebrities added scale and tapped into the most widely recognised of personal aspirations. At the same time it maximised interest in both the name change and the brand's perspective on the world. It also boosted enjoyment scores, critical to creating awareness quickly and efficiently.

In phase three, post-the physical rebrand, specific advertising supporting general insurance and long-term saving products ran to drive consideration in specific sectors.

Surpassing targets

1. The migration campaign

The key result for the migration programme was that it was delivered on time and under budget. The scale of the project was immense and the fact that the programme progressed without any significant problems is testament to the diligence and effective teamwork of the programme managers and their teams in the business units and the central programme office, as well as the impact of the campaign.

Some specific achievements for the migration programme included:
- The company communicated directly about the rebranding to over 13 million customers.

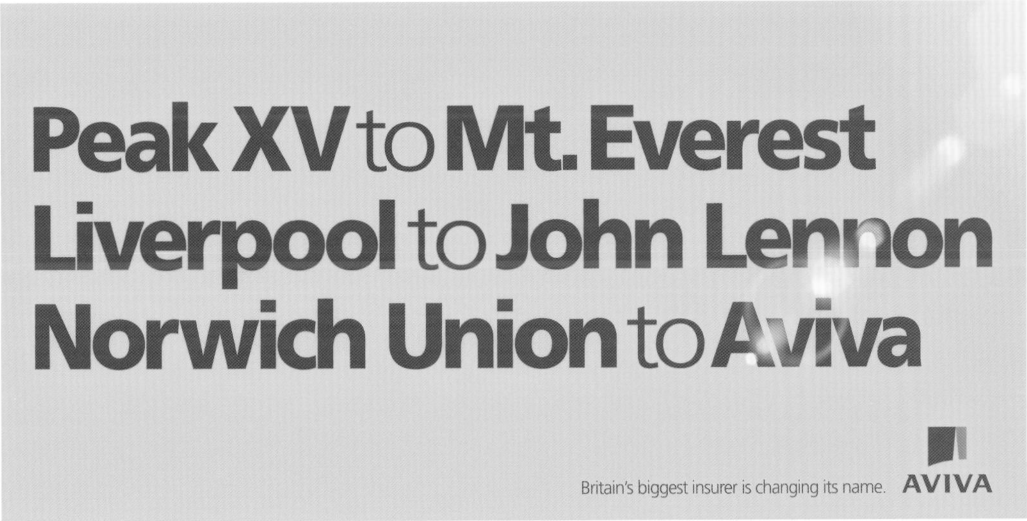

Peak XV to Mt. Everest Liverpool to John Lennon Norwich Union to Aviva

Britain's biggest insurer is changing its name. **AVIVA**

Figure 4. Example of the advertising

From a small corner of England to the 4 corners of the world.

Figure 5. Example of the advertising

- Over 30,000 external email addresses and 35,000 internal email addresses changed.
- The company updated external signage on hundreds of buildings and thousands of internal signs.
- 4,500 system-generated documents and at least 5,000 pre-printed documents changed.
- Around 30,000 staff passes were updated.
- All intranet, internet and broker/independent financial advisors sites were updated to the new Aviva name and brand identity.
- 49 legal entity names, 900 bank account names and over 970 fund names were updated
- All front-line employees were retrained.
- Corporate merchandise, learning and development materials, sponsorship etc. were all redone.

The project's biggest risk was that the business would lose customers in the three biggest markets as it moved away from established brands. This risk did not materialise thanks to the excellent work from the migration programme teams and the various functions they supported. The company knew from a dedicated call centre set up for migration that customers were not confused by this rebrand and on the whole were positive about it. In the UK, customer complaints regarding migration were only 0.005% and similar results were seen in Poland and Ireland.

2. Winning hearts and minds

Taking the 54,000 Aviva employees on this journey was clearly no mean feat, and one that was also crucial to the success of the rebrand. It is worth looking at a snapshot of the UK communication programme that was part of the name change activity:

- 'This is our story' cinema sessions, where 3,500 Aviva leaders talked about what the name change meant to them, were held around the UK, bringing together staff of all levels to engage with the programme. Brand showcases were introduced in 22 Aviva locations throughout the country to further explain the brand story.
- The actual day of change, the 1st of June, became 'A-day' and was celebrated in all offices as the new brand was adopted around the world.
- A dedicated global intranet, with forums, Twitter functionality, videos and imagery was launched to help demonstrate that this was no mere name change, but the start of something new.

A global employee survey in November 2009 showed that:

- 76% of all employees took part — the highest in its history.
- 79% stated they understood the goal of 'One Aviva, twice the value'.
- 88% stated they were personally committed to achieving the goals of their business unit.
- 62% of employees stated they felt recognised for 'who I am'.

In the UK specifically;

- 79% strongly agreed with the statement 'I understand why we are re-branding to Aviva'.
- 80% strongly agreed with the statement 'I receive enough communication about the rebrand'.

Overcoming cynicism

In a sector that in many cases relies on advice to customers by intermediaries, convincing the often-cynical broker audience that the rebrand was more than veneer was key to Aviva's success. The ICM broker survey in October 2009 in the UK, for example, painted a good picture:
- 61% were positive about the name change.
- 94% were satisfied about the name-change communication.
- 79% had seen the specific broker TV execution.

3. Advertising breakthrough in the UK

According to quantitative brand tracking conducted by ICM, awareness of the brand migration grew from 32% to 79% during the first month of the UK campaign. Despite starting from 4% in December 2008, spontaneous awareness levels beat the April target in March, the June target by April and the year-end target of 52% three months early by September.

Consideration of the new brand over the same period quintupled and overtook Norwich Union's position in August 2009, well ahead of the expected target. Meanwhile, within three weeks of the campaign breaking, 80% of those aware of the advertising associated it with Norwich Union and Aviva,

compared to an industry average of 36%. Other strong indicators included:
- 'Different to other insurance ads' scored 78% (industry average of 54%).
- 'I like the advertising' scored 56% (industry average of 41%).
- Especially noteworthy were key improvements in value perceptions, corroborated by independent YouGov Brand Index data, and in the innovation measure ('reputation for coming up with new products and services') where the Aviva score grew by 65%, beating all the top high-street financial services brands in the wider competitive set.
- Finally, the campaign earned enormously favourable public relations (PR), valued at an additional £1.3 million.

ebookers

08

Creating crossborder consistency in an online brand

Snapshot

An innovative approach to uncovering consumer insights helped the revitalised brand reposition itself seamlessly across Europe.

Key insights

- The business needed to develop a coherent, fresh and harmonised brand across Europe to stand out in a competitive and cluttered online travel market.

- The firm involved managers, staff and customers in finding the right solution — and one which could be built on similarities in the different markets while allowing for local nuances.

- The resulting brand was based on a simple and streamlined design that reflected consumer desire for bookings to be quick, intuitive and hassle-free.

Summary

ebookers.com is a leading pan-European online travel agency specialising in worldwide travel. It offers a wide range of travel products, including a choice of over 250 airlines, more than 86,000 hotels, holidays, car hire and insurance. ebookers.com is part of global online travel company Orbitz Worldwide.

In Europe, ebookers operates in 13 markets. Each of these is at a different stage of development and serves customers with different needs. Back in 2006, the size and positioning of the ebookers brand varied hugely from country to country as a result of its historical development. To benefit from both commercial and marketing economies of scale, the business needed to develop a stronger, fresher and more consistent brand.

The company and its partner, co-creation specialists Promise Corporation, embarked on an innovative crossborder rebranding programme which involved managers, staff and customers. This not only delivered superior results but built internal support and understanding, which led to a more rapid and smoother implementation of the new brand.

Following the launch in mid-2006, the growth in ebookers revenues significantly outstripped the market, unprompted brand awareness more than doubled and increased sales attributable to the brand rose by almost 50% year-on-year (YOY).

A fiercely competitive market

ebookers is one of many players in a European online travel market which has seen an explosion of growth in the last few years. It's estimated there are more than 50 players in the UK alone. Because ebookers was a relatively small player and not as well resourced as many of its competitors, standing out in such a busy market was a big problem as all players fought for supremacy. In addition, ebookers had grown by acquisition, so was composed of many different small businesses, each with their own offering, names, language, and style, and each facing challenges specific to their local markets. For example:

- In the UK, the most advanced European market, ebookers was relatively strong at No.3 in the market.
- In France and Germany, ebookers was virtually unknown, and the word 'ebookers' had no meaning.

In addition, the ebookers business was trying to change focus and shift its emphasis away from flights towards hotels and 'dynamic packages' where margins were richer.

When the Promise team first got together with the ebookers team, it found a brand that was fragmented and lacking a clear vision, and a business that was simply not reaching its full sales potential. One consequence of the way that the ebookers business had developed was an almost complete lack of hard information or insight about its customers. Who were they? What was going on in their lives? What were they looking for? How could ebookers be more appealing to them?

Getting to know the customers

Relying on standard approaches such as focus groups and questionnaires was not going to be effective in this industry. It was unlikely to generate the quality of insights that would enable ebookers to transform its position in the market. So an insight programme was set up consisting of a combination of small groups and large workshops called BigTalk. This brought together ebookers staff and their customers to define jointly what the brand should be like in the future. It was built around groups of 50+ consumers and staff, who worked together over one to two days to share experiences and also work creatively to solve problems.

Having this sort of conversation with customers was a vital step because today's consumers want to be in charge: they want to buy what they want, where they want it and when they want it. Nowhere is this truer than in travel: people used to define themselves by their education or their family or their job. Nowadays they are much more likely to define themselves by their holidays and the experiences they have there. The new travel generation are intolerant of interruptions and unwanted corporate messages or demands for attention. In other words, they want things on their terms.

This approach uncovered fresh new insights in the search for a new positioning for ebookers that would both build on past strengths and help it stand out in the future. Including staff in the conversation was equally important because it meant that the company could harness their creativity and challenge some sacred cows: for example, that the brand didn't matter because consumers bought on price alone or that the old ebookers logo with its bubbles was well-known and valued by consumers.

Reconciling the needs of different consumers in different countries

The European travel market is by no means homogeneous. Here are just a few of the differences:
- In the UK, the biggest market by a mile, people travel as much as they can and as often as they can. They are fearless value hunters with few qualms about buying online.
- In Germany, people like packages and it's difficult to use credit cards online.
- The Swiss are obsessed with planning and getting the quality they expect.
- In France, consumers like websites that feel like paper brochures.
- And in Finland there is a lack of choice as few airlines go there.

Finding a positioning that would work in all these territories and promote growth was going to be tough. The breakthrough came by plotting a continuum across the key European markets, based on consumers' level of familiarity with buying online. At one end of the spectrum were mature markets like the UK and Finland. At the other were markets displaying lower confidence, most notably France. All the other markets could be plotted between the two extremes. Once the difference in maturity was taken into account, much of what consumers look for was found to be remarkably similar.

Time was also spent understanding how the rational components of choice (eg. price) played out versus. the emotional components (eg. discomfort about leaving home). This is where more deep-rooted differences between markets were found. The British are particularly greedy for more and new experiences. The Swiss and Germans are full of potential anxiety about quality.

Finally, a quantitative technique called value mapping was used to test and validate the key drivers of choice in each individual market and across Europe as a whole (Figure 1). This is a technique that identifies what's important to consumers in the decision-making process and then goes on to rank the different attributes with qualitative research. This is then validated with a much bigger sample using quantitative techniques.

This enabled the company to develop the key brand attributes and identify which should be fixed across all markets and which should be more flexible. The fixed elements were attached to the new ebookers brand. The flexible elements were embedded in the communications toolbox that supported the brand.

Creating the brand roadmap

Consumers spend a lot of time talking about two things. First, price. Second, their expectations: how excited they feel or how concerned they are that they will 'get what they expect'. So possible ideas for the brand could have centred around value, trust or quality. They were the obvious solutions. However, using deeper insights, it was decided that the key focus for ebookers should be about making the experience of booking as easy as possible.

The more mature the market, the truer this was. As consumers became more confident they looked to multiple sources to gain information; they didn't need ebookers to excite them and they didn't rely on ebookers to be an arbiter of quality. But they did all want the experience of booking to be quick, intuitive and trouble-free. That didn't mean that value, choice and quality were of no importance but it did mean that the core brand idea — the brand essence — should not be focused on them.

Armed with these insights and a clear sense of what the ebookers brand needed to focus on to be successful, a set of practical tools to help the teams across the company bring the ideas to life was developed. The brand roadmap, seen in Figure 2, created a clear pathway to link corporate strategy, brand strategy and the customer journey to generate brand preference. This clarity was a key output for an organisation where lots of people come from a technology background and were sceptical about marketing.

1. Tone of voice

With so many people producing copy, and the written word being the principal source of interaction for the majority of customers, the language, tone and style that ebookers used was a potential source of brand strength. Detailed guidelines covering tone of voice were prepared with 'worked examples' in different languages. The tone of voice was designed to reflect the personality of the brand and to make sure that an online brand appeared friendly, straightforward, warm and helpful.

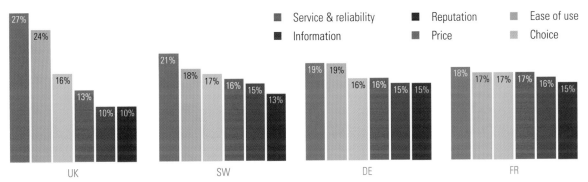

Figure 1. What's important to our customers?
Source: Promise Survey 2006 (UK) and 2007 (SW,DE,FR).
Surveys of 500 users of online travel sites. UK drawn from qualitative consumer groups.

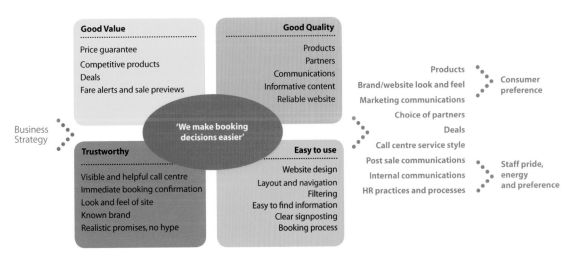

Figure 2. Brand roadmap

2. Brand toolbox

Figure 3 shows the new logo, which reflected the core brand positioning: simple, streamlined and uncluttered.

3. Colour

ebookers' colours were chosen to be bright and strong. There was some flexibility in the palette to enable businesses to continue to use legacy colours that had built significant consumer recognition for a limited time.

4. Shape

Strong shapes create a distinctive visual language and provided a holding device for messaging. There were a lot of shapes because ebookers is a very campaign-led business and needs constantly to update and refresh its messages.

5. Imagery

Imagery focused on atmosphere and character, avoiding those typically clichéd holiday shots. People appeared in the pictures but were secondary to the destination, because customers wanted to imagine themselves there, not see a crowd of strangers (Figure 4).

Record results

The UK relaunch took place in 2006, with other markets following in 2007/8. The outcome surpassed the company's expectations.

- Commercial success. There were eight consecutive quarters of revenue growth in excess of 20% up to autumn 2008 as measured by value of gross bookings, significantly outstripping the growth of most of the competition.

Figure 3. New logo

Figure 4. Example of advertising

Giving the change full backing

Senior ebookers' managers strongly welcomed the crossborder repositioning.

- Customer experience. *"The customer experience online is true to the brand values in all 13 countries where it has been introduced. I think this would have been difficult, maybe impossible, if we had not involved the local marketing teams."* Gilles Despas, managing director, Continental Europe, ebookers Europe.
- Marketing economies of scale. *"In spite of many differences between individual markets, there is now a powerful positioning that works for everyone. This was one of my key objectives at the outset."* Alan Josephs, CEO, ebookers Europe.
- Effective use of marketing resources. *"We've been able to maintain awareness and sales even though we've had to cut our ad spend. I think this is because everything works together better now to reinforce the brand."* Claire Howard-Jones, head of marketing, ebookers UK.
- Internal management and efficiencies. *"Clear brand guidelines mean more professional, memorable and consistent marketing communications, as well as consistency across the customer experience: what you get on the web matches what you get offline."* Matthias Thuerer, marketing manager, ebookers Switzerland.
- A framework to inform human resources (HR) development. *"Developing the brand values into a framework to drive our recruitment and induction plans has helped us to focus and raise standards internally."* Frank Broese, HR director, ebookers Europe.
- A professional and informed approach. *"It's like being able to see in the dark — for the first time, we have reliable knowledge about who our customers are and what they want."* Claire Howard-Jones, head of marketing, ebookers UK.
- A process that led to success. *"We were sceptical at the outset, but working with our customers helped us learn new things and see new possibilities."* Susanna Piri, marketing manager, ebookers Finland.

- Brand awareness. Before brand relaunch, spontaneous brand awareness was 8%. Six months later, awareness had risen to 18%. Prompted awareness was 70% pre-launch and stabilised at 82% with virtually no ongoing advertising support.
- Brand pulling power. Growth of traffic from sources that ebookers attributed to branding (customers searching specifically for the ebookers name) was up 47% YOY by February 2008. Conversion on brand name pay per click was four times that of conversion on normal pay per click. 12% of total traffic now came from people who typed ebookers. com directly into the Google browser bar. Prior to launch this figure was 5%.

All images appearing in this case study are reproduced by permission of ebookers.

Dulux

08

Building on a common insight to create a global brand

Snapshot

By rethinking its approach to cultural differences and finding common ground in the regenerative power of colour, Dulux became a truly global brand.

Key insights

- ICI Paints embarked on its journey from local to global back in 2007 in the face of slowing growth with the aim of operating a much simplified and harmonised brand portfolio and investing in one global priority— Dulux.

- A major needs-state segmentation study, based on both global and local findings, uncovered similarities the brand could build on and gave the global marketing team a shared language.

- Working together this way had the added bonus of helping what were once fierce competitors find a new organisational spirit when AkzoNobel acquired ICI Paints.

Summary

ICI Paints, which was acquired by AkzoNobel, one of the world's leading industrial companies, in 2008, had for some time run as a multi-local organisation with a complex brand portfolio of over 40 brands. Although it had scale and a powerful global footprint, it was struggling to turn this into a competitive advantage,

In 2007, inspired by a universal insight into the 'regenerative power of colour', ICI Paints identified the opportunity to drive growth by building a powerful global brand — Dulux. Over a three-year period the marketing team worked in new cross-border and cross-cultural ways to get the brand to travel successfully, including developing a common marketing language.

The result was the creation of a global innovation strategy for the brand centred around five common platforms and the development of the company's first global communications campaign.

The business derived significant financial benefit from this new global approach, with brand share rising in most major markets.

Laying the foundations

In 2005 ICI Paints appointed its first chief marketing officer (CMO). Until then the organisation had been run as a multi-local organisation, with each of the 50 countries determining its own marketing strategy. There were examples of local success but performance was patchy, the company struggled to leverage good ideas and, more importantly, growth was slowing.

The task for the CMO was twofold: improve the performance of the marketing organisation and create competitive advantage from global scale. Its major competitors were local or regional players, so global reach and scale set the company apart. However, its multi-local operating model was limiting its ability to realise this advantage.

A pivotal question the company asked itself was whether it could win against its competitors through simply building local capability and leveraging best practice. Or was there actually an opportunity to create advantage through building a global brand? The Dulux name was present in many markets but it was far from being a global brand.

To answer this question the company first had to develop a common language across the marketing teams and start looking at the market through the same lens. So ICI Paints embarked upon a global needs-state segmentation study. This was a globally-led initiative but developed through a highly inclusive process through which the segmentation model was built 'bottom up' : developing and validating hypotheses with the local marketing teams and then coming together to share learning. The study was conducted in 27 countries and identified that, despite the many assumed differences in markets, the same consumer segments existed across the globe with common needs.

The quantitative study was further enriched by an ethnographic study across the top 10 markets where rich insights into the segments were captured through video diaries and in-home interviews. Some gems of local differences were uncovered and the team learned that taste is certainly subjective. However, the commonality among the needs of consumers whether in China or Brazil, India or Poland was astounding.

For the first time the company had a common framework and a language to describe its market that was understood and embedded in its marketing teams across the globe. This became a powerful tool in the development of a global marketing organisation and a first step in uncovering opportunities to develop global strategies.

Finding common opportunities

The next stage of the journey was the co-creation of a global brand portfolio strategy. Each market arrived independently at a remarkably similar brand portfolio strategy, targeting the same segments with just two or three brands required to deliver the businesses growth objectives. Within these portfolios one brand positioning — the Dulux brand positioning — was identified by all as the major opportunity for growth. This was a key milestone as, until then, the company had been managing more than 40 different brands in as many different ways. Now it could focus its resources on a simplified and harmonised portfolio with one global priority.

At this point a global brand team came together and, through a series of workshops, began to share business objectives, market trends and dynamics, consumer understanding, brand portfolio strategies and views on Dulux brand positioning. While the marketers would describe insights and brand positioning in subtly different ways, it was now becoming obvious that the team shared many common objectives. They were targeting the same three segments globally and uncovering a powerful, universal insight upon which a global brand with scale could be built. Critically, this was the realisation of the team and not an imposed view from the top.

The power of innovation

Having identified that the team members were trying to build the same brand, they could rapidly move into the convergence of strategy and leverage of ideas. A common model was created for the Dulux brand architecture that immediately unlocked the potential to transfer existing innovation ideas across markets.

For example, in Europe a strong 'aesthetic pillar' had been developed for the brand, but in Latin America this was a complete gap in the brand's architecture. Within months the Coral Decora range was created and launched in Brazil (Coral is the name for Dulux in Brazil) and generated 2% incremental sales in the first year.

In Asia an opportunity was identified to strengthen the 'performance pillar', leveraging concepts from the UK such as 'Light and Space' (a paint that makes rooms look brighter and feel more spacious). This was launched across five markets within the year. And a concept based on 'super durability' that had been successful in the UK was developed and launched across France, Brazil, and many of the Asian markets. It has been estimated that the total impact from such innovation leverage generated more than

€250 million of incremental sales for the business in 2007.

Furthermore, the convergence of brand strategy allowed the company to develop five globally-aligned innovation platforms which are now driving the development of a global innovation portfolio. By December 2009 the brand's innovation pipeline contained 10 – 15 cross-regional projects with a focus on breakthrough innovation as compared to the > 50 incremental local initiatives of two years ago.

A whole new world

In January 2008 the world changed dramatically. ICI Paints was acquired by its biggest competitor, AkzoNobel, followed rapidly by the global economy going into meltdown. The company not only faced the major challenge of integrating two large companies which had been at war for decades (with a combined turnover of €5 billion) but the markets were in freefall: builders stopped building, people stopped moving and consumers stopped buying paint.

The business imperatives became clear. To grow, the company needed not only to leverage the global scale to win share from local competitors, but the focus now had to turn to category growth through igniting the passion for decoration. The company also wanted to encourage the growth of a new spirit in the organisation, and one in which the two former companies were unified by a common purpose. Working together to create a global Dulux brand with a global purpose proved to be the perfect platform through which these new imperatives could be tackled.

Adding colour to people's lives

The universal insight that had been uncovered for

Dulux was that *'Our surroundings have a powerful influence on how we think, feel and live. We feel good when they reflect who we are and who we want to be. Dulux's role is to inspire and help people to create beautiful homes and communities through colour. We believe that in doing so we can lift spirits and bring people together. In fact, we sell 'tins of optimism' not just tins of paint'*. This was articulated through the brand idea of 'adding colour to people's lives'.

The South East Asia marketing team was immediately inspired by this idea and created a cross- market campaign for Dulux Weathershield that focused on how Dulux transformed a community from a world of grey to a vibrant and colourful community filled with joy. This more emotional approach (backed up by a clear product functionality) proved to be much more effective than the previous campaigns, yielding above average cut-through and persuasion and was seen as new, credible, relevant and unique.

Encouraged by the work in South East Asia, the global team began working with the Brazilian team who were looking for a way to challenge the market leader Suvenil. The Asian work was researched in Brazil and again the company found that the advertising had the potential to be effective as it created a strong emotional bond and a stimulus to paint.

Moreover, the social and community bonding aspect of the creative was particularly valued and with this insight the idea started to build. Because, in addition to testing advertising creative based on community stories, the team researched a campaign which celebrated how the company was transforming communities for real –'our people, our paint, our brand transforming Brazil one neighbourhood at a time'. The audience's reaction showed this was a winning idea (see 'Brightening up the neighbourhood').

Brightening up the neighbourhood

The 'Coral Community' campaign began in the summer of 2009 with the transformation of several neighbourhoods and communities in Sao Paolo and Rio de Janeiro. But these weren't just events created for advertising purposes. The whole company was engaged in preparing the projects, working with the local community to seek their ideas, engaging with local celebrities and dignitaries to build newsworthiness, talking with customers to gain local distribution and, of course, actually painting the building and then — because it was Brazil — celebrating with a party (Figures 1 and 2).

These events created significant PR coverage (including the mayor of Sao Paolo being interviewed on national TV) and by the end of 2009 the company had achieved more than €1.5 million's worth of free coverage. The transformations were filmed for a TV campaign the following year

However, the impact extended much further than the brand. The company in Brazil had faced significant challenges through the integration of ICI Paints and AkzoNobel. The community programme began to unify the company and create a renewed purpose and spirit. This began to translate into tangible benefits through gains in distribution and market share growth for the first time in years. Coral grew 3% points to 22.5% volume share in 2009.

Becoming truly global

The pace at which the idea of 'adding colour to peoples lives' was travelling was fast, with teams inspiring other teams. The company appreciated that it had a powerful concept. But this energy and passion for the idea needed to be grounded and channelled to use it as a platform for a global brand. In the summer of 2009 AkzoNobel embarked on a process to create a global communication and activation campaign for the brand — a pivotal milestone in the journey from multi-local to global.

Through the process of campaign development the company confirmed that demonstrating the 'regenerative power of colour' was a powerful strategic platform for Dulux because it was relevant, competitive and, most of all, it was a truth from within the business.

- It was relevant because audiences could be helped to recognise that small steps could make a big difference and understand the regenerative impact colour or a fresh lick of paint can have.
- It was competitive because the company believed it had an opportunity to distinguish itself not just through what was said but how it was said: not what we say but how we say it.
- It was true because it was actually at the heart of the organisation. The company had been actively transforming communities for decades but, until it started working globally, it hadn't realised it.

Figure 1. Brightening up in Brazil

Figure 2. More colour in Brazil

Let's Color
project

By now it had arrived at the stage of bringing to life how it could 'add colour to people's lives' (from the small lick of paint in an apartment through to the rejuvenation of communities). With EuroRSCG London a global campaign idea was created under the slogan 'Let's Colour' that straddled activation, content, social media, advertising and beyond. Let's Colour was a creative expression and a collective call to action that embodied the visionary spirit of 'adding colour to people's lives'.

In 2010 the campaign was taken to France (Figures 3 and 4) and the UK (Figures 5 and 6 overleaf) along with Turkey and South Africa. (It was set to be rolled out globally in 2010). Local resources were combined to create global assets operating to the principle of fewer, bigger, better and proving to have the potential to be more effective than if the company had continued to work locally.

An additional benefit was that the idea inspired the organisation. Following the model of Brazil, every business was now creating 'Let's Colour' community programmes, whereby every year AkzoNobel would work to transform the communities where they lived and worked. Furthermore, the company embarked on a programme of colour training for all its employees so that they all could learn how to add colour to their lives in their own homes.

Figure 3. France

Figure 4. France

Impressive performance

The previous few years had been challenging for the category with market volumes down 6% in 2009 versus 2007. However, the Dulux brand share performance had been more encouraging, with volume and value share gains across the priority markets. In addition, all top 10 markets showed share growth — particularly in the UK, France and the emerging markets of Brazil, Argentina, Indonesia and Vietnam.

Figure 5. The UK

Figure 6. The UK

All images appearing in this case study are reproduced by permission of AkzoNobel.

Chapter 9
Organising for Good Marketing

Troy Warfield
Vice President of Family
Care, Europe,
Kimberly-Clark

This chapter highlights two important areas integral to success in improving organisational capability. The first is the role of leadership in terms of owning, cultivating and shaping the people agenda, be it through recruitment, development, engagement, motivation, recognition and/or reward. Crucial to delivering this is the importance of creating the employee value proposition (EVP) and aligning that with the external perception of the brand.

The second is recognising that 'marketing' is and can be a highly effective 'transformational' business solution, tackling difficult organisational issues. The word 'transformational' is key. At Shell there were two separate marketing challenges to address. One was to attract more highly-skilled recruits by strengthening the external perception of the brand. The other was to transform the capabilities of the internal human resources (HR) organisation to enable it to deliver an EVP that was aligned to this new external representation of the brand.

ICI Paints wanted to transform its organisation to become more brand-led and customer-centric. It took a leap of leadership to commit to doing that through enhancing marketing capability, from creating a global marketing leadership team, to a global marketing capability academy through to driving a common language across the organisation that resulted in growth in sales, profits and market share.

McDonald's had two issues to deal with. One was an external negative perception characterised by the term 'McJob', referring to the perception of people outside the organisation to roles within McDonald's. The other was to achieve higher engagement and retention levels. McDonald's actively campaigned to make the external world understand the benefits of a McDonald's career — which in turn enabled employees to feel prouder of the brand internally. This was accompanied by some tangible EVP changes, with HR innovations such as more flexible contracts and educational opportunities.

All three case studies illustrate the success that organisations can leverage when they combine powerful and visionary leadership, with a clear agenda on both people, and their brand. The marriage of the two areas, brought together by a very clear, compelling and aligned EVP, ensures that organisations can unleash the power of their people.

Shell

09

Better marketing for a more desirable employer brand

Snapshot

A comprehensive marketing capability programme had a significant impact on Shell's ability to attract the best people.

Key insights

- Shell had to find a way to double the number of new and highly-skilled recruits in the face of strong competition and weak brand equity.

- It decided to undertake an ambitious programme to develop the marketing capabilities of its recruitment team.

- Sharpening up their marketing skills, while also strengthening the image of the employer brand, transformed perceptions of the company as a valued employer while costs dropped significantly.

Summary

Shell is a global group of energy and petrochemical companies with around 102,000 employees in more than 100 countries and territories. In 2004, with the world's soaring demand for energy, Shell needed to rethink its approach to recruitment in order to boost the number of highly-talented recruits it was able to attract. That meant doubling the number in a year and expanding this even further by 2008.

But persuading large numbers of high-quality people to change their perceptions of the Shell employer brand and join the group would be a challenge. Brand equity was weak while the recruitment team was internally focused, operated in country silos, and not oriented around its customers — the candidates. The problem was that the recruitment team lacked excellent marketing skills and processes.

Pioneering the use of best-practice marketing approaches in the recruitment process transformed the company's candidate attraction ability. Not only were targets exceeded, but recruitment costs decreased significantly.

Setting ambitious goals

By 2006 Shell was facing some hard truths:
- There was a step change in the demand for energy, as the world population soared and the geography of demand shifted eastward.
- Energy supply was struggling to keep pace, causing a race to identify new, sustainable, sources of energy.
- Increasing environmental pressures meant finding more responsible energy solutions.

Addressing these truths and growing the business required an ambitious business strategy, delivered by an expanded and talented workforce. Since 2006, the focus of Shell's business strategy had been on finding more and different types of energy. People were to be a key enabler of this strategy, and an unprecedented capital investment was accompanied by an emphasis on recruitment. The company needed large numbers of new and highly skilled employees in disciplines such as engineering and finance, and in new and competitive geographies like India and China.

The business set itself challenging targets:
- In 2005 it had recruited 2,697 employees. In 2006 the target more than doubled, to 5,440 new recruits.
- The three-year picture was to be even more ambitious: 14,000 new recruits would be needed between 2006 and 2008. Fewer than a third of that, 4,151, had been achieved in the previous three years, 2003-2005.

It was the job of the recruitment marketing team to attract these new employees and convert them to choose the Shell employer brand over other multinational competitors. It was a massive challenge: Shell's employer brand equity was weak, the employer brand proposition meant little more than salary packages, and the 'customers', the potential candidates, were ever more demanding, with the best being spoilt for choice as the recruitment market had grown hugely competitive.

Shell thus had to double its results while reducing costs. The business expected the recruitment team to demonstrate cost-effectiveness and maximise its return on investment. This was a classic marketing dilemma. In the face of strong competition and weak brand equity, how could the number of new candidates be doubled cost-effectively? It demanded much sharper marketing approaches.

But there was a distinct lack of marketing skills in the recruitment team, many of whom had a background in human resources (HR). While some steps had been taken to introduce marketing disciplines with a marketing planning process, the team recognised the need to make a substantial improvement in marketing capabilities — and to do so rapidly — if it were to meet these ambitious goals.

Developing a robust framework

Working with the specialist marketing capability consultancy Brand Learning, the Shell team began by developing a pioneering capability programme, Shell 'xchange'. This was a blend of marketing skills development, process creation and knowledge management for non-marketing specialists.

The first step was to design a marketing capability framework which identified the skill areas needed to deliver the business strategy. The analysis generated ten areas which were prioritised to develop a marketing capability plan (See 'Enhancing capabilities').

Enhancing capabilities

The Shell marketing capability framework highlighted the following key areas:
- Living the brand
- Brand development
- Channel
- Product
- CRM
- Creative communication
- Co-ordinated campaigns
- Marketing strategy and planning
- Marketing efficiency and effectiveness
- Information to insight

By interviewing business stakeholders within and outside of marketing, and by analysing the issues raised in the new marketing plans, the team identified two capability priorities:
1. To create a motivating customer (candidate) experience driven by insight and which would help to retain candidates and deliver a better return on investment. This involved several capability areas, including gaining insights and co-ordinating campaigns.
2. To develop and learn how to leverage a differentiated brand positioning which allowed the company to attract the best candidates with relevant and differentiated benefits (reducing reliance on factors like salary).

1. Creating a motivating candidate experience

Establishing a motivating candidate experience from the moment someone heard about Shell to the moment they joined the company required a coordinated approach across all the recruitment disciplines. It was not enough to ensure that marketing communications resonated with prospective employees. Instead, marketing, operations, recruiters and line managers all needed to work together. To do this required a leap from the typically 'Shell-centric' perspective, to becoming 'candidate-centric'. That might sound obvious, but for an operation with 300 people, working on five continents and receiving up to 600,000 applications each year, it was no easy feat.

First, the candidate journey was defined by applying a classic brand funnel approach to the world of recruitment. A workshop run with members of each recruitment discipline helped build up the understanding of the importance of candidate-centricity. This was followed by creating a candidate journey model, which was subsequently described as "the bedrock of our business approach" (See 'The candidate journey').

The candidate journey

The candidate journey followed a defined path:
- Prompted/spontaneous awareness
- Positive interest
- Action
- Mutual assessment
- Hire
- Coming on board

- A website and learning programme were designed to help embed the processes and candidate-centred philosophy.
- Clear key performance indicators (KPIs) that revolved around candidates were set, while the 'candidate experience survey' was established to measure performance and identify improvements. These became core KPIs on a recruitment dashboard.

Having developed the overall journey, the team identified the key moments of truth, gathered insights into candidate needs at these moments, and assessed how well they were being addressed. This was new territory for an HR team, so the marketing concepts and tools used to build capabilities at each stage of this journey proved invaluable.

The next stage involved a series of marketing capability initiatives to improve the candidate experience:
- The organisational structure was changed to put candidates first. Instead of operating in separately-managed functions based on specialisms (marketing, operations and recruiting), one function was set up — recruitment — with strategic, structural and cultural emphasis on collaboration and joint ownership of the candidate experience.
- Processes were refined and standardised to ensure cross-functional alignment along the candidate journey, with clarified roles and responsibilities to avoid duplication or candidates being 'lost'.

Fixing the recruitment process

Research demonstrated that candidates found the recruitment process frustratingly slow — particularly between being assessed and receiving an offer. Several would drop out at this point, switching to more agile competitors. This lack of speed had been justified by referring to the number of Shell stakeholders involved in hiring decisions and the number of candidates who had to be reviewed. Now, however, the team members challenged themselves to overcome internal constraints and improve the candidate experience. This was a particular issue for graduates in Europe. In 2007 they had had to wait an average of 81 days between final assessment and receiving an offer. This was reduced by 50% to 39 days by 2008. Candidate satisfaction improved significantly.

2. Developing a differentiated brand proposition

The second capability was to develop a differentiated brand proposition and the skills to leverage it effectively. Working with Brand Learning, the Shell team built a shared understanding of what makes an excellent employer brand, and embarked on a process to identify what the Shell employer brand should stand for in the hearts and minds of customers — candidates and employees.

Qualitative and quantitative research was commissioned in six countries to probe people's attitudes towards Shell as an employer, including both internal and external audiences. Based on the insights this generated, an employer value proposition (EVP) was created for graduates with a new brand idea, validated in further research and then rolled out globally.

The roll-out process involved enhancing the marketing capabilities of several thousand employees. All marketers needed to understand the proposition, why it was important and how to use it in their markets. However, to be effective, it also needed to be understood across the business. Brand understanding had to be built among all involved in recruitment — from engineers in Aberdeen to lawyers in Malaysia. This was delivered with an extensive multi-channel programme, including virtual classrooms, conferences and brochures.

The successful implementation of the graduate EVP was followed by the development of an EVP for 'experienced' professionals in 2007 /08, tailored to a different target audience with different motivations and expectations.

These EVPs were then actively used to develop new communication campaigns, refine recruitment tools and processes, and to guide the messages everyone gave candidates. To ensure that costs were managed effectively, an 'ad creation tool' was introduced which allowed local markets to create tailored versions of the global campaign using a simple website. It ensured the new EVP was consistently communicated to candidates without incurring excessive creative agency costs.

Markets could tailor messages and use targeted channels which in fact delivered better quality applications and reduced costs per recruit compared to the national press on which the company had previously relied.

Broadening the reach

While the main focus in 2006-8 had been on developing these two crucial capabilities, the company was also investing in developing other broader marketing skills. A series of virtual classrooms were created in the capability programme, xchange, and supported by on- and offline toolkits to teach people marketing fundamentals. This built up knowledge of the core principles of marketing among everyone in recruitment. It covered the skill areas of the candidate journey, insight, segmentation, brand positioning, brand activation and marketing planning.

Recognising the importance of strengthening marketing leadership, the key managers in recruitment were sent on The Marketing Society's Marketing Leaders Programme, which they found inspiring and helpful practically.

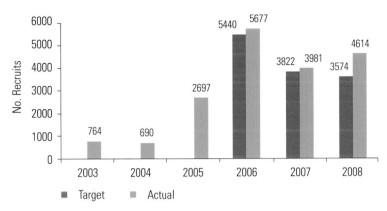

Figure 1. In 2006-8 targets were exceeded and the number of recruits more than trebled

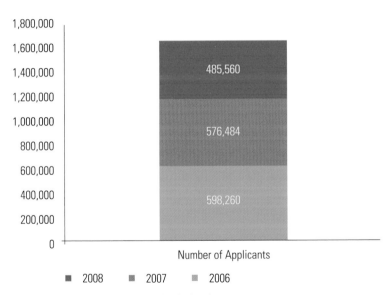

Figure 2. 1.6m applicants were attracted to the brand

The brand resurgent

The challenge was huge: to double the number of new and highly skilled recruits to Shell cost-effectively in the face of strong competition and weak brand equity. The HR team had little marketing experience in the face of a business hungry for new talent. By building the marketing capabilities with Brand Learning's specialist support and pioneering the application of classic marketing approaches to recruitment marketing, the company achieved impressive results.

- Recruitment targets were surpassed every year between 2006 and 2008 which resulted in massive growth (Figure 1).
- 1.66 million applicants were attracted to the Shell brand (Figure 2).
- The marketing budget and marketing cost per hire were both reduced by focusing on the customer — the candidate — and finding efficiencies in communicating the EVP (Figure 3, overleaf).
- The customers reported improvements in their brand experience, which was driven largely by improvements in process efficiency (Table 1).

Table 1

	2006	2008	% change
Overall customer experience score	3.55 out of 5	3.7 out of 5	+4%

- Perceptions of Shell's employer brand continued to improve. Research showed that the Shell employer value proposition was motivating more people to consider Shell as an employer against competitors and they were now more likely to recommend Shell to their friends.
- Enhanced marketing capabilities meant that staff could be developed and promoted into other marketing roles across the business. Between 2006 and 2008, 20% of the recruitment marketing team were promoted into other marketing roles, from marketing Shell Lubricants to corporate communications.

The company had overcome the perception that its recruitment team were not 'proper marketers' because they were in recruitment marketing. This turned out to be very motivating to the team, as was the investment in building their marketing capabilities.

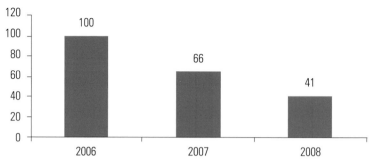

Figure 3. Marketing cost per recruit fell to 41% of 2006 levels

McDonald's

09

Instilling a renewed sense of staff pride

Snapshot

A far-reaching and innovative programme had a major impact on employees' confidence and motivation and banished outdated perceptions of jobs at the company.

Key insights

- In a service business motivation of staff is critical and McDonald's has been making a concerted effort in the last few years to change the 'McJob' tag from a criticism to a compliment.

- This has included a series of imaginative human resources (HR) initiatives to bring to life its employee value proposition and give staff pride in what they do, as well as offering educational and training opportunities.

- By the end of 2008 almost 80% of employees were proud to work at McDonald's, while staff turnover had decreased significantly.

Summary

McDonald's is the leading global food service retailer with more than 32,000 local restaurants serving more than 60 million people in 117 countries each day. More than 75% of McDonald's restaurants worldwide are owned and operated by independent local men and women. However, the retailer had suffered from the perception that jobs at McDonald's offered few benefits and were of low prestige — symbolised by the derogatory 'McJobs' label.

McDonald's in the UK decided to fight back. Starting in 2006, it embarked on a concerted campaign to challenge inaccurate perceptions of jobs and careers at McDonald's in order to build the confidence and pride of its 72,000 employees, whose engagement and motivation is crucial to its customer-focused business.

In addition, the organisation undertook a vigorous external communications campaign to change perceptions of work at McDonald's. By 2008 the number of employees who felt proud to work at McDonald's increased from 60% to 79%, while staff turnover decreased significantly (See Chapter 4).

Laying the groundwork

Since the author Douglas Coupland popularised the phrase 'McJob' in his 1991 book *Generation X* to describe 'a low-pay, low-prestige, low-dignity, low-benefit, no-future job in the service sector', the label became embedded in the public consciousness.

This was despite the fact that the label was far from the reality of McDonald's employees' experience, with 95% believing their training and experience would be valuable to another employer. But misconceptions of the value of work at McDonald's had the potential to affect employees' confidence and pride significantly, as well as motivation and morale.

When David Fairhurst was appointed McDonald's vice president for people in late 2005, one of his main motivations for joining the company was a desire to change these inaccurate and outdated perceptions of jobs at McDonald's. At the heart of this aim was a strategic need to build the confidence and pride of McDonald's workforce, ensuring they had the skills and motivation required to provide excellent customer service — key to McDonald's overall commercial performance.

The 'people' strategy he set in place aimed to build confidence and pride among employees by:

- Creating HR innovations for employees that would bring to life McDonald's 'employee value proposition', which focuses on providing improvement opportunities, flexibility, an energising environment and continuous learning for all employees.
- Educating and exciting McDonald's 72,000-strong workforce about these innovations so they could get maximum value from them.
- Telling the outside world about the reality of work at McDonald's in order to change inaccurate preconceptions, thus improving internal confidence and pride by reinforcing the message externally.

In January 2006, McDonald's embarked on a long-term, four-phase campaign to achieve its strategic objectives:

1. Independent research to identify the levels of satisfaction among its workforce as a basis for subsequent activity.
2. A concerted campaign to roll out a series of HR innovations to employees and external audiences, putting forward irrefutable evidence that McDonald's offers valuable, highly-skilled jobs and careers.
3. Active campaigning on behalf of McDonald's workforce to transform the perception of jobs and careers at McDonald's.
4. Celebration of the employment opportunities available at the company.

A carefully-crafted strategy

Phase 1: Independent research

Each year the company asks its employees for comprehensive feedback on their experience, from support and resources available, to respect and recognition, and learning and development opportunities. These insights are collected via an independently-conducted employee survey. In 2008 this was completed by 89% of employees.

However, in early 2006, having just set in place the new 'people' strategy, McDonald's commissioned an independent academic study in addition to its employee survey into the impact of work at McDonald's on young people. This was conducted among 500 people, including young McDonald's employees, their friends, parents, teachers and managers. The research, by Adrian Furnham, professor of psychology at University College London, proved that employment at McDonald's had a positive transformative effect on young people compared to other jobs, by boosting their confidence, communication skills and career prospects.

This gave the company confidence that its strategy was grounded in strong and accurate insight, and it thus prepared the way for the roll-out of a series of HR innovations.

Phase 2: HR innovations

In January 2006, McDonald's began developing and launching a series of HR innovations, with each one designed to embody an element of its employee value proposition.

Friends & Family Contract

The company prides itself on its flexibility as an employer, offering opportunities which help employees cope with the modern-day demands of juggling family life. In 2006 it launched the Family Contract, which enabled two family members who work in the same restaurant to cover each others' shifts without prior notice. In mid-2007 this was extended to friends and re-launched as the Friends & Family Contract.

Figure 1. OurLounge

The contract was communicated to the 1,200 restaurants, while excitement about the idea was built by finding employees from around the organisation who embodied the benefits of the contract — for instance, twins who covered shifts for each other while studying towards university exams. These case studies formed the basis of articles in the employee magazine *MDUK*. The company also created excitement by announcing the contract externally, putting case studies at the heart of the story. The *Daily Telegraph* published the story on the front page, positioning the company as an innovator in flexible working. In total, the announcement generated 55 million opportunities to see/hear the story.

OurLounge

In late 2006, McDonald's launched an innovative career and lifestyle website for its employees called OurLounge. The site was created with considerable input from 150 employees to give them the information, advice and support to enhance their personal and working lives (Figure 1).

OurLounge enables employees to study online from any PC and gain nationally recognised GCSE-equivalent qualifications in maths and English. This basic skills training is set in the wider context of a range of other helpful lifestyle information and advice, from film reviews to advice from external experts on topics like buying a house and communication skills. OurLounge also hosts a number of discounts available only to employees, including driving lessons and reductions on Apple products. In 2007, 'McTime' was added to the site. This tool enables employees to check and sign up for shifts via OurLounge, meaning they no longer need to check these details with managers by phone or by physically visiting the restaurant.

At the launch those employees involved in the development of the site were thanked with a party at the popular Sugar Reef bar and restaurant in central London, with hourly-paid crew members invited along with the McDonald's executive team.

Since its launch, OurLounge has become the chief communication tool between McDonald's and its 72,000 employees. Employees can access the site from home or via the PCs provided in the crew rooms of its restaurants. By the end of 2008 65,000 employees had signed up to OurLounge and 2,560 were studying towards GCSE equivalent qualifications.

The McDonald's A-Level equivalent

The natural next step from OurLounge was to develop externally-recognised qualifications for management training. In January 2008, McDonald's was one of the first three employers to be given the authority by government and the Qualification and Curriculum Authority to award its own A-Level equivalent qualification in shift management. The qualification was piloted in 2008, and up to 2,000 trainee managers were set to complete the qualification in 2009.

Phase 3: Active campaigning

In adding to developing a series of innovative tools and benefits for employees, a key element of the company's 'people' strategy focused on actively campaigning on behalf of employees to encourage people outside the organisation to reconsider their views of work at McDonald's.

'Not bad for a McJob'

The first step in this campaign was to launch the bold, disruptive 'Not bad for a McJob' ad campaign, which examined the benefits of working at McDonald's and rounded off with the phrase 'Not bad for a McJob'. This was the first time McDonald's had reclaimed the derogatory 'McJob' label, and the ads provided a strong platform for McDonald's to explain the reasons why it was campaigning for people to reconsider their views of jobs at the company.

Importantly, it also enabled the company to send out a clear signal to employees about the value and recognition they deserve. Senior management took the time to host regional conferences to brief franchisees and restaurant managers on the campaign in advance of launch, and collateral was produced for staff to explain the aims of the campaign. In addition, buzz was created about the campaign for both internal and external audiences by displaying it on the iconic billboard at Piccadilly Circus.

McJob petition

The next step in the active campaigning was a high-profile public petition asking dictionary houses to reconsider the definition of 'McJob'. Because this was the company speaking out on behalf of staff, it was crucial that they understood the reasons for launching the campaign.

The executive team undertook a nationwide, regional tour over a four-month period to discuss the campaign with restaurant staff, as well as local customers, media and stakeholders. They travelled to 40 different towns across the UK and helped ensure that the employees understood the value of the petition.

The company wanted the petition to be accessible to employees, so, in recognition of the fact that over half of the staff are under the age of 21, text and online signing mechanics were developed alongside conventional books placed in restaurants. The petition gained more than 100,000 signatures from employees, stakeholders and members of the public and attracted public support from 35 MPs and a high-profile coalition from the worlds of business, education and skills. In addition, it generated over 500 pieces of media coverage across 26 countries.

Phase 4: Celebrating McJobs

Thanks to the investment in HR innovations for staff and campaigning for reappraisal on their behalf, opinions of 'McJobs' began to shift. In 2008, this meant the company could shift its focus from defending 'McJobs' to celebrating' McJobs'.

Designer uniforms

Having undertaken a major investment in modernising the restaurants, employee uniforms were next. McDonald's recruited renowned fashion designer Bruce Oldfield to create the new uniforms, thus demonstrating to staff the high value placed on them (Figure 2).

It was crucial that the uniforms were fit for purpose and popular with staff. Therefore, an internal consultation was launched several months before rolling out the uniform nationally. This included a wearer trial across 80 UK restaurants.

Employees were invited to feed back their views, which were taken into account before the final designs were approved.

In order to build excitement about the uniforms, an internal competition in which employees could win a trip to Warsaw was launched as well as a place on the catwalk at a fashion show to reveal the new uniforms at the company's annual general meeting. According to a staff survey commissioned as part of the consultation, 67% of employees believed the new uniforms were more modern and professional than the old ones and nearly half said it made them feel more confident.

'My McJob'

In August 2008 the company replaced the 'Not bad for a McJob' advertising campaign with its successor 'My McJob', which illustrated the career benefits available at McDonald's through the voice of its own employees. The campaign was made relevant to employees by inviting them to contribute to its development. Via OurLounge, employees were asked what they loved about their 'McJob'. The company then selected 12 representative responses and used them as the basis of the advertising creative approach, with each employee's comment attributed to them on the poster.

Figure 2. New employee uniforms

In the week following the 'My McJob' ad launch, the number of applications for hourly-paid crew positions more than doubled to over 1,300 per day and daily applications for management roles rose from seven to, on average, 32 applications.

Making a decisive impact

By the end of 2008 the results had exceeded expectations in a number of areas.

Employee engagement and motivation

- Since the 'people' strategy was set in place the number of employees who felt proud to work at McDonald's increased from 60% (Your Viewpoint independent employee survey, 2004) to 79% in 2008.
- 83% of employees would recommend working at McDonald's to a friend and 95% believed that their experience and training would be useful to other employers (an increase of 3% since 2006).
- By 2008 the confidence of McDonald's employees had increased by 10%, which contributed to McDonald's highest-ever customer service levels and 11 consecutive quarters of commercial growth.
- According to Professor Adrian Furnham's independent study, nine out of 10 young McDonald's employees showed high levels of satisfaction and commitment to their jobs — substantially higher than other workplaces where comparable studies were undertaken. Two-thirds believed their opportunities for promotion were better than their friends', with the average among their peer group only 25%.

Recruitment and retention

- In the same time period the average tenure of hourly-paid crew members increased to over two years, and to almost 11 years among restaurant managers.
- Staff turnover was at an all time low.
- McDonald's was attracting on average 1,300 applications per day for hourly-paid crew positions.

Learning and development

- 65,000 employees signed up to OurLounge and 2,560 were studying towards GCSE equivalent qualifications by the end of 2008.
- Following the successful pilot in 2008, up to 2,000 trainee managers were set to gain an A-Level equivalent qualification in shift management.
- 80% of restaurant managers and one in five franchisees started as crew.

External recognition from active campaigning

McDonald's concerted campaign to encourage reappraisal of jobs and careers at McDonald's generated over a billion opportunities to see/hear in the media between 2006-08. The campaign attracted support and recognition among high-profile stakeholders including former Prime Minister Gordon Brown, former Skills Minister David Lammy MP and business groups such as the CBI and British Chambers of Commerce. McDonald's HR innovations were also recognised by organisations including *Financial Times* Best Workplaces/Great Place to Work Institute, Business in the Community, Working Families and Where Women Want to Work. Finally, for three consecutive years, David Fairhurst was recognised by his HR peers, winning awards such as HR Director of the Year and Most Influential HR Practitioner.

All images appearing in this case study are reproduced by permission of McDonald's.

ICI Paints

09

Benefiting from a full marketing makeover

Snapshot
A complete reorganisation of marketing capabilities helped
ICI Paints become a global leader in decorative paints.

Key insights

- With the arrival of a new chief executive in 2004 ICI Paints was determined to re-orient itself to become a more brand-led, customer-centric company.

- It achieved this through a comprehensive global marketing capability project developed with the full commitment of the marketing leadership team.

- The results were boosts in both revenues and market share by December 2007.

Summary

ICI Paints was bought by AkzoNobel, one of the world's leading industrial companies, in 2008. The combined business is the world's leading global coatings manufacturer and the number one in decorative paints and performance coatings, as well as being a major worldwide supplier of specialty chemicals.

ICI Paints had traditionally been a product-driven paints manufacturing company and had grown organically through a strong brand presence in a limited number of markets and through various local acquisitions. In 2003, however, the business was slowing down, with the share of its leading paints brand, Dulux, declining in several key markets. At this stage, it was not clear where future growth could come from.

In 2004, a newly appointed chief executive, David Hamill, outlined an ambitious growth agenda for the company to grow sales revenue by at least 4% per annum over the next three years with an incrementally higher rate of profit than rate of sales.

By December 2007 ICI Paints was the global leader in decorative paints, having achieved a compound annual growth rate (CAGR) in excess of 5% between 2004 and 2007, compared to an average 3% CAGR over the previous three years. Central to success was a global marketing capability initiative that was supported and endorsed by a committed marketing leadership team.

Taking stock

In 2003 ICI Paints was a product-driven paints manufacturing business characterised by low rates of growth that depended as much on the growth in key markets than the performance of its brands.

While some of the brands had carved out powerful and distinct positions in their marketplaces, many more were poorly differentiated. The lack of a brand portfolio strategy meant that the available resources were spread too thinly, with many brands inadequately supported.

The company had isolated marketing tools and processes that were applied with varying degrees of skill around the world. Some pockets of excellence existed, but with limited transfer of best practice they remained isolated success stories. At the heart of the issue was the lack of both a common strategic marketing framework that would provide focus and clarity of direction and a capability agenda that would drive the performance of the marketing function.

With a number of leading brands starting to lose share, the business was looking increasingly vulnerable to any decline in the decorative paint markets worldwide.

Setting out the strategic vision

With the arrival of a new chief executive, David Hamill, in 2004, came the recognition that marketing needed to play a more strategic role in transforming the business into a brand-led, customer-centric organisation, and one that could achieve sales revenue growth of at least 4% per annum.

A new marketing vision was articulated: 'Lead the business in delivering sustainable, profitable top-line growth through developing world-class marketing capabilities and performance globally'.

The marketing function aimed to be a source of competitive advantage for the company. For this ambition to be realised, ICI Paints needed to create fewer, bigger, stronger brands with wider distribution. This was an aspiration which, in turn, relied on a more capable, professional, accountable and engaged marketing function.

With a clearly-articulated ambition and challenging business objectives, the company set out to develop a transformational marketing capability agenda that involved:
• Re-orienting the organisation for the future by building a strong global marketing leadership team that could drive the overall business agenda.
• Developing the ICI Way of Marketing by identifying best practice where it existed and establishing a common approach to marketing.
• Planning the marketing capability change initiative by prioritising capability development needs and planning a global process, skill and culture development programme to foster marketing excellence.
• Tackling key strategic business issues by defining a clear brand portfolio strategy focused on building fewer, stronger brands and providing clear direction to the rest of the business.
• Developing operational marketing excellence by delivering a superior brand experience for all customers and consumers.

Re-orienting the organisation for the future

David Hamill recognised that having a strong marketing leadership team would be critical for shaping a winning marketing strategy and meeting the business objectives. He appointed Kerris Bright as chief marketing officer, who then created a marketing leadership team that comprised both the regional marketing heads from the six operating units and a number of functional leaders in key marketing disciplines (insight, innovation etc).

This powerful team formed the first marketing governance body for key strategic decisions as well as the marketing capability initiative that was to follow. They aimed to ensure that best practice would be co-developed, deployed and refreshed across the organisation.

Following that, the Advance Marketing Academy, led by Karen Jeffery, was established to plan, develop and execute the marketing capability transformation programme. Working in conjunction with the marketing leadership team to ensure alignment of key stakeholders, the Academy was also supported by regional programme co-ordinators who could ensure global applicability of a common ICI way of marketing.

Brand Learning were appointed as the marketing capability consultancy partner to ensure that the company was tapping into external best practice and expertise.

Planning for marketing capability change

The central challenge was to create a step change in the marketing capability to make marketing a key source of competitive advantage. Only then would the marketing community be able to deliver the strategic direction and executional excellence required to revitalise business performance.

The first task was to create a common marketing capability framework that would define the key skill areas that were required for marketing excellence.

This was translated into a robust process capability audit tool (PCAT) which articulated what world-class marketing processes looked like in order to develop a shared vision for excellence. This tool allowed the business to score performance on a 10-step maturity scale against world-class performance in a number of key elements.

When the self assessments were undertaken for the first time in 2004/05, they produced an aggregated average level of just 3/10. While disappointing, this finding was not altogether surprising and it enabled the company to set an ambitious goal to raise the score to 7/10 by 2010 (Figure 1).

Crucially, the PCAT enabled the company to prioritise the capability gaps within the marketing function. A key implication of the first audit was the recognition that there was an urgent need to address the relative weakness in strategic marketing skills such as insight, market strategy and planning and brand equity development. These skill areas became the first area of focus in the capability programme that ensued (Table 1).

Table 1

2004/2005	UK	Asia	North America	Latin America
Insight	3.5	3.5	3	3
Marketing strategy and planning	3	3.5	2.5	2
Brand equity development	4	3.7	2.5	3

2004   2010

Figure 1

Having identified the key capability gaps using PCAT, what was then required was a means of addressing them in a way that clearly linked to business priorities. This led to the development of a marketing capability programme strategy and plan with the input and endorsement of the marketing leadership team. (See 'Getting the right ingredients in place').

Getting the right ingredients in place

The key elements of the marketing capability programme strategy and plan were:
- Modules focused on strategic marketing capabilities in the first phase (2004-5) and operational marketing capabilities in the second phase (2006-7).
- A live-action learning approach to apply learning to real business issues. This required senior marketers to acquire and apply the skills to develop a brand portfolio strategy for their market via a series of facilitated workshops.
- Tailored content to build senior leadership skills as well as middle/junior professional skills.
- Tailored content to reflect business-to-business (B2B) and business-to-consumers (B2C) business needs.
- The development and deployment of ICI trainers to embed the ICI Way of Marketing.
- The creation of Advance Lite programmes for general managers and other functions to foster a customer-centric culture within the organisation.

Developing the ICI Way of Marketing

This would be a way to provide a common language for marketers within ICI, and also to embed an integrated, best-practice way of working throughout the company. It sought to combine best practice from within the organisation with external, world-class marketing thinking. A simple set of processes and tools were developed, with active involvement from senior marketers and leading practitioners to ensure their engagement and commitment.

Delivering the programme to the organisation started with high-impact leadership workshops designed to engage and align the marketing directors across the world. This was quickly followed by an extensive roll-out plan to the professional level. The roll-out was also supported online with a toolkit that provided easy access to latest thinking.

A critical factor in the success of the programme was that it was used to address directly the burning strategic issues facing the business through the creation of, and alignment to, a common language and common thinking framework. The most urgent priority was the development of a global brand portfolio strategy for each of the six operating regions.

A live-action learning programme was developed to put capability-building for key teams on a fast track. The teams learned about the associated tools and processes (from the creation of a need-state segmentation to the development of market maps and implementation plans) and then applied them to their own region. Over a period of six months each region was able to determine which brands it needed to build and how these should be positioned in the marketplace.

Figure 2 shows the 2005 identification of the company's global segments.This process enabled ICI Paints to begin focusing the portfolio to concentrate resources behind building fewer, more powerful brands. For example, in Poland the media budget, which had been shared previously across both Dulux and the locally acquired brands Pillak and Ekonowinka, was now concentrated entirely behind Dulux.

Branding renaissance

By early 2006, brand positionings had been developed for all master brands within the ICI Portfolio.

The use of a common tool to express these positionings enabled the company to identify key areas of overlap, both in how a master brand such as Dulux was positioned in different areas of the world, and also among other brands that were targeting the same segments. Synergistic positionings for Dulux and other leading brands began to be created in order to fuel higher levels of growth and to realise other associated cost benefits across the marketing mix.

Having improved the strategic marketing capabilities in order to develop brand portfolio strategies, the next priority for ICI Paints was to translate the positionings of the master brands across the marketing mix successfully. The PCAT revealed that brand communication and activation was a key area of focus — in particular, the creation of big ideas that would be brought to life through integrated media plans.

In the UK an award-winning integrated campaign — 'We know the colours that go' — was developed and translated across multiple channels (e.g. TV, online, and public relations). This campaign resulted in the highest-ever level of people spontaneously recalling a Dulux ad and also dramatically improved the brand's health (See Chapter 6). For example, the proportion of people claiming that 'Dulux is an expert at putting colours together' increased by 2I% in one year alone. Moreover, given that the core end-user insight behind the campaign held true in other parts of the world, the campaign was rolled out to other markets like Ireland and Poland.

Transforming the business

The impact of this marketing transformation on ICI's business performance was very significant. The company achieved the challenging stretching commercial targets set in 2004 with revenue growth of over 5% p.a. while increasing the profit-to-sales ratio (Figures 3 and 4, overleaf). Underpinning this performance were significant improvements in brand advocacy across the world — one of the key drivers of the turnaround in market share performance.

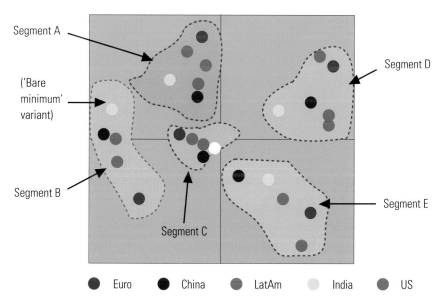

Segment A

('Bare minimum' variant)

Segment B

Segment C

Segment D

Segment E

● Euro   ● China   ● LatAm   ○ India   ● US

Figure 2. Identifying global segments

The latest PCAT results in 2007, which had moved up to between five and six from three in 2004, demonstrated the strong progress the company had made towards its vision for 2010 to achieve a score of seven (Figure 5). This was thanks to the significant improvements in the discipline and rigour of the marketing activities.

A further significant benefit of the initiative was a positive impact on recruitment, motivation and retention in the marketing community. For example, in Asia, 44% of marketing vacancies were filled internally in 2007 compared to 0% in 2005. In the annual UK survey to assess employee engagement, the grand mean score for the 90-strong marketing community improved significantly from 3.59 to 3.87 between 2006 and 2007.

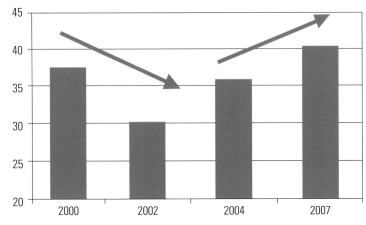

Figure 3. Share by value RSP (retail sales price)

Key lessons

Some of the key lessons from the company's experience included:
- Investment in marketing capabilities can have a significant impact on marketing and business performance.
- The leadership of the company must be fully involved to drive through the necessary changes in behaviour.
- Things don't happen overnight. A sustained commitment to change over the long term is needed.
- Linking learning to real-life business issues can 'turbo-charge' performance on the job.
- Focusing on fewer, stronger brands can transform business performance.

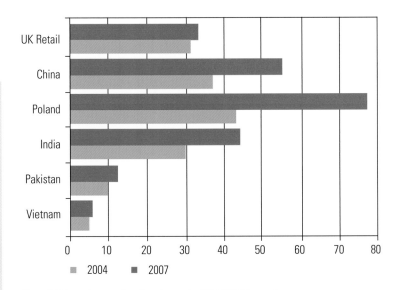

Figure 4. Dulux volume market share by country 2004-2006 % growth

Figure 5

All images appearing in this case study are reproduced by permission of AkzoNobel.

Chapter 10
Social Marketing

Sheila Mitchell
Marketing Director,
Department of Health

Achievements of recent years have seen a true coming of age in social marketing, demonstrating that the particular challenges of this discipline can be met head on and deliver results within the overall framework of marketing activity as impressive as those of any other sector.

But people still ask: what exactly is social marketing? Social marketing applies most of the techniques of marketing in the financially-driven world of business to goals that are concerned with societal good: health, environment, education, safety etc. Whereas most commercially-orientated marketing is concerned with behaviour change (e.g. buying) that brings immediate and tangible benefits, the benefits social marketing deals with are often no less real but very much longer term. Along with usually very much lower budgets, another factor that distinguishes the challenges of social marketing from the business world is that it frequently finds itself dealing with deeply-entrenched behaviours that are often perceived as both pleasurable and comforting — behaviours in fact that in some instances commercial marketing has the somewhat easier objective of indulging and reinforcing!

Each of the three case histories here has its distinctive achievement and tells us something useful about social marketing. The British Heart Foundation really scored by engaging its target of 11-13-year olds by making healthy living fun with an online game. Keep Britain Tidy reached beyond its target of 18-24 males by recruiting non-littering peers to shame the litterers into taking responsibility for fast food litter. It also demonstrated the benefits of aligning stakeholders such as local authorities and the fast food outlets themselves. Finally, Jamie Oliver's enduringly impactful initiative on school dinners showed the results that the combination of a powerful media partner (Channel 4) and a high profile personality adept at campaigning can deliver.

In seeking to draw out the lessons for us all from the best of recent social marketing, the following would seem to be among the most salient:
• Social marketing goes beyond being a communication function and should ultimately be embraced by those planning public policy and service configuration.
• Achieving the optimum alignment of partners/ stakeholders is essential. Get the tone of engagement right: avoid nagging and make it fun!
• Effective lobbying and campaigning — including the use of high profile personalities — can often be an integral part of social marketing. Recognise that long-term behaviour change is difficult to measure and ensure robust interim proxy measures are in place.

Channel 4

10

Sparking a national debate on nutrition

Snapshot

The compelling combination of a culinary icon and a social marketing campaign triggered the start of a food revolution.

Key insights

- An inspired partnership of Channel 4 and TV chef Jamie Oliver took on the huge challenge of tackling the significant rise in childhood obesity through a radical TV series.

- Built around the high-profile TV programme, the multi-channel campaign departed from the norm by fusing programming into the marketing mix.

- The result was not only a massive leap in government funding, but it netted Channel 4 an impressive 148% return on investment.

Summary

Today's generation of children is the first in history to be expected to die before their parents as a result of long-term health and diet-related problems. The problem is that school dinners provide a significant proportion of children's diets, and over the years, cost-cutting had seen food being offered on the basis of cheapness rather then nutritional value.

One of the more imaginative approaches to tackling this disturbing trend began in 2005 with the inspired pairing of TV chef Jamie Oliver and Channel 4. The result was an integrated campaign which was built around a high-profile TV programme and which had an impact far beyond the programme alone.

Not only did Channel 4 benefit commercially, but, even more importantly, the campaign achieved its goal of attracting increased government funding for school dinners of £280 million.

Championing change

The direct and indirect costs of obesity are estimated to be approaching £7 billion a year. This is particularly disturbing in regards to children:

- Children now wear trousers two sizes larger than in the 1980s.
- Obesity has tripled with 31% of children now overweight or obese.
- 94% of 7-10 year olds consume more saturated fat than recommended.

In 1978 the government had set out to halve expenditure on school dinners to £190 million, leading to food being provided on the basis of cheapness rather than nutritional value. Various individuals and groups had tried to influence local and national government policy on this issue but with little significant or widespread effect. For meaningful change to take place, the children needed a champion to make school dinners an issue of national interest.

The desire to inspire change and create national debate are central to Channel 4's brand values and remit. Channel 4 was thus a natural media partner for TV chef Jamie Oliver in his crusade to change the state of school dinners. At the core of the partnership would be an innovative 360-degree integrated campaign built around a TV series. This was to be a new generation of integrated campaigns fusing programming into the advertising and marketing mix — akin to a cause-related advertiser-funded but programming-led approach.

Shining the spotlight on school dinners

The big challenge was to make the topic of school dinners a ratings success. This would not be an easy task. School dinners might smell of many things, but certainly not of ratings success. To make a commercially viable campaign and a real difference to the health of the nation required the full marketing clout of both Channel 4 and Jamie Oliver to catapult this to a matter of national debate.

While having Jamie on board was crucial, it was no guarantee of success. Only a series on the same scale as 'Lost' or 'Desperate Housewives' could have the required impact — a tough call given the subject matter.

A series of discussions between Channel 4 and various other stakeholder parties led to a coalition of partners with the brief to deliver from scratch one of the highest profile TV series of the year, and to build around this an entire campaign for change. The objective was very ambitious: to secure £280 million additional funding for school dinners from the government.

A campaign team was brought together consisting of a rainbow coalition of stakeholders. Specific, measurable targets were put in place:

- Commercial payback for Channel 4.
- Minimum spend of 50p per plate for school dinners (an increase of 43%).
- The introduction of enforceable nutritional standards and greater food education.

The campaign strategy is illustrated by Figure 1 overleaf.

Banging the drum for school dinners

Jamie Oliver's celebrity, let alone the subject matter, would simply not be enough to attract viewers or generate positive press coverage. To capture the public imagination, advertising had to establish Jamie's School Dinners as a high-profile, flagship Channel 4 series rather than a worthy factual docu-series featuring a famous chef. Large audiences had to be delivered from the start, at least in line with the 3.7 million viewing average for the slot. Because Jamie's School Dinners was to be only a four-part series, there wasn't time to build the audience through the quality of the series. Advertising had to deliver viewers from the start.

Promotional airtime began on 9th February, 2005, with Jamie's plea to the nation being defaced by the kids' graffiti in the TV trailers. The weight of airtime increased up until the first show in the series. A heavyweight national outdoor campaign made use of 'chameleon' sites for 48-sheet and 96-sheet posters, which changed every evening so that they appeared to be graffitied with the kids' hostile messages (Figure 2).

In quality broadsheet magazine supplements, front and back images of Jamie Oliver on consecutive pages were used to show the kids playing pranks behind Jamie's back to sabotage his campaign. There was also a dedicated cover wrap for *Observer Food Monthly* magazine (Figure 3). Meanwhile, to provide support and galvanise action for the campaign, a dedicated website was developed: www.feedmebetter.com.

Finally a paid-for direct marketing pack was developed containing detailed advice, recipe cards, campaigning tools, etc, for schools, dinner ladies and parents.

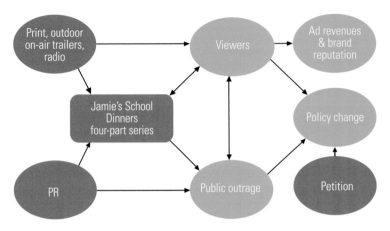

Figure 1. The campaign strategy

Figure 2. Posters

Spreading the word

Pubic relations (PR) had to attract millions of viewers, plus make school dinners an issue of national importance and put it on the agenda item for every newspaper and politician. There were three broad phases.

1. Managed PR by Channel 4

The single biggest risk was that using Jamie would backfire, with cynical journalists focusing upon his actions and motivations rather than the bigger issues involved.

So the brief was to keep journalists on message, place sound bites, and enable them to get involved in the campaign itself since their participation would be critical to success. This managed PR took a very clear problem / solution campaigning focus:
- This is a key social issue about the state of school food (*not* a Jamie programme).
- This is what Jamie did/found out.
- This is the recommended solution.

PR activity began at the same time as the advertising in order to create as much 'pull' to the programme as possible.

2. Supporting PR driven by the media

Once the series had begun in a blaze of publicity, the press began to run with the story. PR throughout this stage was critical in providing information and resources to journalists, escalating this from a TV series to a serious national issue.

Figure 3. *Observer Food Monthly* cover wrap

3. The petition

A key part of the PR plan was the development of an online petition in partnership with Poke and Jamie Oliver's team at www.feedmebetter.com. This petition was intended to generate 30,000 signatures for Jamie to deliver to Downing Street.

A big breakthrough

Pre-transmission advertising delivered notable ad awareness. Series awareness also reached record levels for Channel 4, with 94% total awareness prior to transmission. In addition, record levels of awareness were generated per £ spent, as Figure 4 shows.

Ad awareness was synchronised with PR and press coverage, with 35 major articles written before transmission, spanning a breadth of titles including almost all the popular and broadsheet newspapers, plus bbc.co.uk and Radio 1.

Integrated advertising and PR ensured record levels of awareness which directly followed through into viewer interest, with 1.1 million viewers above average for the slot. The campaign generated first episode audiences per £ spent in excess of Channel 4's most famous blockbuster series of 2005 (Figure 5). Between February and April 2005 the campaign website achieved over 10 million hits — a figure that would have been significantly higher were it not for the servers melting down due to the levels of unexpected demand. The website achieved a massively higher reach than its nearest equivalent to date, which was the Soil Association's 'Food for life' campaign.

The website focused upon a petition which exceeded its original target almost tenfold, with a total of 271,677 signatures and 3,000 letters sent to MPs.

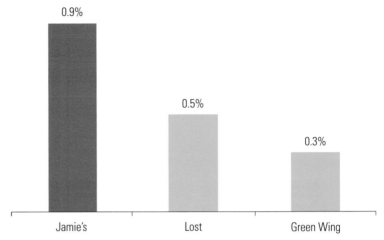

Figure 4. Awareness per £1k spent on paid-for media
Source: Channel 4 (Hall & Partners)

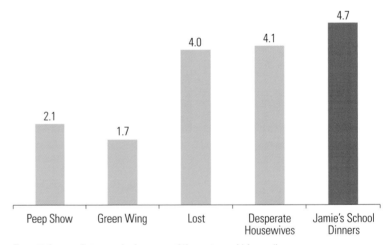

Figure 5. Average first epesode viewers per £1k spent on paid-for media
Source: Channel 4 sales/OMD

The petition was delivered to Downing Street on 30th March, 2005, an event which was the top news item on all the TV news bulletins that day.

Winning on every front

This was one of Channel 4's highest ratings winners of 2005, which made it a 'must have' series for any TV buyer looking for young, upmarket light TV-viewing adults. It was therefore classified as a 'special' by Channel 4 ad sales, a classification which added a 50% premium to the advertising revenue, equating to actual revenues of £6.69 million.

The campaign made school dinners headline news and a national talking point. Between January and June 2005 there were a total of 1,016 articles with mentions of Jamie's School Dinners, including 21 key leader articles. Evaluation of print media coverage showed the PR value was worth at least an additional £14.1 million.

The total campaign, including the production of the entire TV series and all the costs of media and production, cost just £4.52 million, which was a tiny fraction of the total marketing budgets of 'junk food' advertisers aimed at kids. The campaign surpassed targets in a number of ways:

- The TV series itself delivered a total advertising surplus of £2.18 million above total costs — a net conventional return on investment of 148%.
- As a direct result of the publicity generated by the campaign, the government announced a £280 million funding increase, with £220 million to deliver a minimum ingredient spend of 50p per meal for primary schools and 60p for secondary schools, backed with minimum nutritional standards.

- The campaign revitalised Jamie Oliver's brand image, taking him from celebrity chef to a truly national hero and champion of change.
- The campaign helped Channel 4 meet its remit of inspiring change and creating national debate about key issues, and as such was of significant (but intangible) value to the Channel 4 brand.

British Heart Foundation

10

The power of an online game to influence behaviour

Snapshot

An entertaining online game encouraged children to fight the flab by making it fun to equate what they eat with their health.

Key insights

- The British Heart Foundation (BHF) mounted a major campaign to tackle the growing childhood obesity crisis based on a clever insight: children like to learn through play.

- The result was an unconventional online game Yoobot which engaged the target audience of 11-13 year-olds while at the same time subtly educating them about the impact of healthy lifestyles.

- The Yoobot game had a major impact on this hard-to-reach young target audience, with 85% of users saying that it had made them think more about eating better and doing more to keep healthy.

Summary

The British Heart Foundation (BHF) was founded in 1961 by a group of medical professionals who were concerned about the increasing death rate from cardiovascular disease. In 1986, the BHF became more involved in public education, and in 1990 moved into rehabilitation.

One of its main campaigns has been the Food4Thought initiative, designed to help tackle the UK's obesity crisis in children. As part of this programme it decided to try and engage with children directly.

The result was an entertaining online game called Yoobot, which allowed children to create a miniature version of themselves that they could then play games with, feed and watch it grow older. Showing the direct connection between food and health worked: 85% of the game's audience said that Yoobot made them think more about what they ate while almost three-quarters said they would eat more healthily.

Tackling a national problem

The current obesity crisis is likely to cost the National Health Service (NHS) £50 billion by 2050, according to a 2008 report by Foresight. Currently, one in three children are obese or overweight and if the trend continues, it is predicted that a staggering 90% of today's children will be overweight or obese by 2050. An unhealthy diet and/or being obese increases the risk of type-2 diabetes, high blood pressure and coronary heart disease — the UK's single biggest killer. The resulting increase in life-threatening diseases is predicted to cost the NHS a crippling £50 billion a year.

In 2005 the British Heart Foundation (BHF) set up its Food4Thought initiative, which aims to tackle this through giving children the tools and information they need to make healthier, more informed food choices from an early age and thereby reducing their risk in later life. In 2008 it decided to mount a campaign to encourage 11-13 year old children to take greater responsibility for their own health by:
1. Engaging them with the issue.
2. Educating them about the future consequences of their current food choices in a personal, relevant way.
3. Empowering them to take control of their diet and make healthier dietary and lifestyle choices.

Getting the attention of an indifferent audience

Faced with a limited budget, the BHF had to be selective about which children to target. It decided on 11-13 year olds, who, having just entered secondary school, were starting to express freedom of choice in both their dietary habits and wider lifestyles. This life stage represented the ideal opportunity to influence and shape their long-term attitudes towards food.

However, several factors made 11-13 year olds an extremely difficult group to educate about health. Firstly, regardless of age, children tend to live in the moment. This means threats to their adult health feel remote — for now, they feel invincible. Secondly, linked to this, is the common misconception that 'if you're healthy on the outside, you're healthy on the inside.' So, although most of them know junk food is bad for them, they eat it anyway.

The need was thus to find a way to engage with these children for long enough to absorb and act upon the key messages. An invaluable insight pointed to the solution: that children tend to avoid anything that looks or feels like 'education'. Many health education messages are built on 'single-minded propositions' ('eat 5-a-Day', 'smoking causes cancer') based on adult-imposed rules and so fall into this trap. But this isn't how children like to learn. Instead, they like to play, explore and experiment with the world, learning rules and how to interact. In other words, they want to discover problems and solutions on their own terms.

With this in mind, the BHF set itself two key strategic principles for the eventual solution:
• To help children learn, it had to encourage in-depth engagement and exploration.
• It had to feel like it was theirs, rather than something created and imposed by adults.

By this point it was obvious the answer couldn't be conventional. Whatever the channel, traditional advertising relies on single-mindedness and authority to deliver its message. The BHF strategic principles demanded complexity and co-ownership.

The solution: no adults allowed!

The need for an immersive environment where 11-13 year olds felt at home led naturally online. Children of 11-13 are digital natives — they feel online is their domain as they begin to use it for homework and social networking. And the natural genre within the online world is gaming. If a game was used for education, the lesson could be naughty, mischievous, funny, irreverent and free from the didacticism of the adult world. Online gaming is a channel where kids genuinely play and engage with content, and have 'ownership' of it. This made it the ideal medium for exploration, discovery and learning.

The resulting game, called Yoobot, was launched in November 2008. It allowed children to create a free digital, mini-version of themselves at www.yoobot. co.uk. Personalisation was key to make the exercise engaging and relevant, so they could upload a photo and give their Yoobot their own face. Users were further able to recreate their world, customising room decorations, clothes and hairstyles (Figures 1 and 2).

As the game had to be entertaining and playful, Yoobots would burp, snore, fart, break-dance, grimace and wave as well as send funny poems, one-liners, complaints and virtual birthday gifts to users by SMS and email. This gave the Yoobot a sense of personality and life that the user could relate to.

Most importantly, children could experiment on their Yoobot by setting its diet and activity routines, learning which foods were healthy or unhealthy. In particular, game play was accelerated to bring future problems into the immediate world, with one human day equating to three Yoobot years. Kids could rapidly see over the course of days the real impact of their food and lifestyle choices to their short, medium and long-term health.

For example, Yoobots could develop both internal and external health problems including weight gain, heart disease, diabetes, and high cholesterol and blood pressure, with daily health alerts. These health problems could be explored further in 'The Lab', where children were given the opportunity to change their lifestyles – or not – and continue to watch the future unfold before their eyes. Effectively, children were given the chance to create an educational

Figure 1. The Yoobot site

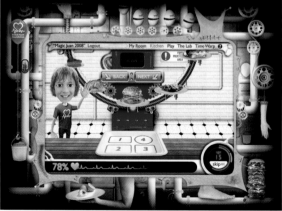

Figure 2. The Yoobot site

experience as complex as they desired. Once their Yoobot died, the game featured an 'autopsy', allowing kids to see the effects of the lifestyle they chose. They could then investigate healthy recipes or lifestyle tips via bhf.org.uk, and were encouraged to play again.

Getting the children's attention

Beyond the appeal of Yoobot itself, success largely hinged on the ability of the communications mix to tell children about it and create a real desire to have their own Yoobot. The media strategy was thus informed by two additional research insights:
- Children are true connectors when it comes to discussing things they like. They are indiscriminate about their sources of recommendations, happily accepting/passing them on to peers.
- Yoobot could not expect instant credibility as entertainment prior to release because it wasn't a recognised game or genre from a known games manufacturer.

The strategic platform was therefore to 'provoke desire for Yoobot by making it a subject for playground banter' through:
- Creating credibility pre-launch.
- Launching with a bang.
- Enabling sharing and discussion.

A multi-channel, multi-phased approach was used to reach children in their most common environments: online, at school and in front of children's television. Highly-targeted digital media in 'kids only' channels was employed to drive traffic, specifically targeting areas where children would be looking for entertainment/games.

A high-profile offline campaign helped to generate 'banter'. Elements were deliberately complex and multi-faceted. showing a wide range of features within the game and providing talking points. This included:
- School six-sheet posters delivered to 1,200 schools nationwide (Figure 3).
- Launch-day direct marketing packs, distributed to the desks of one million school children.
- In particular, television advertising on popular kids' channel Nickelodeon was employed to add a sense of scale, intrigue and credibility.

Playing a winning game

The original objectives were to engage, educate and empower. It fulfilled all three successfully.

Objective 1: Engage

More than one million Yoobots were created in just two months exceeding the initial target of 150,000 by 550%. Approximately 400,000 of these registrations were in the target age range (about 19% of the 2.16 million 11-13 year olds) while about 90% were under 14.

Figure 3. School poster

This strong result was in part due to the highly-targeted media strategy, which resulted in 40% of the 11-13 target being aware of Yoobot. This high awareness fuelled playground banter, with Yoobot becoming a 'must have' game in the run-up to Christmas:
• 68% of users talked about it with friends, family or in chat rooms.
• Yoobot was the third fastest growing UK search term at launch (just above Britney Spears).

It proved so popular, in fact, that were it a commercial game it would have joined the elite group of 11 games that have achieved 'Diamond' status (selling one million units in the UK) and the 48 that have achieved 'Double Platinum' (600,000 units). The success as an entertainment property was due to the fact that children enjoyed playing the game:
• 76% thought Yoobot was brilliant/very good and well worth their time.
• 68% of users logged in at least once every couple of days, 85% at least once a week.
• The average site visit lasted six minutes.

This means 68% of users actively engaged with an educational message for roughly 20 minutes a week. But did they actually absorb and act upon the key messages?

Objective 2: Educate

Yoobot definitely made kids think more about their diets. 85% of users said the game had "made me think more about the food I eat and do more to keep healthy" — 24% higher than the previous Food4Thought Junkmonkeys campaign. It also helped children realise that their current diet had an important effect on their future health.
• There was a 14-point increase in the kids who understood that "At my age the things I eat are important and can have an impact on my health and my long term health".
• There was a significant uplift in those feeling that their diet and health was something they should be thinking about now (Figure 4). Children even learned about the specific diseases linked to obesity (Figure 5).

Objective 3: Empower

Success at engagement and education made the issue important to children:
• 72% of the target now said they "think about my diet a lot, it's important to me" — a 25 point increase pre-to-post (from 47%).
• 63% claimed they wished they ate more healthily — up 22 points from 41% pre-wave.

This, in turn, led to all-important behavioural changes: 70% of users said Yoobot had made them eat more healthily. This implied that of the one million+ registrations, 730,000 had already taken steps to eat more healthily (Figure 6).

As a result there has been a significant uplift in those feeling their diet and health is something they should be thinking about now (not seen for previous campaign)

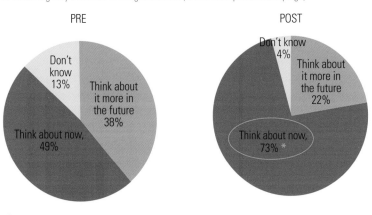

PRE

Don't know 13%
Think about it more in the future 38%
Think about now, 49%

POST

Don't know 4%
Think about it more in the future 22%
Think about now, 73% *

(*) Indicates a significant shift

Figure 4. Concern about health and diet - now vs future

And this is underpinned by greater understanding of what the health consequences are.

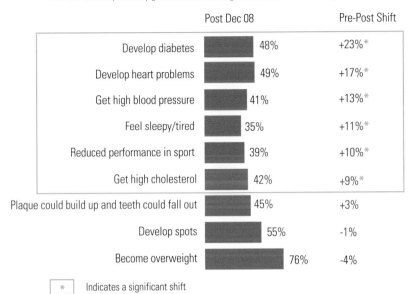

	Post Dec 08	Pre-Post Shift
Develop diabetes	48%	+23%*
Develop heart problems	49%	+17%*
Get high blood pressure	41%	+13%*
Feel sleepy/tired	35%	+11%*
Reduced performance in sport	39%	+10%*
Get high cholesterol	42%	+9%*
Plaque could build up and teeth could fall out	45%	+3%
Develop spots	55%	-1%
Become overweight	76%	-4%

* Indicates a significant shift

Figure 5. Long term consequences of eating unhealthy food
Source: Hall & Partners Europe

These changes in attitudes have followed through to behaviour with 70% claiming to eat more healthily, reduce their junk food consumption or ask their parents for healthier food.

	Eat healthier food*	Speak to my friends/family about health	Forward the Yoobot game to friends	Continue playing the game	Reduce the amount of junk food I buy or eat*	Ask my parents to give me healthier food*	Do more exercise
Yoobot	51%*	45%*	45%	44%	43%*	43%*	41%
Previous Campaign	28%	28%	n/a	n/a	28%	21%	30%

Total 'Eat more healthily' = 70%
(Previous campaign 42%)

* Indicates a significant difference from F4T3

Figure 6. Behaviour: already done - Yoobot vs previous campaign
Source: Hall & Partners Europe

A pronounced return on investment

This Yoobot campaign was also very cost-effective. At a cost of £1.85 for each of the 730,000 children who reported changing their diet, Yoobot was cheaper than other intervention methods. For example:
- School initiatives, such as free school meals, cost hundreds per child per year.
- Restricting junk food advertising is estimated to cost £3.20 per child, per extra year of good health. Even if Yoobot was repeated annually, this still equates to at least a 42% saving over restriction.

Furthermore, the financial savings from Yoobot during 2015-2050 could be estimated using obesity prevalence/cost projections:
- NHS costs of obesity alone: £5,800 per person.
- Total wider costs of elevated body mass index: £40,600 per person.

It follows that to break even the campaign would need to change the long-term behaviour of just:
- 33 people based on NHS costs.
- 233 people based on wider costs.

It would therefore require just 1% of the 730,000 to convert their dietary improvements into long-term healthy habits for the 2008 campaign to pay for itself 30 times over.

Building on success

By 2009 the BHF decided to mount an even more ambitious campaign by promoting a new game, Ultimate Dodgeball, to get children to be more physically active. Pre-launch the BHF again reached out to teachers through a compelling direct mailing, offering them a pack which contained lots of suggestions for fun, including cool dance moves and interesting recipes, along with everything the school would need to play a Dodgeball game or tournament.

It also introduced a new personality to the Yoobot site: the Yoonot, which acted as the Yoobot's alter ego, encouraging it to eat junk food and be lazy. The user could only defeat the Yoonot in an online game of Ultimate Dodgeball. The campaign culminated with National Yoobot Day on December 21, 2009, where children were given the opportunity to 'make their Yoobot famous' by entering a competition where they could win the chance for their Yoobot to appear on Nickelodeon.

The results of this second campaign were equally impressive.
By February 2010:
- 40% of those using Yoobot had returned from last year.
- 60% of children said Yoobot made them want to exercise more regularly.
- 63% of children said Yoobot made them want to eat healthier food.
- 72% said Yoobot was excellent/ very good.
- 28% had played Dodgeball either at home or at school.
- 60% enjoyed playing Dodgeball and would do so again and 88% had something positive to say about Dodgeball.

- One in six went on the Yheart website after seeing Yoobot. Yheart is the young people's site at the British Heart Foundation.
- The Yoobot site received almost a million visits in the two months after campaign launch.
- Half a million Yoobots were created in the first four months after the launch of Food4Thought5.

All images appearing in this case study are reproduced by permission of the British Heart Foundation.

Keep Britain Tidy 10

Achieving a fast reduction in fast food litter

Snapshot

Keep Britain Tidy's campaign played on young men's desire to appear desirable by equating dropping litter with looking like a pig.

Key insights

- Keep Britain Tidy found that the main litter offenders, young men of 18-24, were nevertheless keen to not be seen as dirty or unhygienic.

- The campaign likened them to pigs to show them how others see them when they litter.

- The campaign also enabled the charity to discuss with fast food companies their making a long-term reduction in food litter.

Summary

Keep Britain Tidy is an environmental charity and the anti-litter campaign for England. Research in 2007 revealed that fast food litter is one of England's biggest litter problems, with 24% of streets strewn with fast food. The Keep Britain Tidy litter segmentation report highlighted two important issues: that 18-24 year old males were the most likely group to drop litter and that issues of desirability were very important to this group.

In response to the research the campaign targeted 18-24 year old males. Litter droppers were likened to pigs to show them how others see them. Advertising mediums used included six-sheets, bus shelters, phone boxes, A3 posters in key locations, admirrors in restrooms, A4 adverts on toilet doors and pig snout stickers on mirrors.

To engage with the target audience a supporting dirty pig website was created which encouraged people to upload pictures of friends and family and add pig noses to them. Engaging with the fast food industry and key local authorities about the problem of litter was also an important aspect of the campaign. It proved highly effective, with a 31% reduction in litter at survey sites.

Honing in on the target

Keep Britain Tidy conducted market research in 2007 which revealed that fast food litter is one of England's biggest litter problems, with 24% of streets being strewn with fast food. The research also showed that 18-24 year old males were the most likely to drop food litter so this was the audience to target. They lived in England, were more likely to smoke, and had a complete disregard for the consequences of dropping litter. This audience fell into Keep Britain Tidy's 'Am I bothered' litter segment.

However, this target audience was also deeply concerned about sexual desirability and were embarrassed if other people thought they were dirty or unhygienic. So the organisation decided to use a creative approach with the strapline 'What does dropping litter make you look like?' alongside the image of a male and female depicted as a pig. It was felt that this route would have a significant impact on this image-conscious age group.

The total budget for the campaign was £238,000. This was broken down as follows:
• Agency budget (creative, design, artwork): £72,935.
• Booking advertising space: £159,404.
• Printing/production: £2,689.
• Public relations (PR) and a launch event in London: £2,000.

Covering all the bases

The campaign ran for four weeks and was integrated across a variety of channels. The outdoor advertising campaign featured two posters: one of a young female and one of a young male depicted as pigs with pig snouts, accompanied with the strapline 'What does dropping litter make you look like?'

(Figure 1). Media used included six-sheets, bus shelters, phone boxes and A3 posters placed in key locations. Ambient media was also used, with advertising being placed indoors, primarily on admirrors in washrooms, as this was the location the target audience was most likely to be looking at themselves. A4 posters were also placed on toilet doors and pig snout stickers on mirrors.

In addition, the organisation partnered with 10 local authorities to ensure campaign delivery on the ground, as well as wide regional coverage. Campaign partners were chosen to have wide geographical reach and included Colchester Borough Council, Trafford Council, Gateshead Council and the London Borough of Islington. The participating local authorities partnered the campaign by holding a launch event and placing A3 posters and A4 window stickers in key locations, A4 stickers on bins and stickers on mirrors. They also conducted pre and post-campaign litter counts to measure the effectiveness of the work, which showed a combined 31% reduction in litter.

In addition, local authorities were encouraged to engage with local businesses and request that they sign up to a voluntary 'Food on The Go' pledge and display campaign posters in their windows. The feedback from participating councils was very positive, with 100% of those involved reporting that the major fast food retailers (such as McDonald's, Greggs, KFC and Subway), as well as independent outlets in their areas, had shown their support.

The web was used as a promotional tool and a bespoke website was created to run alongside the campaign. The web address was promoted throughout the campaign and those visiting the site could upload pictures of their friends and family and add pig noses to them.

Figure 1. Advertising campaign

Naming and shaming

Manchester University undertook some research on behalf of Keep Britain Tidy to look at the relationship between key brands and litter. The research found that the public's opinion of major brands was greatly reduced once they saw those brands littered on the street. In response to this Keep Britain Tidy conducted a branded litter survey which counted the most littered fast food brands found on England's streets.

The top ten manufacturers/retailers were then named and shamed through the media. The branded litter found to be most prevalent was from McDonald's (53%), Greggs (20%) unbranded fish and chips (13%) and KFC (6%). The charity wrote to the chief executives of the companies named detailing a list of suggested initiatives for reducing litter, and invited them to write back and suggest ways they could work together.

On the day of the campaign's launch the media were invited to attend a special launch event in London, which again named and shamed fast food manufacturers/retailers. The event featured specially-made giant beef burgers and fast food wrappings, which ensured excellent media interest.

Hitting the mark

The campaign was highly successful. In terms of short-term success, it showed immediate correlation between the campaign and the impact of litter as it brought about a 31% reduction in litter at survey sites. The campaign messaging was well understood, with 45% of respondents saying they thought the key message was 'Don't drop litter', 23% interpreted it as being 'Put your litter in the bin' and 65% said that 'If you drop litter it makes you look like a pig'.

Contacting both Greggs and McDonald's chief executives by letter was also highly fruitful, with the companies responding with long-term strategies to reduce litter. Greggs was planning to change its packaging messaging to communicate to its customers that they should put it in the bin. The company also held Big Tidy Up clean-up events across England (the Big Tidy Up is a campaign run by Keep Britain Tidy which invites any member of the public, groups and businesses to hold litter clean-ups). Discussions with McDonald's also resulted in the company improving litter cleansing outside its stores.

In terms of PR, the campaign was very successful. The campaign PR launch event in London generated media coverage worth £6.8 million, and reached an audience of 122 million people worldwide. It was featured on national television, including BBC Breakfast and BBC Newsround, and the story made page leads in five national newspapers and regional and commercial radio stations.

As Keep Britain Tidy is an environmental charity, the environment was considered throughout the campaign. Paper-based mailings were avoided, particularly untargeted direct mail. All printed materials were produced on evolution satin 75% recycled stock, certified by the Forest Stewardship Council (FSC) and were recycled afterwards.

Chapter 11
Marketing for Sustainable Consumption

Jo Daniels
Marketplace Director,
Business in
the Community

'Marketing for sustainable consumption' is a difficult one because it poses a fundamental challenge to our business models, including the nature of marketing and what constitutes success. Currently business success is defined by growth and often selling higher volumes of products and services. But this is not ultimately sustainable. The earth simply doesn't have enough resources to be able to carry on producing these goods nor cope with the waste as we throw them away. It also, however, presents a real opportunity for marketers.

Marketers have the chance to redefine what we 'need' and move us from a society that values materialism to one that values experiences; selling services instead of products. We need to be thinking about what we market and how we market in order to create profit for the business and positive societal change. And importantly — at the same time as enhancing the quality or value the customers are receiving.

These case studies show the unique and powerful role marketers can have in being able to create change by engaging in the innovation to create more sustainable products and services and then influencing consumers to come on the journey with them.

Marks & Spencer is one of the best examples of a company that has put sustainability at the heart of its business with its 100-point Plan A. This gives the company the credibility to talk to their customers about changing their behaviour 'to do the right thing' because it has done the heavy lifting on their behalf. Procter & Gamble, too, has made sustainable product innovations before promoting 'turn to 30°' to its consumers washing with Ariel.

Both companies are influencing consumers by raising awareness and providing simple actions to empower and enable behaviour change. They keep their message fresh, evolving and adapting their approach to ensure it continues to resonate with consumers.

These haven't been 'flash in the pan', stand-alone communications campaigns. They are sustained approaches which are credible, tangible and have achieved real results for the business. It has built their brands, changed the relationship with their consumers and encouraged more sustainable behaviours for a better future for us all.

Ariel

11

Getting people to change behaviour for the greater good

Snapshot

Ariel's campaign to get consumers to wash clothes at lower temperatures persuaded them that they could do something to battle climate change.

Key insights

- A strong commitment to promoting sustainability led to a breakthrough campaign which encouraged consumers to save energy by washing at lower temperatures.

- The second wave of the campaign advanced this message by showing how small steps can make a big difference to the planet.

- A tightly-integrated approach led to significant change in consumer behaviour in terms of washing temperatures.

Summary

Ariel is one of the leading brands in the portfolio of Procter & Gamble (P&G), which markets more than 300 branded products around the world. As a sector leader of the Dow Jones Sustainability Index, P&G has an established track record of promoting environmental sustainability through its Live, Learn and Thrive corporate cause campaign and through its brands to 'ensure a better quality of life for everyone, now and for generations to come'.

The Ariel 'Turn to 30°' campaign, which first launched in 2006, was one of the first P&G brands in the UK to capitalise on mainstream environmental awakening. It promoted washing at 30 degrees rather than the previous standard 40 or even 60 degrees. However, by 2007 there was a much more crowded competitor environment, with retailers and competitors communicating a diversity of sustainable messages and in cases, mimicking Ariel's original 'Turn to 30°C' message.

Nevertheless, the second wave of the campaign in 2007 helped Ariel maintain ownership of the issue in consumers' minds. Furthermore, it delivered strong volume uplift and contributed to an increase in the number of loads washed at 30 degrees.

Educating consumers to help the planet

October 2007 marked the 170th year that P&G had been in business. Over that time, growth had stemmed from keeping faith with P&G's core principle of sustainable development: 'Ensuring a better quality of life for everyone, now and for generations to come'. The organisation had a long heritage as a sustainability leader, and remained committed to improving consumers' lives through its brands and by contributing to the sustainability of the planet and communities in which its employees lived and worked. Over the past decade, P&G had made a significant impact through its 'Live, Learn and Thrive' corporate cause campaign and, by using the trusted relationship its brands had with billions of consumers, continued to champion domestic behaviour that contributed to the greater good.

As a brand, Ariel itself had been associated with encouraging the UK's children to lead an active lifestyle and take up tennis. From 2006 this focus became less social and more environmental in its sustainability messages. Its commitment to reducing packaging and water usage, as well as its dedication to reducing the energy used in the production stage, had made it one of the leaders in its field.

Analysis of Ariel's Life Cycle Assessment (LCA), which measured the product's environmental impact from cradle to grave, showed that the highest amount of energy was used in the home: heating the water in the wash cycle. In response to this, in 2006 Ariel developed a message which emphasised the importance of washing at lower temperatures — 30 degrees C — to help 'do a good turn' for the environment.

Before the launch of this campaign, consumers believed that they needed to wash at high temperatures in order to get good results, which proved an entrenched barrier to adopting more sustainable cold-cleaning behaviours. However, Ariel's superior Cold Clean technology meant consumers benefited from excellent cleaning at low temperatures, while still saving energy and promoting more sustainable laundry practices (Figures 1 and 2).

Figure 1. Pack shot

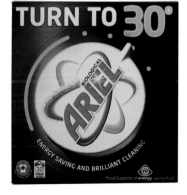

Figure 2. The 'Turn to 30°' campaign

Broadening the message of sustainability

In year two of Ariel's 'Turn to 30°' campaign, Ariel challenged consumer perceptions even further on this point, which in effect also helped with an increase in differentiation and branded recall. This route provided a meaningful improvement to the business in terms of energy efficiency by spreading a 'sustainable behaviour' message generally.

The decision to run the campaign in partnership with the Energy Saving Trust (EST) for a second consecutive year was important in bringing about long-term behavioural change but brought fresh communication challenges for the brand team as well.

Ariel's challenge was not only to educate consumers that they could get good results at low temperatures, but to widen the context by creating direct links between energy saving and climate change (communicating the small steps we can take to make a difference) and thus generate a much stronger, more high profile call to action while still inspiring and empowering consumers.

Integrating for maximum impact

The messages were complicated and needed a tailored approach, so communications planning ensured that different media communicated different messages, which ultimately added up to a totally integrated plan centred around one central call to action. (Figures 3 and 4)

The success of the second wave campaign stemmed from:
• Using a variety of media to emphasise the different aspects of the campaign while maintaining a balance of the media mix so that the overall message of 'Turn to 30°' was still clear.

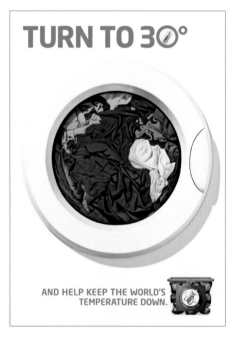

Figure 3. Example of the campaign

Figure 4. Example of the campaign

- Using the website as the central hub of the campaign — important for the green audience to feel that their contribution was part of a broader commitment.
- Leveraging TV to communicate complimentary, multi-messages with striking creative on global issues followed by personal testimonials from well-known faces linked to washing and energy saving to enforce the call to action.

There were a number of specific activities.

- The internet was the central hub of the campaign. It was a bespoke site to support all campaign messaging (doaqoodturn.co.uk) and served as an interactive hub to track and inspire information-seekers on sustainability issues.

Figure 5. Ariel Excel Gel

Figure 6. Ariel Excel Gel

- TV copy (30" and 10"): 'polar ice caps' communicated energy-saving and the message of Ariel performance in a striking, poignant way and generating a call to action, while celebrity endorser Helena Christensen encouraged the nation to turn to 30°.
- Packaging: a limited edition Ariel packaging revived from the previous campaign provided a call-to-action for consumers.
- EST partnership: Ariel maintained the partnership with the EST to quantify credible energy-saving benefits of washing at 30°C. The EST logo was communicated on TV, packaging, in media partnerships, through public relations and online.
- Media partnerships: with core press, online and broadcast media to provide cleaning reassurance and deliver complex sustainability messages.
- Media relations: with the support of the EST, Helena Christensen, Joanna Yarrow and Oliver Heath, speaker placement opportunities occurred in prestigious green pages, and with journalists renowned for their focus on energy saving in the home.
- Road show: 10 key UK shopping centres were visited by the Ariel 'Do a Good Turn' house. Visitors could explore a sophisticated mock-up of an energy-efficient house and obtain tips and advice. Energy doctors from the EST were on hand to complete free and personalised energy-saving audits of their home. Consumers were encouraged to sign up to 'do a good turn'. A partnership with local radio stations and local media relations increased awareness and boosted footfall.
- In-store: there was additional activity in various retailers to support the initiative and communicate the energy-saving message.

For the second wave campaign, all resources where possible were made from recycled materials or sustainable forestry, while the entire campaign was carbon offset.

Making a big difference

The Ariel 'Turn to 30°' second-wave campaign stood out because:
- It engaged with and encouraged consumers to see how doing a simple thing at home could help the planet.
- It served to create a sense of belonging around small-step activism by building a communal membership centred around Ariel's pledge website. This was particularly important for the 'green audience' that made up 64% of the population. They wanted to do something for the environment but were often discouraged if they thought that no one else was bothering or that their small change didn't add up to have a significant impact. A sense of group mentality was instilled through the 'Turn to 30°' website, which tracked pledges and provided regular news feeds of sustainability-related information.

Data from the Habits and Practices Study showed that before the start of the campaign, only 2% of wash loads in the UK were washed at 30 degrees. By the end of Ariel's 'Turn to 30°' second wave, customer perceptions had been successfully changed as shown by an independent survey conducted in August 2007, which revealed that since Ariel's bid to get the nation to wash at 30°:
- 48% of women linked Ariel with washing at 30°.
- Nearly half of the UK population claimed that the Ariel campaign had made them more likely to try washing at 30 degrees with Ariel.

In addition to this, independent research by IPC Green Matters 2007 attributed high brand linkage between Ariel and 88% of those that now washed at 30°C. This highlighted that, despite a more competitive marketplace, a combination of credible messaging, an enhanced message and stakeholder and customer support paid dividends for the second wave of the Ariel 'Turn to 30°' campaign.

The campaign was thus not only responsible for consistent behavioural change and volume sales uplift since, but received widespread stakeholder and industry accolade for putting energy saving on the mainstream agenda.

Continuing the crusade

Since the 'Turn to 30°' campaign, the Ariel brand has continued its leadership in encouraging sustainable consumer behaviour in the laundry category. Launched in 2009, Ariel Excel Gel is a breakthrough detergent designed from scratch to deliver outstanding cleaning even at low temperatures and can clean as well at 15°C as at 60°C. To find the optimum formulation for the brand, over five million formulations were tested by R&D experts, with only 30 meeting the success criteria. This provided the ultimate mix of ingredients to form a stable and high-performing gel (Figures 5 and 6 on previous page).

In fact, *Which* magazine called this new formulation better than any other laundry detergent ever tested, even at a much lower temperature.

Washing at low temperatures is the single most important thing people can do to lower CO_2 emissions while doing laundry. Cold-water washing campaigns such as the Ariel 'Turn to 30°' have helped cut 58,000 tonnes of CO_2 emissions by educating consumers to save energy.

Marks & Spencer

11

Pioneering a sustainable business

Snapshot

Marks & Spencer has put sustainability at the heart of its business.

Key insights

- For Marks & Spencer (M&S) going green has meant not just transforming every part of its business but trying to change the attitudes and behaviour of its 25 million customers.

- A carefully-planned, three-stage approach has worked by convincing, not cajoling, people to do the right thing and change behaviour.

Summary

M&S is one of the UK's leading retailers, selling clothing, food and homeware. In 2006 the company became determined to put sustainability at the heart of its business. It set out to transform every aspect of the company, from sourcing products to relationships with suppliers, shoppers and the wider world.

To succeed, it would have to change the attitudes and behaviour of every one of its 25 million shoppers. Since its inception it has passed through three distinct steps. The first step, 'Look Behind the Label' raised awareness and approval of a whole range of initiatives — and the brand itself.

The second step, 'Plan A', involved a more thorough reappraisal of M&S, and set out a five-year plan involving 100 commitments. After only a year, it had reached many of its goals and achieved significant recognition from opinion leaders. But it still didn't change the average shopper's behaviour.

It was the third step, 'Doing the Right Thing', that accomplished this by 'normalising' the aims of Plan A and expressing them in a way that seemed right and proper to mainstream people. In a relatively short time the measured attitudes of a million shoppers had changed, moving from a passive, defeatist approach towards a more actively sustainable, optimistic one.

Facing a changing world

For well over a century, and long before words like 'sustainability' entered the vernacular, M&S had been quietly practicing a whole range of ethical business practices. For example:

- A hundred years of long-term, mutually-beneficial relationships with suppliers.
- Fifty years of smoke-free shopping.
- Forty-five years of energy-efficient thermostatic fridges.
- 'A returns' policy unmatched for generations.
- Free-range eggs long before most people knew or cared what the phrase 'free-range eggs' actually meant.

But times had moved on. By the early years of the 21st century things had reached the point where, without drastic action, it would be hard to imagine any kind of decent future for forthcoming generations. For M&S it was time to do something more about sustainability.

In 2006, it took a long, hard look at its ethical and sustainable activities as a whole, and set out to 'move them up a gear' and to gather support behind them. Its aims were to change the business from root to branch, and through this to help change lives and, in as far as it was able, to do what it could to help change the world for the better. This was never going to be a quick fix.

Nor, realistically, was it ever going to be something that could be fully achieved completely, or to everyone's complete satisfaction. A journey is the best way of looking at it. By the end of 2009 it had been a journey that had passed through three distinct steps. Each step moved M&S and its partners towards a better place — although there was still a long way to go, and there probably always will be.

Listening to the customers

A number of studies had been conducted into what consumers thought about sustainability and the environment, and, broadly speaking, they coincided. Generally, 20% didn't care and weren't interested. The rest (80%), said they did care — to some degree — and to some degree thought that being 'green' was the 'good' or 'right' thing to do.

However, only a minority (10%) actively went out of their way to do something about it. The main bulk said they might do something if it was easy and didn't involve making sacrifices (35%) or that they didn't see what difference it would make anyway (35%) (Figure 1). Making millions of shoppers less defeatist, and more willing, was never going to be an easy task.

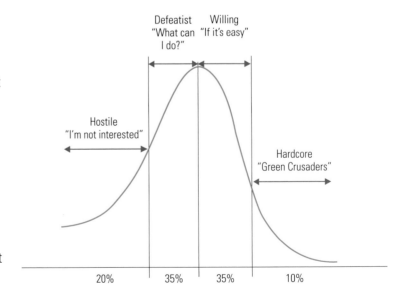

Figure 1. What consumers think about sustainability
Source: TGI

Figure 2

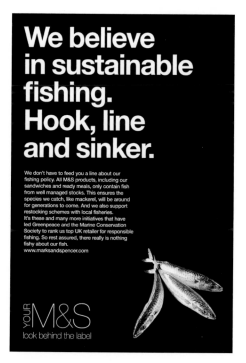

Figure 3. Raising awareness about sustainability

Embarking on a long journey

Step One, 2006: Look Behind The Label

The first step was about raising awareness and encouraging approval. For socially and environmentally-aware consumers 'Look Behind the Label' drew attention to a range of things M&S was doing, from sourcing Fairtrade to environmentally-friendly textile dyes (Figures 2 and 3).

This programme resulted in increased awareness and approval of M&S initiatives, particularly among opinion formers and the ethically-aware. Highlights included:

• Voted Britain's Greenest Supermarket by consumers and most popular with socially/environmentally-aware shoppers.
• Evidence collected by Citigroup analysts suggested that 'Look Behind the Label' was the most successful campaign M&S had ever run.
• Compassion in World Farming's Good Egg Award for free-range eggs.
• Top of the Marine Stewardship Council League for sustainable fishing.
• RSPCA Good Business Awards for best fashion retailer.

But the company felt there was more to be done. 'Feel good' awareness and approval among people who are already concerned about ethics and the environment was a good thing, but it didn't always translate into tangible change in the world. What needed to be done was to move people from just feeling something to actually doing something — from awareness and approval to engagement and commitment.

Step Two, 2007/8: Plan A

The next stage was about engaging and attracting commitment. In 2007, after a process involving stakeholders both from inside and outside the business, M&S set out its new plan: 100 commitments, in five 'pillars', to be accomplished in five years. It was called Plan A because, the argument went, there was no Plan B. It was to encompass all of the big issues in the business and across the entire value chain. The end of all this would be a transformation of M&S itself, its business practices, its relationships with customers and suppliers and its dealings with the world at large. Few, if any, major retailers had ever done anything like this before.

The pillars of Plan A were:

1. Climate change: to make M&S's operations carbon-neutral.
2. Reducing waste: to have zero waste going to landfill through reducing and recycling bags and packaging.
3. Sustainable raw materials: to source the most sustainable and renewable materials available.
4. Being a fair partner: to improve the lives of hundreds of thousands of people in the supply chain and their families and communities.
5. Health: to help thousands of employees and customers choose a healthier lifestyle.

Plan A had to be much more than a 'feel good' campaign. It required engagement and commitment from M&S itself and from customers. It meant making difficult decisions. People who had become accustomed to getting as many plastic carrier-bags as they liked for free would suddenly find themselves having to bring their own shopping-bags from home (like their mothers used to do) or else pay 5p a bag.

They would be expected to see the point of it, and think it a good thing, rather than a rip-off or a nuisance.

The achievements of the initial phase of Plan A were notable because it began the process of bringing about tangible change, including:

- Reduced 10,000 tons of packaging.
- Diverted 20,000 tons of waste from landfill.
- Saved 40,000 tons of CO2.
- Saved 387 million food carrier bags (an 83% reduction).
- Used 1,500 tons of recycled polyester (equivalent to 37 million bottles).
- Organic food sales 2007/8 up 40% compared to 2006/7.
- Saved 100 million litres of water.
- Generated £15 million for charities, including £1.6 million raised for Breakthrough Breast Cancer and £600,000 raised to educate 15,000 children in Uganda.

In addition, recognition from opinion-formers continued to grow. Not only did the company receive a whole range of environmental and ethical awards but it managed to get significant opinion-former involvement in the Plan A Climate Change Quilt project. Over 5,000 people contributed to the website, including message patches from Twiggy, Myleene Klass, Jemima Khan, Geri Halliwell, Tom Aikens, Philip Glenister, Noemie Lenoir, Zac Goldsmith and Sir Ian Botham, as well as top executives from charities such as WWF and Oxfam.

But there was more to be done. Plan A had created extremely high levels of engagement and commitment among both staff and internal audiences and 'Green Crusaders', while it made people in general feel better about the company. However, what it didn't do was to get enough mainstream customers to change their attitudes and behaviour significantly. A lot of people still didn't understand Plan A. They suspected that the 5p carrier bag policy was a cunning way of benefiting M&S — despite the fact that the profit was donated to an environmental charity. More needed to be done to change mainstream attitudes and behaviours.

Step Three, 2009: Plan A: Doing The Right Thing

This was about going mainstream and getting to those people who weren't the active, committed Green Crusaders and who felt happier being comfortable, fitting in and doing what's generally considered to be normal, acceptable and right. But 'normal, acceptable and right' is a moving standard. Twenty years ago people sat with their children in buses and train carriages filled with a thick fog of cigarette smoke and no-one thought twice about it. Twenty years ago, people bought battery eggs, and anyone who made a fuss about free-range was thought to be a bit odd.

2008 awards and recognition for Plan A

- World Environment Centre Gold Medal for International Corporate Achievement in Sustainable Development 2008
- British Renewable Energy Awards Pioneer Award
- Property Executive Sustainability Award for Excellence (Pollok Store)
- Retail Interior Award — Green Store of the Year (Bournemouth)
- RSPCA 2008 Awards — Cosmetics winner; Ongoing Commitment to Change Award; Fashion Winner; Best Large Retailer and Food Winner; Best Supermarket Award

2009 awards and recognition for Doing the Right Thing

- Joint winner 2009 Consumer Focus 'Green to the Core' supermarket league table
- Retail Leadership Award 2009, Greener Package Awards
- Fashion Commitment Award 2009, RSPCA Good Business Awards
- 2009 Winner Environmental Investigation Agency's supermarket refrigeration table
- 2009 Winner Pesticide Action Network UK supermarket pesticide league table
- 2009 Most Ethical Retailer, *Cosmopolitan* Magazine Awards
- High Street Recycling Champion 2009, Letsrecycle.com Awards
- Environmental Initiative of the Year in the 2009 International Wine Challenge Awards
- Top 100 in Ethisphere World's Most Ethical Companies
- Regular analysis from CIU department showing M&S as the most ethical/green retailer

M&S needed to find out how to:

1. Normalise Plan A. That meant re-framing or re-positioning the commitments so that they would be seen by the public at large as the 'default' choice of normal, right-thinking people like you and me, rather than the active hobby-horse of rainbow-clad people with dreadlocks who lived in yurts and constructed their own wind-turbines out of bits of old bicycles.

2. Talk about the benefits. It had to be made into a win-win situation, not seen as a puritanical sacrifice. Ethical food and ethical fashion should stimulate someone's desires first and their conscience second.

The 'normalising' idea, when it came, came from consumers themselves. In research, the same phrase kept coming up time and time again: Doing the Right Thing. As in, "I just want to do the right thing." There are any number of people who might, or might not, decide to take part in something called 'Plan A', but there are very few people who don't want to be seen to 'do the right thing'.

To put it another way, the thrust of the argument behind the campaign changed from objectivist ("It's a fact that we need to deal with these issues.") to approbationalist ("All right-thinking people think this is a good thing to do, and they'd feel good about you for doing it.").

This made it feel a lot more friendly and normal. Then there was the job of making it seem not just normal and friendly but desirable, and for this there was a deliberate communications policy of always using 'Doing the right thing' in combination with examples of the benefits and pleasures offered by M&S quality (Figures 4 and 5).

Figure 4. Doing the Right Thing campiagn

Figure 5. Doing the Right Thing campiagn

The Oxfam Clothes Exchange programme

This was the UK's largest clothes recycling initiative. Customers were encouraged to donate their old M&S clothes to Oxfam, in return for which they got a £5 voucher. People felt virtuous for having done the right thing, pleased with their £5, and good about M&S quality after learning that the clothes they donated had a high value to Oxfam on account of being so well-made and long-lasting.

This third stage resulted in the following achievements:

- Began the process of changing mainstream attitudes and behaviour, resulting in a less defeatist attitude, with a million more shoppers willing to do something (Figure 6).
- Continued reduction in carrier-bag usage, doing away with 400 million bags and raising £1.2 million for its partner, environmental regeneration charity Groundwork.
- Over a million people donated M&S clothes to Oxfam and collected their voucher. 3.2 million M&S garments were recycled and £2 million raised for Oxfam.

M&S set out on a journey whose aim was to build a better business that improved lives, changed attitudes and behaviour and made the way we live better and more sustainable. Although it is a journey possibly without end, the first three steps achieved remarkable results.

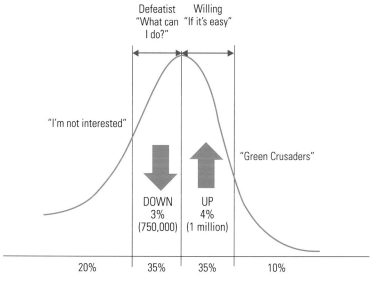

Figure 6. Changing consumer views
Source: TGI

Appendix

The case studies in this book have won or been highly commended for the following Marketing Society awards. The names of the original agencies involved (where applicable) are also included.

Organisation	Category	Year
Ariel *Agency: Hill & Knowlton*	Ethical	2008
Audi UK *Agency: Bartle Bogle Hegarty*	Long-term marketing excellence	2010
Aviva *Agency: Abbott Mead Vickers BBDO*	Marketing teamwork	2010
British Gas *Agency: CHI & Partners*	Brand revitalisation	2010
British Heart Foundation *Agencies: Various*	Digitally-led marketing(SME)	2008
BT Business *Agency: Swarm@RKCR/Y&R*	Brand revitalisation B2B	2009
Change4Life *Agencies: M+C Saatchi, in-house*	New brand/Not-for-profit	2010
Channel 4 Jamie's School Dinners *Agency: 4Creative*	Cause-related marketing	2007
Dulux *Agency: Abbott Mead Vickers BBDO*	Marketing communications	2008
Dulux *Agency: In-house*	International brand marketing	2010
ebookers *Agency: Promise Corporation*	International brand development	2009

GlaxoSmithKline *Agency: In-house*	New brand or business	2010
Harlequins FC *Agency: Bamboo Marketing Communications*	Marketing on a shoestring	2010
Hovis *Agency: MCBD*	Brand revitalisation	2009
ICI Paints *Agency: Brand Learning*	Marketing capability	2008
Keep Britain Tidy *Agency: In-house*	Not-for-profit	2010
KFC *Agency: Bartle Bogle Hegarty*	Brand revitalisation	2007
Magners *Agency: Young Euro RSCG*	New brand	2007
Marks & Spencer *Agency: RKCR/Y&R*	Long-term marketing excellence	2010
Marks & Spencer *Agency: RKCR/Y&R*	Sustainable consumption	2010
McDonald's *Agency: Leo Burnett*	Marketing achievement	2009
McDonald's *Agency: In-house*	Internal marketing	2009
More Th>n *Agency: Stephens Francis Whitson*	Customer relationship marketing	2009
NHS Blood and Transplant *Agency: Abbott Mead Vickers BBDO*	Customer insight	2010
O_2 *Agency: VCCP*	Brand extension	2009
Pedigree *Agency: TBWA\London*	Cause-related marketing	2009

Appendix continued

Sainsbury's *Agency: Abbott Mead Vickers BBDO*	Marketing communications	2009
Shell *Agency: Brand Learning*	Marketing capability	2009
Sky *Agency: WCRS*	Customer insight	2007
Thinkbox *Agency: In-house*	B2B marketing	2010
UPS *Agency: McCann Erickson*	Digitally-led marketing	2009
Virgin Atlantic *Agency: RKCR/Y&R*	Long-term marketing excellence	2010
Waitrose *Agency: MCBD*	Brand extension	2010
Walkers *Agency: Abbott Mead Vickers BBDO*	Marketing capability	2010

Index

Sponsors

Aviva

Aviva - 300 Years of Insight

We're the world's sixth-largest insurance group and the biggest in the UK, with 46,000 employees that everyday serve 53 million customers worldwide.

We are committed to delivering one distinctive experience for our customers. Wherever they are, we want them each to feel that "no one recognises me like Aviva". Our global consumer research reveals that most of our competitors are particularly bad at recognising people's individual significance. This research also tells us that small human touches can make a huge difference to a customer's experience. Our aim is to make recognition the familiar quality that distinguishes Aviva from our competitors - just as Apple means user-friendliness and FedEx means reliability.

"We know insurance isn't just about policies and pensions; it's about people. That's why we're making our customers the big picture, putting a spotlight on them and our people. Putting customers at the heart of everything not only makes sense for them, it makes good commercial sense too." (Amanda Mackenzie, Aviva's chief marketing and communications officer)

We are working hard every day to build the company around what our customers want from us. That's why Aviva now ranks among the UK's top ten most valuable brands, according to the 2010 Brand Finance Global 500 survey and that success is something we are looking to replicate across the world.

BT

BT operates in over 170 countries and is one of the world's leading communications services companies. BT is a major supplier of networked IT services to government departments and multinational companies. It's the UK's largest communications service provider to consumer and business markets and is made up primarily of four customer-facing lines of business: BT Retail, BT Global Services, Openreach, and BT Wholesale.

BT operates in a thriving, multi-trillion pound industry that spans the whole world. In recent years the global communications market has been focused on convergence, whereby the boundaries between telcos, IT companies, software businesses, hardware manufacturers and broadcasters have become intertwined to create a new communications industry.

BT has evolved from being a supplier of telephony services to become a leading provider of innovative communications products, services, solutions and entertainment products. BT's business customers range from multinational, multi-site corporations to SMEs and start-ups.

More than 80 per cent of the FTSE 100 and 40 per cent of Fortune 500 companies rely on BT for networking, applications and system integration. The National Health Service, Procter & Gamble, PepsiCo, BMW, Emirates, Fiat, Microsoft, Philips, and Unilever are just some of the organisations working with BT.

BT has been a driving force behind the success of 'Broadband Britain'. Thanks to the company's investment, nearly every home in Britain now has access to broadband and in September 2009, BT announced plans to more than double the availability of its fastest fibre broadband service.